Testimonials for *Start & Run Your Own Record Label*

"In this new world of music, a book like Start & Run Your Own Record Label *is essential reading! Our gospel and jazz clients are independent on purpose and plan to stay that way. They know that their future music business depends on controlling their own fate, and books like this help us all realize we can do it!"* —Eric Copeland, producer, creativesoulonline.com, Franklin, TN

"Regardless of which facet of the music industry you are involved in, if you want to succeed, there is only resource guide you will need: anything written by Daylle Deanna Schwartz. She has consistently rewritten music industry bibles. Start & Run Your Own Record Label *is one of her books that have launched, and guided, a long list of successful music careers."*—Cheryl Harvey Hill, journalist/album reviewer, countrystarsonline.com, Las Vegas, NV

*"*Start & Run Your Own Record Label *offers immense value and necessary lessons for those who decide to make entry into the music industry their goal."* —Israel Vasquetelle, publisher, insomniacmagazine.com, Orlando, FL

"I read Start & Run Your Own Record Label, *and I did exactly that. The book helped me develop my label. It afforded me the opportunity to make a living writing music for TV and film as well as touring college campuses. I am eternally grateful!"*—Elza, singer/songwriter, Squirrel Girl Inc., Mamaroneck, NY

"Daylle was maybe the very first to throw herself full force into the cause of encouraging independent musicians to seize their own power in the marketplace. Her commitment helped spawn a revolution—direct communication between dedicated artists and their audience. As the marketplace keeps evolving, Daylle continues to shine her probing light on fresh possibilities. Thanks to her research and inspiration, we have both nuts-and-bolts and spiritual support for having fun with this, whatever our genre—so we're going for it in classical, too!"—Robert Stallman and Hannah Woods, Bogner's Café label, Philadelphia, PA

"I have read Start & Run Your Own Record Label *at least a dozen times and love the fact that Daylle is keeping up with the ever-changing music industry with new editions. This book is essential and a staple for anyone wanting to know the right way to put out music."*—Jay Ronan, CEO, Blue Duck Records, Boston, MA

"I have attended many seminars, and have read numerous publications on do-it-yourself promotion. Daylle's book Start & Run Your Own Record Label is the most comprehensive, hands-on, nuts-and-bolts guide to understanding the music industry. A must-read!"—Mark Regula, Ivory Tower Project, Howard Beach, NY

"Start & Run Your Own Record Label puts the keys to releasing your and others' music in your lap. This manual is encouraging to a songwriter."—Tftka Dawidalle aka daggakarab, Everett, WA

"I started my own label after reading this book. It gave me a sense of 'this can be done' rather than 'oh my God, what am I doing?'"—Nathan Temby, Merica Records, San Francisco, CA

"Start & Run Your Own Record Label is a great reference for anyone in the music business to keep on hand. Even if you think you know it all, this book quickly clarifies any foggy moments. As a former label GM (Popular Records/ BMG, West End Records), now publicity/marketing company owner, I find it a perfect complement to This Business of Music."—Andy Reynolds, president, Penetration, Inc., New York, NY

"Daylle has a straightforward way of explaining the business. However, while making clear all the work and effort entailed in making things happen, she also inspires and instills the belief that it is indeed all possible. This is an informative and motivational book that everyone serious about putting their music out into the world should read, and then keep rereading."—Michael Gilboe, Copperheadz Productions, New York, NY

"I want to create my own label in Europe, and this book is a bible for those who want to start their own record company and develop it to the max."—Vincent Habryn, Gravelines, France

"Daylle's book has been a guidebook to success for me and my small label. With my zeal for success and her ideas and testimony, I've been able to turn my dreams into a living reality!"—Matt Allison, recording artist and indie label owner, Capetown, South Africa

START & RUN YOUR OWN
RECORD LABEL

3rd Edition

Winning Marketing Strategies for Today's Music Industry

START & RUN
· YOUR OWN ·
RECORD LABEL

3rd Edition

DAYLLE DEANNA SCHWARTZ

Winning Marketing Strategies for
Today's Music Industry

BILLBOARD BOOKS
an imprint of Watson-Guptill Publications
New York

Senior Editor: Amy Vinchesi
Project Editor: Ross Plotkin
Production Director: Alyn Erans

First published in 2009 by
Billboard Books,
an imprint of Watson-Guptill Publications
Crown Publishing Group,
a division of Random House, Inc., New York
www.crownpublishing.com
www.watsonguptill.com

Library of Congress Control Number: 2008935965
ISBN-13: 978-0-8230-8463-0
ISBN-10: 0-8230-8463-9

Printed in the United States
First printing, 2009

3 4 5 6 7 8 9 / 17 16 15 14 13 12 11

*This book is dedicated with love to my sister, Carla Herman,
for her consistent support and encouragement and for showing
by example that women can be very successful in the business world,
and to my wonderful brother-in-law, Doug Landy,
for being a supportive member of my family.*

CONTENTS

Chapter 21 Effective Digital Marketing   *286*

Chapter 22 Some Advice from the Pros   *319*

ACKNOWLEDGMENTS

First, I want to thank God and the Universe for all of my blessings. I wouldn't be where I am today without my faith. This book wouldn't have reached its fruition without the support of many people. I'd like to acknowledge everyone who helped me. I consider all the following folks part of my blessings!

I've said it before, and I'll say it again: The music industry is known for its cutthroat reputation, yet the folks who took time to share their experience and knowledge prove how many wonderful people are in this business. You're all terrific! Thank you to everyone I interviewed for sharing your knowledge and experience with me. You were all such a pleasure to talk to and are definitely an inspiration for others who want to start and run a record label.

Thank you a million times to (in alphabetical order): Lee Abrams, Stephanie Furgang Adwar, Esq. (Furgang & Adwar, LLP), Andy Allen (Alternative Distribution Alliance), Philip Antoniades (nimbit.com), David M. Bailey, K. Banger (The Dirt Department), CJ Baran (Push Play), Sue Baran (Push Play), Alan Becker (RED Distribution), Rich Bengloff (A2IM), Jonatha Brooke (Bad Dog Records), Ansel Brown, Tony Brummel (Victory Records), Michael Bull (Caroline Distribution), Jed Carlson (ReverbNation), Mark Carpentieri (MC Records), Rudy Chavarria (Rude College Promotions), Cliff Chenfeld (Razor & Tie Music), Edward Chmelewski (Blind Pig Records), Jay Cooper, Esq., Rolando Cuellar (Roland Entertainment), Damon Dash (Roc-A-Fella Records), Laura Duncan (WTTS), El-P (Definitive Jux Records),

Eric de Fontenay (MusicDish & Mi2N), Jason Feinberg (On Target Media Group), Jesse Fergusson (Definitive Jux Records), Tom Ferguson (*Billboard*), Juni Fisher (Red Geetar Records), Martin Folkman (*The Musician's Atlas*), Mark Fox, E. A. (Fox Tax), Keith Grimwood (Trout Fishing in America), Ellyn Harris (Buzz Publicity), Christopher Harrison (DMX), Paul Hartman (*Dirty Linen*), Michael Hausman (United Musicians), William Hochberg, Esq., Rita Houston (WFUV), Eric Hutchinson, Lydia Hutchinson (*Performing Songwriter*), Ezra Idlet (Trout Fishing in America), Brad Jefferson (Animoto), Philippe Kern (IMPALA), Seth Kibel (Azalea City Recordings), Michael Koch (Koch International Corporation), Scott Krokoff (Hypochondriac Records), Beth Krakower (CineMedia Promotions), Jeff Krantz, John T. Kunz (Waterloo Records), Onno Lakeman (Red to Violet), Scott Lapatine (*Stereogum*), Trudy Lartz (Nielsen SoundScan), Gregg Latterman (Aware Records), Bob Lefsetz (*Lefsetz Letter*), Karen Leipziger (KL Productions), Jon Lowy (Echospin), John Luneau (Palm Pictures), Steven Masur, Esq. (MasurLaw), Geoff Mayfield (*Billboard*), Todd McGee (Groupie Tunes), Sean Michaels (Said the Gramophone), Michael Mollura (Music Connection), Robb Nansel (Saddle Creek Records), Jennifer Nielsen (YouTube), Anthony Orlando (Feuer & Orlando), Panos Panay (Sonicbids), Mark Pellegrini (Wikimedia Foundation), Steve Penta (White Light Productions), Matthew Perpetua (Fluxblog), Rick Purcell, Esq. (MasurLaw), Jim Pettid (Media Services), Ed Razzano (Ricall), Mark Redfern (*Under the Radar*), Fern Reiss (expertizing.com/publishinggame.com), Dick Renko (Trout Records), John Robinson (Shaman Work Recordings), Susan Rush (Pinnacle Records), Anslem Samuel (*XXL* magazine), Jane Siberry (Sheeba Records), John Simson (SoundExchange), Derek Sivers (CDBaby), Arty Skye (SkyeLab Sound Studio), Eric Speck (Ace Fu Records), Jim Sullivan (newengland.com), Jim Testa (*Jersey Beat Fanzine*), Peter Thompson (Vital Distribution), Marc Urselli, Jason Van Orden, Tony van Veen (Disc Makers), Kelly Vandergriff (Five Times August), Israel Vasquetelle (*Insomniac* magazine), Valerie Vigoda (GrooveLily), Susan Walker (Tried & True Music), Ken Weinstein (Big Hassle Media), Bill Werde (*Billboard*), Jay Woods (New West Records), Lisa Worden (KROQ), Dan Zanes (Festival Five Records), Walter Zelnick (City Hall Records).

I could write a long paragraph about each of these, but space is limited. I must say a special thanks to people who went above and beyond to support my efforts as an educator. Thank you, Daniel Glass (Glassnote Entertainment) (and his incredibly helpful assistant, Adam Herzog), for inviting me to visit your office filled with dynamic energy. I'm still in awe of what I learned and observed! Thank you, Jeff Price (Tunecore), for your continued support and friendship and for creating a service that helps indies to empower themselves through digital sales. Thank you, Tim Westergren (Pandora), for sharing your inspiring story with me and making so much time to chat. Thank you, Ingrid Michaelson, for making time during your busy tour schedule and for proving how powerful having great music can be! Thank you, Perez Hilton, for making time in your very busy day to share suggestions for getting online attention for good music and for helping spread the word about it. Thank you, Rev. Moose (CMJ), for being so supportive over the years and for sharing your vast wisdom. Thank you, John Szuch (Deep Elm Records), for contributing your wealth of experience and for proving a label that's passionate about music and its artists can succeed. Thank you, Dave Roberge (Everfine Records), for imparting so much from your successful endeavors and for giving me the honor of knowing that my books have helped you get there.

The music industry has shown me lots of friendship. Thank you, Wallace Collins, Esq., for many years of friendship and support and for allowing me to share your legal knowledge. Thank you, Rich Hardesty, for continuing to share your amazing accomplishments and for becoming a good friend in the process. Thank you, David Wimble (*The Indie Bible*), for your friendship and for being my angel whenever needed. Thank you, Ellyn Solis (Vermillion Media), for your long-time support and for helping enlighten my readers. Thank you, Ryan Kuper (Redemption Records), for continuing to share your knowledge and for becoming a friend. Thanks to Cheryl Hill (number-one country music fan!) for all your support. Thanks also to the Moonstruck Diner on Second Avenue (*best* diner in New York City!), especially Hedia, for pampering me with great food, caring, and attentive service when I come in with my laptop and stay for hours.

I feel very blessed to have had the privilege of getting to know so many supportive industry people! Thank you all once again!

INTRODUCTION

The music industry changed noticeably from the first edition of *Start & Run Your Own Record Label* in 1998 to the second in 2003. The Internet has changed the playing field dramatically. More people than ever before are taking the independent route. And there are more opportunities than ever for making money once you have a finished product. I don't want to just help you figure out how to release a record. That's the easy part. I want you to make money from it! So I did my best to gather as many new resources as I could find to provide the most ammo for accomplishing that.

I've rewritten and expanded this edition to reflect the current climate of the music industry in relation to independent labels. It includes many new interviews with an assortment of fantastic people who provide fresh ideas for successfully starting and running a record label. Of course, the biggest addition is several huge new chapters about how to market and promote digitally. The Internet offers options that we've waited many years to see develop. You can take advantage of digital marketing and promotion, even if you don't have a lot of cash.

I won't delude you. There are no miracle formulas for creating good music and marketing it successfully. Competition is stiffer as more people release music. Technology makes it cheaper and easier to create and sell music. The reality is, anyone can start a record label—i.e., call themselves one—but running it successfully is what strikes most people out of the ballgame. It takes work and perseverance, GREAT MUSIC, money, and patience to stay in the race. Have I hammered in the impression that it's not easy? Sorry—you'll have to work your butt off to succeed. But, when all the pieces are in place, opening your own record label can be a very satisfying endeavor.

This book was hard to write. My readers' needs vary. Many of you are new to the industry, while some are pros. Many of you have teeny budgets, while others have extensive financing. You're producing music in a variety of musical genres, requiring different strategies to market and promote. Many of you want a CD as a vehicle for attracting a deal with a larger label, to book gigs, and make money on the road to a record deal. Some of you are starting a label as a long-term business, for your own music or to market unsigned talent. I hope that as you read *Start & Run Your Own Record Label* you'll take from it what serves you and understand that I've included as much information as could fit, to cover a variety of needs.

To maximize your chances for success, immerse yourself in your music. I provide knowledge and tools to get a label running, but you have to plug in the specifics about the music you're marketing. Start compiling a list of publications and blogs that might review the music or profile your artist. Get active on websites with social networks and opportunities for exposure—now. Become aware of stores that might sell your products. Read trades to learn what's going on in the industry. The more knowledge you gather, the more prepared you'll be. If you learn everything you can about your genre, you can apply what's in this book to your music, with the best chance for success.

Successfully running a record label is doable, if you want it enough. I was a teacher. No experience. No contacts. No knowledge of the music business. While teaching in a New York City public school, my students laughed when I said I could make a rap record. Why not? These young people said I wasn't the right color or sex. So I had to prove that limitations can be overcome or they'd grow up allowing stereotypes to block them. Determined to prove they can be broken, I learned how to rap and eventually was labeled the "rappin' teach."

When I recorded "Girls Can Do," the kids loved it. People made promises, then disappeared. I paid folks to shop my music and hired consultants who gave crumbs instead of an education. My students got angry and advised revenge on those jerking me around, offering to slash tires and do other nasty things to those who didn't play fair with me. I decided to prove it's better to use the energy behind anger to do something positive for yourself. In my quest for a positive revenge, I opened Revenge Productions, then Revenge Records. It began of a fruitful career—very sweet revenge.

Clueless, I worked very hard to start Revenge Records and endured costly mistakes. Eventually I learned enough to establish my label. My first record was "Girls Can Do." A local distributor got it into stores. My second rap was "Wrap It Up." It sold more. I learned from every mistake. Sales enabled me to pay expenses from label income. My third record established Revenge. I wrote "Never Again," a dance track, and signed my first artist. It took off quickly in DJ circles. Distributors called me! Large labels offered to pick it up. I took a deal that gave credibility to my label and to me as a songwriter.

I continued signing artists, selling lots of records, and learning about the music business. People asked me for accurate information on breaking into the music industry. I put together music biz seminars and have been teaching them ever since. I also speak in colleges and at music conferences. My first book, *The Real Deal: How to Get Signed to a Record Label*, is in its second edition. That book led to *I Don't Need a Record Deal! Your Survival Guide for the Indie Music Revolution*.

If you get discouraged, remind yourself that if a teacher with no knowledge or contacts can start and run a record label, you can too! The "secret" is signing/having GREAT marketable music, learning the biz, and working your butt off. People whine about having day jobs, so time is limited. Hello! This is a business. You won't get more out of it than you put in. When I began, I taught full-time and ran a summer recreational program. I didn't sleep much but did the work. No one cuts you slack for having a day job. There are no shortcuts for the working class. A record label is a commitment. Start VERY slowly, and be realistic. If you want a record label, prepare to work hard. You must begin with GREAT music, or you'll never get out of the box.

From the get-go, network like crazy, both on- and offline. Get to industry seminars. Talk to everyone. Go to clubs and meet DJs, performers, and fans. Get friendly with folks who work in record stores that sell your genre. They were my best friends when I opened Revenge Records. Who knows more about selling music than those selling it? My friends in stores listened to my demos and advised me on what to release. They pushed my records and hooked me up with industry contacts. I wouldn't have successfully operated Revenge Records without their friendship and support!

The record industry has been in a slump. People say, "Forget opening an indie label. Business is bad." On the other hand, indie labels are heralded as the best way to break new music or get attention for talented artists who can't get a record deal. Yet I was warned it's not worth it anymore.

So why bother reading this book? Because opening your own label gives you a shot at breaking music that may have no other outlet. Because indie music breaks every day. Because it's a better shot than shopping music to a major. The most negative folks have been in the record biz for a long time. They remember how the industry was and want to market records as they used to. Things have changed, but many "old timers" haven't. So they see the industry negatively.

In contrast, those starting new labels are paving their way in today's market. Rather than fighting to fit into the old system, they're creating new options for marketing music. Many newer indie labels have found alternative marketing strategies and loyal fans. These indies effectively take advantage of all the online tools and opportunities. Watch your perspective. Lament the old days when stores were more helpful and CDs sold better, or jump into the digital revolution and learn new ways to successfully market music! Enough indie labels have proven that it works.

I've talked to many heads of indie labels of all sizes, who share their knowledge and experience in this book. I believe that an indie label is the best way to break new artists. To do this, prepare to bite the bullet, work extremely hard, have money in the bank or a day job, and be totally passionate about the music. Opening your own label is a chance to control the destiny of music you love. Passion is the fuel that keeps many going.

Today's market offers more opportunities to make money as an indie than ever. MUCH MORE! As most music is edged out of commercial radio, consumers hunger for music they love, not what they're told they must love because it's all they get. A big advantage that indie labels have over the majors is they can sell a fraction of what majors need to, to turn a profit. A major might drop an artist who "only" sells 30,000 records, or even 430,000, but an indie can make a decent profit with much less than those numbers. A major label's overhead is substantially greater: The promotional fuel needed to drive the big machine costs stupidly spent mega-dollars. Indies can keep costs down and therefore sell many fewer units and feel happily solvent.

Educate yourself as much as possible. I'll refer to my other titles throughout the book. I've been criticized for doing it. I've seen review comments saying I should put everything in each book. Sorry, but I want each title to have new info. This book already stretched my word limit, so there was no room. *The Real Deal: How to Get Signed to a Record Label* has more detailed, basic info, focusing on artist development. The chapters on networking, finding managers, agents, etc, and basics of a press kit are much more detailed, and it gives an overall education about how the industry works. There's also a resource list at the back of the book.

I Don't Need a Record Deal!: Your Survival Guide for the Indie Music Revolution focuses on how to create a whole variety of income streams. It has a huge section on licensing music, putting both a domestic and European tour together, and many alternative venues that aren't clubs but that pay better money, with dozens of interviews with people who do these things. I also have a full chapter on avoiding music-related injuries and one on how to get your head in the right place—how to build confidence, ask in ways that get results, handle rejection, develop the fortitude to persevere, etc. It strongly complements *Start & Run Your Own Record Label*.

The key to being successful as an indie label lies in finding your niche market and working it in every way you can. Indie music is selling very well. VERY! I'm not asking you to take my word. That's why I interviewed the heads of many labels and indie artists that do it. Some might sell better online than in a chain of record stores. Some sell mainly by touring. The college market has been kind to indie music. Commercial radio hasn't. If you can accept the music industry as it is, and learn to work around the big major machines, you can find a comfortable home for the music you want to market. It is possible to break through the BS of the system.

There are more inexpensive marketing and promotion tools than ever. Releasing music digitally is easy and <u>cheap</u>. Many labels just do that. So your overhead can be nil! Now there are fewer excuses you can use for not getting your music out! The biggest expense is time. Believe me, I know how tough that can be to make. But when you're driven by your passion for your music or the music of other artists, you have to make it. If you're prepared to work hard to develop a fan base, or work with your artists to achieve it, and do as much as possible to promote and market them, you have a chance of joining the ranks of those who are happily running successful indie labels. The tools to achieve this are on the following pages.

CHAPTER 1

Deciding to Start a Record Label

D o you have a great act you believe in? Are you frustrated by the lack of response or crappy offers from record labels you pitch? The allure of a major label gets overshadowed by the reality of those deals: Few artists make much money on major labels, most get low priority, promotional support is scarce, and artist development is history. So what can you do? Take charge by releasing music yourself! Sonicbids founder Panos Panay says if you're an artist who wants to go the indie route, do it! He explains:

> *Artists today may never be an Elton John or Madonna and sell fifty million units. But ultimately, I believe that as an artist you have the tools and ability to make a living out of playing music and doing what you're great at. That starts with recording your own stuff and putting it out on your own, which is controlling your destiny. Cost of production, marketing, and distribution has gone down tremendously. You no longer need to look elsewhere for the quality production, distribution, and promotion that major labels used to give. It's foolish for an artist today to always look to someone else to help them. You owe it to yourself to be the driver and CEO of your own business. That doesn't mean don't hire other people to help. It means that the era when you were entirely dependent on someone else to be able to practice what*

you're good at in life is over. You are in the driver's seat. It's paramount, in my opinion, that artists educate themselves about the world out there, invest in learning about the new playing field, and capitalize on it.

People start their own record labels for various reasons. Some common ones are:

- Wanting a CD to promote music to attract a record deal
- Wanting to stay independent and have a product to sell at gigs, pitch for use in films and television, and sell
- Wanting to own a label as a vehicle for discovering and developing talent
- After having worked in the industry for years, wanting to use one's hard work and contacts to establish one's own business

Why Start Your Own Label?

Because you can! More than ever, independent record labels are experiencing success on many levels. Jim Pettid, owner of Media Services (www.mediaomaha.com), a CD and DVD manufacturer says:

I really believe that independent labels are the future of music. The major label business plan is slowly becoming obsolete. The independents are at the front of the pack, able and willing to recreate the music business plan to make it work for not just themselves but for artists and fans.

The music industry has changed dramatically since my last edition. Eric Speck, founder of Ace Fu Records (profile in Chapter 3), says, "I think the music industry has changed more in the last five years than it has in the last twenty-five years on how things are done from deals, to how bands are marketed—the whole process." There are many small labels; collectively, they represent an impressive presence in the music industry. Bill Werde, executive editor for *Billboard* magazine, explains:

The indie market share is growing as the major label market share shrinks. The blockbusters of yesteryear seem to be a thing of the past. The top-selling albums now sell two to three million copies, not five, or eight million copies like they once did. So the huge stars are getting smaller. In comparison, the smaller stars are getting a little bit bigger. We're now in the age of the niche star, where you can have a nice career selling 100,000 to 200,000 copies of your release if your business model is adjusted. Right now I think a lot of the smartest innovations in the music business, the most creative ways of launching a career and selling a record, are largely happening in the indie space.

Many people think major labels completely dominate the music industry. Many labels are part of their bigger entity. It's the same with indies. When independent labels are looked at together, they're a sizable presence in the music industry. Rich Bengloff, president of A2IM (www.a2im.org), an organization for independent labels, says:

The Independent music label sector now comprises over 30 percent of the music industry's market share in the U.S. and has, based on Nielsen SoundScan, increased as a percentage of the .U.S. marketplace in six of the last eight years.

Many artists are choosing not to chase record deals since there are many more ways than ever to market on their own. Jeff Price, founder of spinART Records and Tunecore, a digital distribution company, says that the resources are available:

I had no background when I started spinART. It was trial by fire. As long as you approach starting a label understanding how you can do it in a cost-efficient manner, there are turnkey solutions that have others doing a lot of the work for you. I believe finding a company (like a record label) to exploit your music is on its way out. The services-and-products model is on its way in. You can go to a website and get music industry in a box.

If you do this, you're not alone, A2IM offers support and benefits to indies. Bengloff explains:

A2IM *is a not-for-profit organization that serves the independent music label community as a unified voice, representing independent music labels' interests in the marketplace, in the media, on Capitol Hill, and as part of the global music community as a member of the World Independent Network, an organization with nineteen participating country trade organizations. A2IM's support for the independent music label community is done via lobbying, messaging commerce opportunities, and providing member services, including education and participation discounts for events and services. The organization's board of directors is comprised of a diverse group of the music labels, in terms of label sizes, genres of music, and geographic locations.*

Major labels don't nurture acts. Artist development ranges from slight to nonexistent. Indie labels are considered the most innovative segment of the industry, usually the first to start a trend. According to Werde, indies have more flexibility:

Indies tend to have fewer rights issues. Small companies can be a lot more nimble than giant corporations. Major labels' hands can be a little more tied with what they can do in terms of leveraging an artist's catalog or an artist's current release. Everything tends to be a little more stipulated or ironclad. I think the indies have been quicker to experiment. Maybe they have less to lose based on their top-line revenues. Their business models are geared a little differently as well. Major labels are still looking for those blockbuster albums to sustain the ones that don't hit that way. I think indie labels are taking a more project-by-project view of success. For each album that comes out, they consider how they're going to get a return investment on it. They're less willing to drop a few balls in order to hit a home run with just one or two.

Majors need to sell MUCH bigger numbers than an indie, which can be solvent with a fraction of those sales. Indies recognize there are many great artists who may not sell the kind of numbers the majors want but are still worthy of being released. Not every artist will sell a half million albums, but there are many thousands of artists who can make a full-time living by selling much fewer records. According to Jeff Price:

> *Major labels need to have grand-slam home runs, or a record is deemed a failure. The definition of success for independents varies, depending on how big or small the act is. There's only one definition for the majors. At spinART we thought on the lines of whether the act was profitable, or did we at least break even? Did they have a future?*

Rolando Cuellar, founder of Roland Entertainment, saw great potential for his thirteen-year-old cousin, rapper Baby Jay. He believed his guidance could help him make a huge positive impact on young people. Baby Jay was bullied in school, came from a broken home, and saw his brothers incarcerated. Yet he pushed himself to do well in school, and his rap lyrics reflect a positive path. Through networking, Cuellar brought Baby Jay to the attention of Peter Yarrow (Peter, Paul & Mary) several years ago and made the "Don't Laugh at Me" video for Peter's organization, Operation Respect, an initiative to combat bullying. Cuellar has gotten Baby Jay onto large stages, into schools in many states, and has generated many other creative opportunities with networking and hard work. Cuellar began in a boy band, handling all the business, booking, marketing, and radio promotions. He says:

> *My attorney said I would succeed in this business, if not as an artist than as a music executive because of my passion, determination, faith, and integrity. When the group broke up I continued my education in music business. I had a vision of finding, creating, and developing positive/clean hip-hop artists for mainstream. I wanted to take hip-hop back to days when music was about social change and making a positive impact, with an innovative, modern sound. Baby Jay's life story was very inspiring. I felt bringing him into schools could make a positive impact. So I made it happen.*

Since beginning work with Baby Jay, Cuellar has signed several more artists and continues seeking creative ways to market them. Opportunities for marketing music are there for those who pursue them! As I elaborated on in my book *I Don't Need a Record Deal!*, there are unlimited ways to create lucrative income streams from musical talent. Independent labels are more concerned with developing talent and are more passion-driven for the music, compared to the major label model of being totally focused on profit. John Szuch, founder of Deep Elm Records (profile in Chapter 3), explains:

> *I was with a bunch of major label A & R reps. They said that anything they didn't feel would go gold—a half million copies— would be dropped or not be considered seriously by the majors, because that's pretty much their break-even point. They're spending gobs of money in the studio, making videos that cost a few hundred thousand, minimum. If we license a record, we can be successful on a financial basis pretty much after one thousand copies are sold. We've never looked at what we release on a sales basis. I've passed on plenty of music that we thought would sell great because we weren't into it and couldn't stand behind it proudly. The smaller artists, with a more limited fan base, need our support too. As long as we love it, we're interested in helping them out.*

Many folks start a label when they can't get signed. Since I couldn't get a deal, I chose to do it myself. Large labels watch indies, which can help you get your foot through a previously locked door. Others start a record label to establish a solid business in the music industry. Hip-hop artist El-P cofounded Definitive Jux Records (profile in Chapter 3) in 1996. His success as an independent is inspirational. He says:

> *We don't want to be on a major label. We are proud of this independent route. This is a long-term plan. We're addicted to the creativity, control, and the hands-on experience of learning how to become an adult as opposed to becoming someone with a patriarch, which is how I look at a lot of artists who are involved with major labels. Once I realized the margins between what you have to sell on a major label and what you have to sell on an independent label to make the same amount of money—once I really broke them down mathematically—I realized I never wanted to be signed as an artist on a major label. For years, no one was saying or even thinking about this. We were the first group to come out and put a voice to that logic and make it a movement. It's not an anti–major-label thing. It's self-empowerment. My goal is to get where I wanted to go on my terms, the right way. And to reap the benefits of my hard work, and also to make the mistakes.*

While a record deal is still considered a brass ring, it can tarnish quickly. Few artists are satisfied and fewer make money. John Robinson, president of Shaman Work Recordings, started the company in 2003. They have a diverse variety of releases, working with musicians including legendary hip-hop artists like CL Smooth, MF DOOM, and Wise Intelligent. He's built a worldwide following via DJ promos, a retail catalog, press, and Internet marketing. Robinson says he keeps going because:

> I am truly inspired by those brilliant artist and great people of our past who came before us and worked so hard to get things to where they are now. I feel that once I give up I fail, and I can't fail!

Since I wrote the first edition of this book, more signed recording artists have left their labels and are taking control of their musical destiny. Some were dropped. Some break their contracts or don't sign again when the agreement ends. Singer/songwriter Aimee Mann chose the independent route. Her manager, Michael Hausman, says:

> Aimee finally realized that it was one of these bad relationships where they were always looking for something from her that she wasn't able to deliver. That was getting in the way of creating music. Creatively she came to a point where she wanted to be free. She actually had pretty low expectations at that point as far as sales. I did a rough budget. We figured we'd start small but ended up doing much better than we thought we would. Not only has it been incredibly successful for her artistically—she can basically do what she wants—but financially it's been more successful as well.

When Hausman realized how difficult it was for individual artists to have their own record companies, he created United Musicians, a distribution, marketing, and promotion co-op for artist-owned labels (see Chapter 4 for details). Recording artist Eric Hutchinson had a label deal that fell apart and learned a valuable lesson. He explains:

> At the time I thought, "here we go, taking off." To have everything fall apart was frustrating. It took a while to rebound and decide if I still wanted to try again. It refocused and reminded me of why I liked doing my music—connecting with audiences and writing songs.

I didn't get into it for glamour and celebrity. Now I understand that things will be up and down, and I have to appreciate when it's going well and not get caught up in it. I always wanted a record deal. I thought it meant that you'd made it. The model is changing. I'm still proud now.

Hutchinson began again with his own independent label, Let's Break Records. After blogger Perez Hilton recommended his album, his buzz and digital sales heated up online. He recently signed a deal with Warner Bros. but says he still thinks of himself as an independent artist since it isn't a traditional artist deal. He's keeping his imprint label, Let's Break Records. Independent success motivates creative deals! Passion for music drives people to start a label. Scott Krokoff recently left his corporate job as a lawyer to begin Hypochondriac Records. He explains:

I am willing to give up a lucrative career as a tax attorney in order to start my own record label and pursue a music career as an independent artist because my heart has always been and will always be in the world of music. It is where my passion lies, not to mention my drive and talent. The money I can make working full-time as an attorney, taking into account the stress and long hours, cannot fully replace the joy I feel when I write a song, play an instrument, perform on stage, or record in the studio.

Daniel Glass (profile in Chapter 3) launched Glassnote Entertainment after holding top positions with Chrysalis, SBK, Universal, and Artemis. He wanted full control with his own label. He explains:

I've been involved with four companies in the past that morphed into something else. Chrysalis was sold to EMI. SBK, which was a tremendous label, was also sold to EMI. Doug Morris and I started a little label called Rising Tide Records, which quickly morphed into Universal. That was a year into our success. And Artemis morphed into an investment model. So I thought, at this point in my life I've been well trained. I couldn't build a company again, see it be sold prematurely, and not be on the controlling end of the creativity, the business part, and the payday. Also, I'd never seen a time when the atmosphere and climate was so perfect for independent labels and intimate, small operations. We had funding and the know-how to attract great artists and a great team.

I must repeat a story from my book *The Real Deal*. Country legend Jerry Jeff Walker had a gold album in 1973 when signed to MCA. In the '80s, he and his wife Susan went to Nashville with his new CD to discuss a new contract. Susan Walker says:

> *I told the head of MCA we had a CD completed and wanted to see if he'd like to release it. He said, as he sat pompously with his feet up, "I'll take it home, smoke a joint, and see if I can figure out a formula." I was furious. It was so insulting to Jerry's artistic integrity. He'd already been in the business for twenty-five years. But that's the way labels are. I told Jerry Jeff, "That's it. We're starting our own label." I want to thank every one of them for not signing Jerry Jeff, because it's been very lucrative for us.*

It's easy to get disillusioned with being signed to a major label. Independent labels can be flexible and get creative with their marketing. Other labels were founded for different reasons. Damon Dash, founder of Roc-A-Fella Records, says:

> *I was a manager first . . . on Atlantic. They didn't know how to market music to the street—they didn't know how to paint that picture or promote it to the people who were painting the picture, so I had to learn it myself. In learning that, I thought I might as well do it myself. When learning the money and point structure, I felt, why should I get 20 percent of twelve points instead of giving out 20 percent and having 80 percent? I was doing all the work for a little bit of money. I was shopping Jay-Z and wasn't getting the response I wanted. People weren't reacting as fast as I thought they should. We pressed up our own white label, which means it's not available commercially. We gave it to DJs and the underground radio stations. They started playing it. Being that we got a response, we put up some money and did a video. Then we got more response and buildup, so we did another white label. Eventually we got one of our records added to radio in full rotation.*

The Upside of Starting Your Own Label

If I had to sum up the advantages of starting your own record label in one word, I would choose CONTROL. With your own label, decisions and choices are in your hands. You may not have the resources that majors do, but freedom of choice and action can give you the edge indies are known for. Larger labels get bogged down in red tape. Indies can act quickly. Majors have more money but often waste it. Today, there are more alternative opportunities than ever. Valerie Vigoda, electronic violinist and singer with the trio GrooveLily explains:

> It's exhilarating, and also overwhelming. There are so many (non-musical) things to do—I find myself working longer hours than anyone I know—but I love it. This is a wonderful time to be independent in music. Consolidation in the industry has put a chokehold on commercial radio, concert venues, and record stores, so the independent music scene is growing incredibly fast in reaction. People are seeking alternatives to the shrinking song lists on their radio dials. New nontraditional music venues, such as house concerts, are popping up everywhere. There are twice as many music festivals in the U.S. as there were only ten years ago! Independent, grassroots promotion is working for more and more artists and bands, many of whom have been dropped by record labels in the past few years. The upshot is, there is a middle ground that did not used to exist! There is a third option, between blockbuster chart hits and penury-independent success.

Independent success. Achieving that is sweet! GrooveLily has now found their way into musical theater as another avenue for their music. Major label success may disappoint. You can sell a half million CDs and not make money. Without selling huge numbers, label support dries up. You can sell 100,000 copies and be treated as a failure. Sell that yourself and you'll be thrilled if you're careful about spending, which you control. Sue Baran, manager for indie band Push Play (profile in Chapter 3), says that so far they've turned down major label offers. She's open but prepared to do it herself, explaining:

> I found the grassroots effort was working, and since I had invested so much personal time into the "Push Play for Purpose" project

[more in Chapter 3], I did not want to stop it midstream. What the major label offered Push Play at that time was something I was already doing for the band. Believe me, I don't disregard a major label offer. If it was a solid offer, something that could actually make the band a living, I would have accepted it. But the timing was not right. Down the road I would certainly revisit any major label offer that was appealing. I know this is a business and money has to be made by the label, but I think that the major label deal offers will get sweeter as the band becomes more accomplished. So, I am willing to wait it out with them and grow the fan base region by region.

Being the boss, you can be more practical about how money is used for promotion. Jay Woods, senior vice president and general manager of New West Records (profile in Chapter 3) likes being able to do artist development:

An advantage is our ability to stay focused on projects for longer periods of time and being more personally involved in all aspects of the business. We get really close to the projects and stay with them for a long time. We don't have the luxury to throw something against the wall to see if it sticks, so to speak. We need everything to have a certain amount of success, or it doesn't make sense for us to do it. Essentially, we're spending our money.

Artists waste a lot of energy convincing people how it should be done. Michael Hausman says, "We decide what to do and do it." You can get a record out quickly instead of waiting for a label to decide. Majors are notorious for producing albums that never see the light of a record store. Releases get stalled. Plus, many artists on major labels get little promotion. El-P likes being able to take chances, rather than using recycled ideas as many labels do:

At the very least, what I come out with is trial and error—learning something. It doesn't appeal to my personality to be involved in a situation where you're an artist and the label is literally like a giant robot with thirty levels of technology and one human somewhere, if you can find them. Taking care of your own destiny is a powerful thing. I believe an independent label has to have a spirit behind it—a philosophy and an idea. If it's, "I want to make money," that

*means that you are simply a chip off of Daddy's block, but without
the resources, and Daddy doesn't want to talk to you. I look at it a
different way. I believe in the consistent release of quality, creative,
artistic, beautiful music—that's my only philosophy.*

Five Times August is the solo project of Brad Skistimas. He's sold over
100,000 digital downloads independently and has gotten many song
placements from his first album on popular TV shows. Kelly Vandergriff,
Five Times August manager, says, "Brad and I both really enjoy and
embrace being independent. Brad is 100 percent in control of everything
he does, and that alone is a huge bonus to doing things this way."
Jay Woods adds:

> *We won a Grammy for our label in 2001. We were thrilled to be
> nominated. That was enough. Delbert McClinton won for best
> contemporary blues, but we were part of it in some way. You walk in
> people's offices and there's a zillion Grammys and gold records. Well,
> we've got one! That's a thrill.*

Ezra Idlet of the popular group Trout Fishing in America says that people
wanted to hear their songs, so they recorded them and made them
available on Trout Records (see profile in Chapter 3): "We thought we
might be able to pick up a little extra change if we did it." Now it's a
thriving label, and he's happy:

> *You see more money on each record sold than you would on a big
> label. You're closer to the accounting process. My wife is doing the
> accounting. That's more secure than somebody that's just pushing
> numbers. When it comes to recording our record, we have more say
> in what goes on it.*

The Downside of Starting Your Own Label

When it comes to starting your own label, I've found that the flipside
of having control can be frustration. It's frustrating when you don't
have a large enough budget to do what you know needs to be done.
It's frustrating when it's hard to get good distribution and sometimes
even harder waiting to get paid. It's especially frustrating when you

have a record that you know absolutely belongs on the radio, and you can't get airplay. If you're also the artist, the frustration of the business side of running a record label interferes with creativity. However, Mark Carpentieri, president and owner of MC Records, says the disadvantage has a bright side, too:

> *You don't have the paternal person writing the check for you or providing a more established background. It's nice to get that kind of extra help or push if you have something that's really cooking. But with money comes demand. Perhaps, in the overall picture, it's best not to have that if you need to adjust quickly or sign who you think is the right artist.*

Singer/songwriter David M. Bailey says his biggest disadvantage is "being completely overwhelmed. Blessings create work. I don't think people realize how much time goes into it." Many of you will start out like I did, as a jack of all trades at the label if you can't afford to pay a staff. I was the "staff" for Revenge Records, from president to stock girl. Ezra Idlet says:

> *It's a lot of work. We had to learn the business, more than I would want. My interest is the music. We see more money out of each individual unit that we sell, but we don't sell as many units. But, we make a living at it. That's good.*

If you want to do it yourself, find ways to do it yourself! You can. I did. They exist. Look at all the indie labels that are surviving. As Valerie Vigoda says, you can find ways to be independent and not be poor. There's never been a better time to take control of your music, or music that you believe in, and create a business around it. Accepting the reality helps you to conquer the pitfalls!

The future of independents has brightened substantially since I wrote the first edition of this book. El-P is certain that independence is the way to go:

> *This is the industry that's based on cult fan base, that's based on grassroots promotion. There is no event marketing. We don't have to come up with splashy, explosive ways to sell a new artist,*

because we know what we're going to do with one. We're going to tour him for a straight year. I'm a businessman. I wouldn't be doing it if it were ethereal—all about heart, struggle, and power. It's more that I believe in my heart of hearts that this is the industry that will be surviving when everything collapses.

And Tony Brummel, president of Victory Records, loves the free spiritedness of the business:

I love putting out independent music. I feel like our founding fathers when I wake up every day, as ridiculous as it sounds, because we really are fighting against a system. We're renegades, rebels, in the trenches, and they're not. It's a fight every day. But we're conditioned to that. It's not something that grinds us down.

CHAPTER 2

Setting Up Your Record Label

Whether you're starting a record label to attract a label deal or sign other artists, you'll have a better shot at success by approaching it as a real business. This may sound intimidating. It did to me. I've included an assortment of resources in this chapter that can make the business of running a label easier. Keep in mind that marketing music, even if it's your own, is a business, unless you don't want to make money. A business mindset instills the right attitude. Developing business sense can mean the difference between making money and running your label as a hobby. Eric Hutchinson adds:

> *I think people fail to take it seriously enough. That's a big problem for me. I consider myself pretty professional. That was really the difference. I started looking at it as a day-to-day job as opposed to a hobby or just some sort of career I was trying to do. How can you show up to a show drunk? You wouldn't show up to the office wasted. But the music industry has somehow decided it's okay to get drunk or do drugs and then go perform. When people don't take it seriously enough, there's a lot of wasted talent out there.*

Setting Goals and Strategies

Many variables come into play in running a record label. Buyers don't magically appear. If you want to sell product, first identify how you'll sell it—without a belief that a good product guarantees sales. The only sure thing is that you need to work your butt off. Taking care of business puts you in a better position to have a record label with longevity. So remove the stars from your eyes and put on your business cap!

Preplanning

Preplanning increases your chances of ending up with a viable record label. Before starting a record label, create long- and short-term goals. Too many folks record music without thinking about what they need to do once it's ready. All they know is that they have good material they want to sell. So they press it up or put it online without a clue about what to do with it. An album can die before it reaches the starting line. Prepare in advance! Opening your own record label, even if it's only to put out your own material, should be approached as starting a business.

Writing a business plan (see below) helps you set goals and define your expectations. It's critical to think ahead. If you're a creative person, it can be painful to force yourself to do business stuff. Biz on the brain definitely makes it hard for me to be creative. I'd much rather someone else handled mine. But life doesn't allow us to skip the business part if we want to make money from our creativity. Dealing with business matters now opens doors for your music later. In the long run, success can free you from a lot of such work. Once you're making money, hire people to handle some of it.

Force yourself to sit down and really think through your goals. Where would you like to be a year after pressing your first record? Where do you plan to sell your records? Who's going to buy them? Will your label be an ongoing business or exist only until you get an artist deal? Do you want to be affiliated with a larger label or stay independent? Do you have access to more financing if needed? Marketing your own music can be profitable, as long as you take it seriously as a business.

Identifying Your Market

The key to a successful record label, in my eyes, is to find your market and figure out how to reach it. Too many folks record an album they love, without giving thought to who the target audience is. The first step in starting a record label is to identify the group most likely to buy your product, such as college students, adults over forty, etc., and the avenue for promoting and marketing your product so that audience knows about it.

Gregg Latterman, president of Aware Records, advises, "Understand who your audience is. Intelligently target that audience."

How will people become familiar with your artist? Is the artist playing in live clubs where CDs can be sold? Will it work on college radio? Determine the outlets for your genre, and gather resources from the onset of the project. Can you fit in outside of traditional markets? Can you develop a good Internet presence? Are you hiring promoters or publicists? This record label game isn't just about good music; it's about finding a market for it and creating a plan to reach those potential buyers. Music lovers won't buy your records if they don't know your artist exists. You must let them know.

Registering Your Company

The first step toward starting your own business is to decide how you want it registered. Should you incorporate or just file a business certificate with your local county? (See below.) Are you working with someone? You better have a written agreement! It can be as simple as a letter stating the terms of everything decided between the two of you, or it can be a formal partnership.

A corporation keeps your company separate from your personal business. Many labels incorporate immediately to protect personal assets from lawsuits. A limited liability company, commonly known as an LLC, offers an alternative to creating a partnership or a corporation. It provides the corporate advantages of limited liability but has better tax options and more flexible partnership arrangements. Determine your needs and possible liability based on your circumstances. If you choose to incorporate or create an LLC, register through the state in which you operate your business. Get specific information from your state.

If you choose not to incorporate, you can register your business with the appropriate office in your local county. Counties vary in their procedures as well as fees. Check your local phone book under the listing for county government offices. Often a business certificate is issued through the county clerk's office. Apply for a business license, follow the instructions on the form, pay the fee, and you'll be issued a certificate that's considered a "doing business as" (DBA) license. Some call it a fictitious name certificate. This enables you to open a bank account in your business's name.

When I started Revenge Records, I spoke with both my lawyer and accountant. After assessing my situation, we decided I didn't need to incorporate right away. For this book, I asked both a lawyer and an accountant to give their points of view on incorporating and to provide more specifics. According to Wallace Collins, Esq., an entertainment/intellectual property lawyer in private practice in New York City:

> As a practical matter, sooner or later you may want to incorporate in order to limit your personal liability. If properly employed, a corporate entity can be used as a shield to protect you and can have certain tax advantages. In most cases, however, it is not really necessary to incorporate at the start of your career. The law of most states does require that, if you use a name professionally other than your personal name, then you should file a business certificate (DBA) in the county in which you reside or do business under that name. Also, as a business matter, the individual members of a group or company may want to enter into a partnership agreement between and among themselves in order to spell out the particulars with respect to certain rights such as songwriting and ownership of the trademark rights in the name. Otherwise, any group of two or more persons operating a business for profit is considered a partnership for the purposes of applying the laws of partnership under the laws of most states. These laws generally employ a rule of sharing evenly in profits and losses, including all assets of the business. As a corporation, you create a separate legal entity that you own as a shareholder but for which you work as an officer and/or director and draw a salary or dividends. In the event that the corporation, despite being properly documented and operated, encounters financial problems, the claim would be against the corporation and its assets and not your personal assets (e.g., the house, car, and boat that you purchased with your salary for the five years that the corporation operated successfully).

Anthony Orlando, a certified public accountant practicing in New York, adds:

> The decision to incorporate most of the time depends on the net worth of the person who is starting the label. If that person has

substantial assets, which may need to be protected, they probably want to incorporate. Incorporating adds a level of both accounting and tax complexity that a small label grossing under $100,000 doesn't really need. Not that it won't do them good, but there are costs and taxes associated with a corporation that they may not need to incur. Operating as a sole-proprietorship is really for accounting simplicity. When it appears a business will gross over $100,000 a year on a consistent basis, you definitely want to start thinking about incorporating. Again, there may not be significant tax advantages, but you do want the personal protection a corporation offers. Another form of business entity that gives you personal liability protection from your business creditors is a limited liability company [LLC]. This is a hybrid between a partnership and a corporation. It shields the owners from liability, and the income or loss is actually taxed to the owners, so there is no separate corporate-level tax. Also, it is much more flexible as far as how profits, losses, and ownership percentages can be split. You can basically come up with any formula you want as long as you put it into your partnership agreement.

Everyone's circumstances are different. Before deciding how to set up your business, I highly recommend consulting with both a lawyer and an accountant. If money is too tight, contact someone at SCORE (more below). Talk over your options and make a decision based on what seems to suit your needs best. Every state varies in its laws and policies, which is why legal advice is important.

I called the IRS and was told that anyone other than a sole proprietor (someone running an unincorporated business with no partners) with no employees needs to fill out form SS-4, an application for an employer identification number (EIN). If tax stuff intimidates you, as it does me, get help by calling the IRS at 800-829-3676. They'll send you a free business tax kit, which explains all forms that may need to be filed. You can also call the appropriate number in your state to get a resale number. That means you won't pay taxes on supplies that will eventually be resold as part of your product.

Don't make a decision to go one way instead of another because you're lazy or uncomfortable about a direction you don't know enough about. When you take one step at a time and learn as you go, business eventually starts to make sense!

Developing Your Business

Once you've decided to start a record label and chosen a direction for your business, your mindset should be the same as that of someone starting any business. Read books covering business in general. Locate free resources.

Business Resources

Many organizations offer support for startup businesses. Search online. The Small Business Administration (SBA) offers quality information. In many large cities, they have a program called Service Corps of Retired Executives (SCORE), a nonprofit organization for which retired busines speople volunteer time to give advice. For more information, check www.score.org. I once went and had a retired accountant to advise me. You can also email a counselor with business questions. All for free!

As discussed in the next section, starting up a new business requires a business plan. There are also resources for writing one. My SCORE counselor helped me. Check adult education programs and libraries for free or inexpensive classes. Check the SBA (www.sba.gov) to see what programs you can use in person or online. Their Small Business Development Centers (SBDC) provide free or low-cost support in writing a business plan. The SBA itself has a free Small Business Planner with valuable information on various topics, including how to write a business plan.

Writing a Business Plan

From a business standpoint, a business plan is essential. It's an outline of what you need to do. Even if no one else sees it, it helps develop steps for getting your label up and running. You'll need one if you try to get financing for your label. Few people or financial institutions will loan money without having seen one. If you're working with a partner, it's good to have all your intentions on paper. Formally organizing goals helps you stay focused. Following typical patterns laid down in business highlights things you should keep in mind. A business plan can be used as a checklist for starting your label. It shows people, including yourself, that you're serious about what you're doing.

How do you begin to write a business plan for a record label? Go to a bookstore and browse through books on business plans. Buy the one you like most. Use what works for you. Key elements that are essential to cover include the following:

- Start with a summary of your project. This should include who you are (e.g., a producer who's worked in the industry for ten years; a musician with a fan base; a studio owner with lots of talent coming through). It should also include short- and long-range goals. Describe your strongest assets for accomplishing each goal. What do you have going for you that will enhance your chances for success? How do you plan to finance your business?

- Provide a brief history of your project. How did you get to the point of starting a label? Specify how your label will be managed. Will you have a staff? Are you planning to hire independent promoters? Be very specific about how the record label will be run and structured. A corporation or DBA? A sole proprietorship, partnership, or LLC? Be very clear about the path your business will take.

- Describe the music industry as a larger picture and how you plan to fit into it. What type of music will you put out, and who will be your audience? Specifically identify your niche. Why will they buy your records? How will your product hold up against competition? How are labels that are marketing similar music doing it? Are you offering something unique? How will you get distribution? What online opportunities are there? How will you price your products? Will you have a budget for advertising or publicity? Answer these for your own reference, too. Just believing in your product isn't enough to market it properly. Thousands of others have the same belief in their music. What sets you apart from them?

- Include a description of all facilities you may use and what equipment you'll need. Will you operate from home or from a separate office? Where will you record your material? Where will CDs be stored? Will you buy supplies to get started? What's your growth potential? Do you plan to expand in the future or just use your label to market yourself? What's your projected timeline? Guesstimate how long you'll need for each step of the process, from the studio to profit. Include any critical risks or problems that may arise.

- Include a detailed financial summary. If you're looking for financial backing, this section is especially important. Estimate the amount of money you expect to need over the next three years, and how much you expect to take in. Create a very specific budget, taking time to list every expense you can think of. Don't forget phone bills; shipping; promotional copies to give away; transportation to get your artist to promotional gigs; printing; press kits; and postage, bank, lawyer, and accounting fees. Check online to estimate costs. Providing financial info is probably the hardest part of preparing a business plan. Be realistic. Estimate higher than you think you'll need to allow for unexpected expenses. Be conservative about expected sales and what your cash flow will be. There's no sense in playing games on paper. Don't be too optimistic in your assessment.

Get help with the actual writing of your business plan. As already noted, there are resources available. Do what you can on your own, and then get support from an SBA, SBDC, other organizations in your area or your accountant.

Choosing a Company Name and Logo

It's good to have a catchy or unique name for your record label, so people will recognize it once you've released some music. When you have artists doing reasonably well, people will pay attention when your label has a new release. Those who've enjoyed acts on your label may want to see what else you put out. It helps if they can remember the name.

Do what you can to check that your choice hasn't been taken by another label. Some folks do a formal search to make sure. There are trademark search companies and lawyers who'll do this for you. Or use a search engine. The Internet makes it easier. If you're planning to run your label for the long haul, the more thoroughly you check now, the safer you'll be.

A nice logo for your label helps brand your identity more. It can be simple—a piece of graphic art that presents the name of your label in a unique way. I designed the letters in Revenge Records to look like lightning bolts and gave a rough sketch to a graphic designer friend. People recognized my label from the logo. I even put it on T-shirts. A nice logo adds to the professional look of your company. An original piece of artwork, however simple, can give your label individuality. If you can't afford to pay someone to design it, try to find a student at a college with a graphics program.

Trademarking Your Label's Name/Logo

If you trademark the name of your company, you'll have protection against others using your name for a record label. Logos and the names of recording artists can also be trademarked. If you consider using a name or logo on merchandise (hats, T-shirts, etc.), get it registered from the get-go to protect against bootlegging.

Trademarks can be registered by state or nationally. Federal registration offers the best protection. You can reserve a name you want to trademark in advance by filing an intent to use it. Don't do this lightly. You have to intend to use it within a reasonable timeframe. Before filing for federal registration, plan to use the mark for interstate business transactions. Only using it locally doesn't qualify you. It's best to do a search to check that no one else has trademarked your name. The U.S. Patent and Trademark Office has libraries to do a search yourself, and now you can also search online on their website at www.uspto.gov.

To register your federal trademark, file an application with the U.S. Patent and Trademark Office in Washington, DC. It takes about a year to come through. Costs run at least several hundred dollars for legal and filing fees. Registering a trademark in the U.S. doesn't offer protection in other countries. If you plan to do business internationally and want protection, apply for trademark status in each country. Laws vary, so consult with a lawyer who's knowledgeable about international trademarks.

Taking Your Business Seriously

Numerous indie labels start each week. It's hard to earn respect. If you have a reasonable budget and serious contacts, you're way ahead of the majority of new labels. If you have a low budget, no contacts, and little music industry experience, looking like a serious business sets you apart from other small labels. Taking your label seriously as a business lets people know you intend to make your label solvent, even if you sell CDs out of a car and live on tuna and Mom's generosity because that's all you can afford. So you and your label share a small bedroom in your cousin's house. Nobody has to know!

When I started my label, I ran it out of a house I shared. Boxes of product doubled for end tables, for lack of space. But I took myself seriously enough to conduct my label professionally. In the eyes of business contacts, I was doing well. Having a separate office generates a more a professional image, but many of you won't have one, at least not at first. In this case, be careful about details. It's hard to take your business seriously when it's also where you play and sleep. But you have to! Don't let others answer the phone you use for business. Nowadays it's easier than when I started because there are so many electronic devices you can just carry with you. Have a businesslike message on your voicemail. Use a cell phone for all business calls if necessary.

Creating a Successful Image

Make every effort to give off an air of success. When anyone other than a close friend asks how your label is doing, reply with a version of "very well, thank you." People want to help those who they think are successful. Don't share your problems. If you create a façade of success, there's a better chance of achieving it. From a spiritual perspective, you get back what you give out. If you treat yourself as successful, you'll have a better chance of it coming true.

I confess—I've stretched the truth. My dad took my first record to stores in Miami. Many took a few copies on consignment, maybe to humor him. When people asked if my record was out anywhere other than New York,

I'd tell them a lot of stores in Miami carried it. It impressed them. When a store in Minneapolis reordered records, I told people my music was doing well in Minneapolis. I didn't lie. I just stretched the truth a bit. It created more interested in my music. They never checked. No one cares much. But when folks hear you're doing well in several cities, they take you more seriously.

If you have no staff, create the illusion of one. When I opened Revenge Records, I was the artist and knew it was unprofessional to represent myself. So I created the names of staff members and signed letters accordingly. I had a marketing person, a publicist, etc. When someone called for one of those people, I'd put on that hat. It got a bit schizophrenic, but it created the façade of a serious business. To this day I use that publicist's name as on my press releases. When someone calls for her, I say she's not in, and I help the caller. Many folks use fake names to market themselves. Few notice later on.

Get into the habit of using "we," instead of "I." "We'll get those records to you tomorrow." "Someone will call you back tomorrow." "We've worked hard with that artist." It gives your business a fuller feeling and makes you sound more like a company. It's a mental thing, but people in this business can be mental. I still do it, even though I don't have to anymore. It's become so ingrained I can't stop!

If you keep putting out the message that you're successful, you create the best conditions for succeeding. Eventually I earned serious respect, which must be earned. When you take your company seriously as a business, others will, too. One day you'll wake up and actually believe the façade you've been putting out to others!

Having High Standards

This is my personal opinion, so take it for what it's worth. I've always tried to live by the adage, "If you can't do it right, don't do it at all." It's hard to get taken seriously. Don't sabotage yourself by doing things halfheartedly. If you can't put your best foot forward, wait until you can. When I released Powerule's video, people were impressed with its quality and took more notice of Revenge Records. My reputation got stronger. Had I put out just an okay video, I'd have been lumped with the other okay labels. The video wouldn't have received the airplay it did. I was told small indies don't get videos played on MTV. I did—regularly!

"Doing it right" doesn't necessarily mean spending a fortune. It means paying attention to details and making sure it's done well. Find a student to do creative work in exchange for credit or a reference. There are many great young people who'd jump at a chance to help, if they take you seriously. Focus your resources in the most important directions, making sure obvious facets are done well. The professional artwork for my label showed. Don't cut corners with visible quality.

Developing the Right Attitude

No matter how much or how little you think you have, you'll get further with a positive attitude. Without this mindset, Revenge Records wouldn't have done as well as it did, no matter how good my records were. Because I was very friendly, people responded in kind. I helped others and others helped me. DJs, people in record stores, journalists, etc. offered support because they liked me. People prefer someone with a smiling face and positive outlook over someone moody, with attitude. Develop a good rapport with everyone. It'll serve you well. Friendliness and sincerity attract good people. If you put out music for the right reasons—because you love it and have so much passion for it—the Law of Attraction helps things fall into the right places. Eric Hutchinson agrees:

> I think that passion is important. That's my own personal philosophy of why things ended up going the way they did. Everything was done for the right reasons. Behind every action was a real passion. I made the album because I wanted to. My friend sent the email to Perez Hilton because she really wanted to. And Perez put it on his site because he really wanted to. That ends up with fans downloading because they really want to.

I personally believe that having a spiritual attitude attracts better people and more satisfying success. Faith helped me succeed. It enables you to hang onto your belief in your music and go the distance. It also helps you to deal with negative people in a positive way. What goes around really does come back to you. Treat folks with respect; many return it. If people screw you, it's *their* problem! Focus on maintaining your integrity, no matter how others act. Be real. Having an attitude won't get folks on your side. When you maintain your integrity and always fulfill what you promise, people remember you as someone they want to deal with. Recording artist Ingrid Michaelson adds:

Be thankful and grateful. Live like it might be gone tomorrow. Enjoy it in the now. Be humble about success. You could be nothing next year. Treat everybody the same and with respect. Be grateful for everybody who comes to your show.

Don't sell yourself short. Sometimes we allow folks to take advantage by undercutting prices and terms of payment if we're afraid of getting nothing. That's not taking your business seriously! Once you create a market for it, you'll be dealt with more favorably. If you allow distributors and stores to manipulate you now, a pattern is set that's hard to change. Some folks will try to jerk you around, but if you hold out for fair terms, those who recognize your potential will come around. If someone believes your record will sell, they're less likely to take advantage. Someone who claims they're "doing you a favor" by carrying your records on unfair terms may not sell them anyway. Let your belief in your music keep you strong. Conduct yourself in faith, not fear! Juni Fisher, of Red Geetar Records, advises:

I learned early on that the music business is a series of opportunities, and the only limiting factor is being afraid to fail. That fear of failing held me back for several years, but eventually I adopted a personal motto: "What would you try if you knew you could not fail?" By getting over that, I was able to approach folks instead of hanging back, to pick up the phone instead of wonder why no one was calling. Sure, I heard a lot of "nos," and still do, but it is not the end of the world; it is now a way to learn to do things better next time.

Respect yourself. Don't consider yourself just a new indie label struggling to survive or be apologetic when approaching people. Confidence makes a great impression (firm handshakes everyone!). If you have a good record and a way to let folks know about it, it will find its way. Don't grovel to get an order or a deal. If you believe in your product and let that belief show, others will get the message. By respecting yourself, you'll be respected. Know your music is worthy of success. Holding your head up proudly makes people take a second look at your label. To earn respect in this business, give it to yourself first.

CHAPTER 3

Road Warriors: Successful Indie Labels

C an an independent label really succeed? Yes! Yes! Yes! While it isn't easy, it's possible. In this chapter, I profile successful labels. Some have a roster of artists, while others market one independent artist or themselves. While they won't argue that having major label resources behind them wouldn't make their label stronger, they're making money and love their independence. I've included this chapter to show by example the variety of motivations and directions for starting and running a record label. Let these labels motivate you! Their common ground is passion for the music they market.

Glassnote Entertainment: Daniel Glass, Founder

Daniel Glass has always been passionate about music. He developed many artists' careers, working as vice president of SAM Records, senior vice president at Chrysalis Records, developing superstars including Billy Idol and Pat Benatar; and at SBK Records, Glass was promoted to executive vice president/general manager. After the consolidation of SBK, Chrysalis, and EMI Records USA, he became president/CEO, where he developed more hit artists, including Jon Secada and Selena. In 1996, Glass and Doug Morris began Rising Tide Records, which later became Universal Records, with Glass as president. He helped break many new artists, including Erykah Badu. Glass says:

> I've always considered myself an independent. I thrive on it; I love the world of it. I only know one way, and that's the independent way. Even when I ran large companies like EMI and Universal, I tried to find independent people, independent spirit, and independent labels, which were the foundation of our company. The great labels were really made up of great independent labels and entrepreneurs.

In 1999, Glass joined Danny Goldberg at his new independent label, Artemis Records, as executive vice president, and then president. Artemis was named the number-one independent label in *Billboard*. From there Glass founded Glassnote, an entertainment company that encompasses Glassnote Records, Music Publishing, and Merchandising. He likes being able to emulate labels he admires, explaining:

> At Glassnote, we try to emulate the labels of the eighties, which we thought were special places, like Chrysalis, where I was for many years, Island Records, and Virgin Records. That's what our template is. Those are labels that were built for authenticity and independence and around touring, with mainly rock artists whose vision they supported. Today, with the advent of MySpace and other online communities, we have an edge. The playing field has leveled because of the online space. Artists and managers now prefer to be with independent labels. They feel they get a fairer deal. There's more transparency and honesty. So the successful independent labels of the present and future are the ones that have great vision and belief.

The Glassnote office has an energetic and friendly vibe. Everyone is in a big room, working together. Glass' enthusiasm for the artists on his label radiates out, and he has the same enthusiasm for his staff. He coaches and mentors them to be the best they can be and tells their stories with great pride. He has a keen ability to see the best in people and to encourage and nurture them to bring it out in themselves. He says:

> We have a very young team here. Each person has amazing potential. It's a true collaborative effort. Physically, we created an office where everyone works in the same room. The open office represents who we

are. It's completely democratic, open and inclusive. I think that's the only way you can be successful—the vibe of a collaborative, team operation. I have the same satisfaction from a hit record as I do from a hit employee, a hit teammate. I love seeing someone blossom and grow. That's how great organizations have done it. You grow people from within.

Glass is very hands-on with his staff. His ambition for Glassnote is to strive for a better batting average. He remembers that when he was at Chrysalis, every record was treated as a potential hit. Glass says:

I'd like to run our company the same way, on a smaller basis—with a high batting average, sometimes batting 1,000, which means if you put out nine records, nine are successful. Chrysalis did everything in-house, like Berry Gordy did. So my dream is as we grow the company to have our artists writing for other artists in the company, to actually sign writers that work for Glassnote to help our writers to write better. I think sometimes as independents we release records that we think are great—A-pluses—but they're B-pluses or A-minuses. A-minuses don't sell. The atmosphere of collaboration makes you better. Here we raise the ante every day. I make people work hard.

Glass and his staff work hard but enjoy it. The ride is just as important as getting to the final destination. Glass advises finding pleasure in running a record label:

It's not a skill, but people aren't having fun. People have been consolidated, bought, and merged by various hedge funds and takeover artists. I think they're not having fun. If you're not having fun, you're not going to be successful. You've got to work hard, but you also have to have fun.

He does!

Cabin 24 Records: Ingrid Michaelson, Founder, Recording Artist

Ingrid Michaelson released *Girls and Boys* in 2005, with a college radio campaign and a few festivals, which created a small buzz. Then she put songs on MySpace. A music licensing company found her there, and they started working together. It also evolved into a management arrangement. After licensing a song to *Grey's Anatomy* in 2006, record sales increased. They chose to go slowly. Sales were more electronic than physical. Then Old Navy used her song "The Way I Am" in a TV commercial. Sales escalated. They got distribution with RED through Original Signal, a small label. Michaelson says:

> *Once the Old Navy commercial happened, we had to step it up. I just wanted distribution. Original Signal stepped forward to affiliate with me. I had to go through a label to get distribution through RED. Original Signal is not my label. They're my distribution label. So the pieces started coming together. We kept the demand higher than the product since we didn't want overshoot it. In the past year and a half it seems to be going pretty fast. We could have made choices to speed things up but kept holding the reins, and still do. We've sold over 200,000 records, and they're still selling. All digital sales are mine.*

Michaelson says their original goal was to see how far they could go—how much power they could get; how much they could build with getting television shows, commercials, and other placements—before signing to a label. They saw that as a new way for an unknown musician to get music out and have people hear it without having to pay. They also liked not having to pay a major label back for recoupable expenses. Their perspective about taking a label deal changed along the way. Michaelson explains:

> *The whole idea was to see how far can we'd get before we signed. The further along I got, the more the idea of actually signing faded away. I still haven't totally crossed that off my mind. I don't know what the future holds. For now, I feel like the way my career is going and the way the major labels' world is going, that I trust myself and feel safe with my own decisions. I know I'm not going to drop myself! While I don't have a $200,000 push behind me, and I'm not getting my face plastered everywhere—all the stuff major labels do—I get to choose where my money goes and what promotion happens. I'm not seeking huge fame, so I don't see a need now. If I can finance myself, why not? It's kind of a no-brainer at this point. But I don't ever pooh-pooh record deals.*

Michaelson has charted on the *Billboard* Top 200 multiple times, getting as high as #63 (also #6 Independent Album, #16 Alternative Album, and #27 Digital Album), and has made the cover of *Billboard*. She's now aggressively doing shows. She says she sort of went backward—selling records before touring. Now she's connecting with the people who bought her music by touring across the country. Michaelson says, "I'm not going to just sell records and not do anything. You have to follow through. I have to connect with people who are fans now. They don't even know what I look like, but they bought my music!"

Everfine Records: Dave Roberge, President

Everfine Records was created as a vehicle for the band O.A.R. Dave Roberge began working with them in 1999. When venues didn't take O.A.R. seriously enough to book them, they'd rent the venue and sell their own tickets. The members of O.A.R. were freshman in college, and Roberge booked around their schedules. He says, "We drew a three-hour radius around Columbus and picked the markets that we could develop." He placed O.A.R.'s product in and around markets where they played. Roberge helped build a street team that went to stores to educate them on O.A.R. He read books to learn the industry and opened Everfine Records in 2000:

> We started the record label in order to give the band higher visibility. They were seeking an identity with regards to having a label. More or less, it came down to a higher level of presentation in terms of the packaging and things like that. When we first came up with the concept, it was to create the impression that the band had a record label. From that, the record label manifested into a much more real situation. Right after we went into the studio there was major label interest in the band. At the time, it didn't make sense to align ourselves with a major label. There was still a lot of growth and development that the band needed to do—maturing as individuals at twenty years old, but also musically and professionally, being understanding and knowledgeable about the industry.

By then they'd moved about 35,000 units of the band's first self-released CD and 20,000 of their second. They sold out big venues with no radio single or video. While not ready to sign, they developed a solid relationship with Lava Records, which led to a meeting with Andy Allen, president of ADA distributors. They entered into a pressing and distribution deal with ADA in February 2001. Roberge says Everfine Records went from being a concept to a fully functioning label with marketing, promotion, publicity, sales, and consumer and trade advertising. They functioned like an eight- or ten-department record label, though still a one-man operation. Roberge credits determination:

> O.A.R. is a band that was constantly told, "You don't fit what the industry standard is." They use this to add fuel to the fire: "Tell us we can't do it, and we'll prove to you that we can." That's my mentality, too. I'm not afraid to take on challenges and think of new ways to approach situations. If you fail, you fail, but you learn from your mistakes. We tell people that for every positive thing that happens for us, there's three or four mistakes behind it that we learned from. We just don't tell anybody about them. You succeed by failing at first, and it shows how resilient you are.

Everfine Records' model is based on artist development. Roberge says, "Everfine Records, in my mind, is almost like a hybrid company in that it's a cross between an artist management company and a record label. We try to develop an infrastructure that could truly support a career-development model." Music and fans come first. Roberge doesn't worry about quarterly expectations or investor pressure. Instead he focuses on building the band. He knows it can take six months or six years. Roberge would like Everfine Records to be a developmental label for a larger one. He loves growing talent:

> I like getting hands-on at the beginning to help develop things because you get to set the tone of what the future is going to hold. Our vision for the record label is having an artist development focus with this band and a grassroots approach in terms of building it up with a micro-marketing strategy, focusing region by region with the band's touring. We're motivated and trying to create a good infrastructure so we can eventually take on other bands and try to take that artist-development approach that is lost at many major labels and employ that region by region. I love being independent. What we want to do is create an identity for the label so that people who pick up an Everfine Record will know it's good.

In 2003, Everfine Records entered into a strategic partnership with Lava Records.

Ace Fu Records: Eric Speck, Founder

Ace Fu is a midsize, independent rock record label. Founded by Eric Speck as a label called Air King Alliance (AKA) at the end of 1997, the first release was a split 7-inch single. When Speck moved to Portland, Oregon, he decided to start anew and called his label Ace Fu. He began his label because:

> I love records. It sounds obvious, but it's that simple. I used to do a radio show and loved learning about the bands and the scene and the labels associated with them. The idea of curating a sound, and a scene, and starting a legacy of music by having my own label became an alluring prospect.

Speck began with about nine hundred dollars to release a 7-inch. It sold out. He released another one that did well. It snowballed. He says there was no initial investment or business plan. He just wanted to put out bands he loved. Speck learned by asking lots of questions of people he knew with labels. Like many who start indie labels, Speck is passion driven and works hard for the love of music. He explains:

> It's a labor of love. If you're successful with your band, think of it as the happy ending, because more bands fail than succeed. The downside is it's not a very viable economic model, especially nowadays. The cost of everything keeps going up, yet record sales and record prices fall. That's why you shouldn't be in it just to make money. You should be in it because you have no other options—and it's what you love to do.

After signing Pinback and moving back to New York, Speck knew he had to beef up the label. He put everything he learned to work and found others to work with him. As sales increased, Ace Fu got distribution from Caroline and continues getting stronger. Speck is hopeful about the future of his label, and indie music. He says:

The future of independent music is strong. The major labels haven't been so strong to react to the changing environment. It's going to be another three to five years before they rebound and are in a better financial state. As they suffer, the independents will be able to function more freely and grow. It's not the best time for any record label, with declining sales. But I think that indies are at a better point than majors and will be for at least three to five years.

Deep Elm Records: John Szuch, Founder

John Szuch always had a passion for music while he worked in the finance business. He decided to combine that passion with his business experience when he quit his job and released his first record on Deep Elm in 1995. As he has learned to roll with changes in the industry, one thing has remained consistent: Szuch's dedication to connecting artists to music fans. He says, "Deep Elm exists as an artist-development–driven record label, not a hit-driven record label. We're there to help artists get their music heard." Szuch believes that the emphasis on great music has been a key to his success:

The label has been successful because we focused on good music versus making money. It's always been a labor of love, so to speak. I wasn't doing it to try to make money. For many years I was constantly putting money into the business and believing in us, our bands, and the records they released. I think that helped us gain a large fan base around the world that continues to buy our records. The same large group comes back and purchases all our new releases.

Szuch read everything he could, went to seminars, and talked to whoever he could to learn. He has grown and learned different ways to help his bands get their music out. His model has changed with the times. His distribution is all digital now, although he does limited CD pressings. Now Deep Elm licenses fully completed records, with artwork and everything fully done. He explains:

We're trying to help bands understand that we're not putting up all the capital for the recording process anymore. So we'll do something on a one-off basis to help bands we like. If they like working with us, they'll continue to work with us. I don't feel a need to have to lock people in for three or five records. The landscape has changed significantly. We've invested lots of money in a band that broke up before the record even came out. Lots of times bands have made promises and we spent money making a great record and they never toured on it or did anything. They thought they could sign with a label, record a record, and somehow become stars, without doing anything.

Szuch and his promotional director provide all label services in-house, on a DIY approach, including worldwide publicity, marketing, radio and tour promotion, street team, graphic design, mail order, and all Internet operations. The Deep Elm website describes the label best: "From ownership to distribution, Deep Elm is one hundred percent independent and intends to stay that way. Indie "Til Death . . . And We Mean It.""

Push Play: CJ Baran, Lead Singer, and Sue Baran, Manager

Push Play is a band with four boys who began playing together when they were sixteen. Two years later they exploded onto the music scene with the help of MySpace, hard work, good music, and a mother who believed in them. It began when lead singer CJ Baran went to a press conference for the Jonas Brothers with his mom, Sue Baran, who manages the band. They had one press kit with two EPs in it and a color picture of the band with them. CJ says at the time they were getting about seven hundred plays on their MySpace page but could not break the barrier. But some quick thinking on Sue's part knocked the barrier down. CJ explains:

I went to the press conference because I wanted to meet with the Jonas Brothers' father and give him the press kit in the hope he might give it to Hollywood Records. When I got there, I realized it was only for VIPs, and I could not get in. But outside in the Time Warner hallway were about a thousand fans who also could not get in. I was initially bummed, but my mom said that this was our market. She ran across the street and made a thousand color copies of our Push

Play picture. She came back, and for the next seven hours I signed autographs. Our MySpace went from seven hundred plays that night to three thousand.

Push Play worked the online sites hard to develop relationships with new fans. They began filling larger venues. Sue Baran wanted to separate Push Play from other independent artists. From the very beginning, she decided it was important to build a foundation that was morally strong. So she asked the boys why they played music for others and what they wanted from their performance. She says:

I got the usual "fame, money, fun," but I also got that they wanted to make a difference. So we formed the "Push Play for Purpose" campaign. I said I would fund it (paying for sound engineer, roadies, guitar techs, tour vans, merchandising, etc.), and it would be to raise funds for a variety of charities across the world. They wanted to know how this would be accomplished. I said it was important to reach out to their peers, to see what community services they were interested in and ask them if Push Play could be a part of it by donating their performance. We were swarmed with teens jumping on the Purpose tour and scheduling us all over the New York tristate area. By doing this, Push Play became somewhat of a household name here and were able to capitalize on philanthropic efforts.

CJ Baran credits the attention to business details for part of their success. He thinks many musicians are artists first and don't have the business sense they need to market and promote their own CDs and manage their careers. He believes having a good manager is imperative. Push Play is grateful to have Sue Baran running their business so they can put their energy into creative aspects. CJ explains:

We find that musicians have to continue to go full circle with everything they do. They have to keep all the branches in their musical operation fully tweaked and healthy. That's what we do. Because my mom is our manager, I know her work ethic is unparalleled by anyone I know. She is relentless in her pursuit for success for us. And because she watches our backs and helps get our music out, we can relax and just create it. That's what we do. We spin the web daily and have so much material to work with right now. We are plugging away at new songs daily and have jamming sessions all the time. Since I have the home studio in my basement, we record everything and then we work on it, consistently tweaking. Our new stuff is sooo much better than our old stuff. We started when we were sixteen with Push Play. Two years is light years when you are this age. We have matured, and our music has matured, my voice in particular.

After I interviewed CJ Baran and Sue Baran, Push Play signed a co-management agreement with Jason Morey, who also manages Miley Cyrus. Sue remains their co-manager.

Red Geetar Records: Juni Fisher, Founder

Juni Fisher got experience while playing songwriter shows in Nashville, after moving there. The idea of doing her own album seemed like one of those daunting things that only other people did. But after seeing friends doing albums, Fisher wondered if she could, too. She spent several years on a recording project. It was then pitched to a label that said it was looking for an artist doing what she was—writing strong songs that were solidly in a western vein. Fisher says, to her dismay, they signed another artist who was her polar opposite—doing bubblegum country music:

The only thing western was they wore a hat and showed a horse on the album cover. That label folded a few months later; seems they were not satisfying the true western music listeners, and sales were dismal. I went on to complete the project months later and decided to pitch it to a folk label that had a western act that was a mainstay of the industry. They listened and said, "We love what you're doing, but how much are you touring?" They were not willing to even talk further until I was working one hundred plus dates a year and had sold 10,000 CDs a year on my own. Then I pitched it to an Americana label and heard "Nice, but too folk for Americana." Another folk label said, "Nice, but too Americana for folk, have you tried western?" In addition to all that, I had been on several really small indie labels, with no success.

A fairly successful songwriter friend heard Fisher's songs and was certain she just needed to find the right niche to make something work. So, Fisher did the paperwork, researched as much as possible, and created Red Geetar Records. Releasing her first album wasn't an overwhelming process in retrospect, though Fisher says it seemed so at the time. Nor was it an instant success. It took four years and a lot of touring for that album to be noticed. Now, Fisher is on her fourth album. The majority of sales come from live performances, at theater venues and festivals. She says:

> With a lot more miles behind me, I am so glad I did what I did. The chance to make a living at music was a great motivator to make Red Geetar Records successful. The sense of pride I get in doing these things for myself is icing on the cake. I was stubbornly determined not to be one of those artists who records a first album, presses 1,000 copies, and still as 950 of them five years later. Success is relative. To some people, because I have won awards and make a living doing music, I am a success. To big label machines, artists like me don't rate a glance. But one thing is for sure. I make my own money, get to keep it, and don't have to rely on a big label team to get me out on the road. I'm very proud of what I've been able to achieve with Red Geetar Records.

Fisher has learned to find a common thread with almost anyone she meets. By doing that, she's developed good personal relationships that helped her get further. She believes the independent music world is all about networking. Fisher is excited yet realistic about being independent, explaining:

> Being independent is both liberating and terrifying at once. I love to be able to tour the places I most want to go and to schedule days in for fun things, but at the same time, there is that tiny voice that still says, "What if I don't get this gig I was counting on as an anchor on this trip to Colorado? How am I going to make this tour work without going in the hole?" It's a wonderful time to be an independent artist, though; we have so many ways to research, and objectives and goals that seemed unreachable just ten years ago are now there for those willing to do the work.

Bad Dog Records: Jonatha Brooke, Owner/Recording Artist

Jonatha Brooke began Bad Dog Records in 1999 when MCA Records dropped her in the middle of a tour with sold-out shows and she chose to keep going. Since MCA owned her masters, she needed a new recording. She recorded her live shows and put the record out herself to keep momentum going. Her manager, Patrick Rains, already had a label and shepherded her through the process. He convinced her to be aggressive in marketing. She learned as she went. They got a distribution deal with Koch, since Rains had a relationship with them through his label PRA Records, and she had a substantial profile. First they hired a publicist. Brooke says:

> It's a ton of money, but it's the kind of thing that can be invaluable to keep my name out there and keep the level of profile that I had established. We hired a publicist to spin the going-independent, bucking-the-trend kind of deal. With Steady Pull, we got some very-high-profile television, and I think the publicity raised the bar a little bit. People were aware of me, and we were able to get Letterman, Conan, and Craig Kilborn. We were in the pipeline.

Steady Pull was the second release on Bad Dog Records. Brooke says she's not averse to partnering with someone with deeper pockets at some point, but she'd never make a typical artist's deal again. She has to own her masters: "I won't ever put myself into the position of not being able to put my record out." Brooke has come to appreciate being independent:

> When you make the decision to go independent, you have to say, "Okay, will this be enough? I know I won't sell 2 million records unless lightning strikes and I win the lottery. Can I readjust my sense of success?" We both said yes. If we only sell 100,000 records in the next few years, that will be okay. We can break even and have a nice little go of it. You're brought up for so long believing that you have to get a major deal and it's the big brass ring. It's the only way you'll succeed, and you want to be a household name. You have to say, "Wait a minute, what's a career? And what is success

in a career?" It was pretty sobering and great to have to realign my thinking and say, "Wait a minute; I am successful and have an amazing career, an amazing audience and fan base." It's totally worth it. I have an amazing life and career, and it's all on my own terms. I just know I'll win the lottery someday!

Victory Records: Tony Brummel, President

Tony Brummel says he was involved in the underground punk scene from a young age and developed relationships with bands around the country. Brummel didn't see many labels assisting these artists in getting their records out. So as a "hobby," he released some records. He began with nothing—no connections in the industry, and no money, figuring things out as he went. Victory Records started with a 7-inch single and built up fast. Brummel says:

> *There was one record after another. The wheels were churning at that point. I was eighteen years old when I started it, and I had to learn bookkeeping, maintaining an accounts receivable, collecting, paying people on time, vendor relations, overall organization of a business, sales, marketing, promotion. Even layout and design. I did everything. Now I have many employees and interns as well.*

Victory Records first distributed by mail order and finding stores that wanted underground rock. Brummel says they also traded records with other labels and sold them at shows. After a year, boutique distributors picked them up. In a few years they were dealing with larger underground ones until RED began distributing Victory and they began penetrating chain stores. Brummel is pleased with his progress:

> *I have a company and job that I love. My hobby turned into my life. I have employees that are either younger or who have kids, and artists that tour the world. That's a pretty rewarding thing to have started as a hobby—as a fan.*

He's hopeful that Victory provides an alternative for their artists. Brummel acknowledges that having a label isn't easy in today's market. Since they control everything, having a major behind him could take

Victory to the next level. He's been courted by them all but hasn't found an offer that works for the label. Brummel sacrificed to get where he is, which helps him appreciate how sweet success is. He proves you can do it from scratch:

> When I started Victory, that was my only source of income. I had the choice—do I buy a bed or desk? For two years, I slept in a sleeping bag under that desk. I never had outside investors and didn't come from a wealthy family. So I put the money the company was making back into the company to keep it going. I'm very happy I had to struggle that way, because I think it helped solidify the foundation for the company, and we've kept growing every year since.

New West Records: Jay Woods, Senior Vice President and General Manager

Cameron Strang (president) originally ran New West Records in L.A. Jay Woods, senior vice president and general manager, had Doolittle Records. Woods says they brought the two companies together in '99 because they had similar philosophies about running an independent record label. Woods says they built their business on a two-tiered philosophy. Developing artists was an essential part of their plan, but they also wanted to sign established artists at varying levels, acts whose music they appreciate. They're known as a roots-rock label with a little bit of country. Woods says:

> New West established itself as real music for real people. There was never a plan to be an Americana or roots-rock label. We wanted to do music that we believed deserved to be out there: good quality stuff. Cameron and I are rockers from way back. We wanted to do what we knew best. I grew up in Texas, so there's some country in me. We want to do good, honest music and to have an environment where all of us here at the label, the staff and the artists, can make some money and love what they're doing.

Woods says that before signing an artist, they look at that artist's marketing potential. Strang worked a deal to be distributed through RED. Now they do about twelve projects a year. Woods predicts that could grow, but he knows his limits. They prefer to devote deserved attention to each project. Woods says enthusiastically:

> I love being independent! It's wonderful. I really do believe I'm the luckiest guy in the world. That's corny and cliché, but think about it. I grew up in Lubbock, Texas. I'm in the music business. I live in Austin and get to do music that I love. It doesn't get any better than that. I'm truly passionate about what I do. I love to come to work. Everybody should be able to say that in their lives, but most can't. It's hard work, a battle every day. I bitch and moan as much as the next guy. But it's rewarding at the same time.

Definitive Jux Records: El-P, Co-owner, Recording Artist

Hip-hop artist El-P says he was kicked out of two high schools and decided to take music seriously. He and his friends pressed up a single and sent it to radio DJs to get the exposure to attract a major label deal. They made an EP. El-P says, "We [Company Flow] threw the record out, and all of a sudden word of mouth was strong on us through the hip-hop underground communities and colleges." Thirty thousand copies sold immediately. El-P says, "It was not something that happened at all on that level. At the time [1996], there was no independent rap scene, at least not the way there is now." Artists performed in front of friends and people in clubs. Their success was contingent on planning every action and doing whatever they could to make it happen. He says:

> Our plan was to put something out, use it as leverage to get a deal with somebody bigger than us to give us exposure; use that as leverage to bring something back into our company and not have to use them for exposure. We mapped it out. We were getting so much money because we put none into promotion. We were working at [a mail order place] and sending our records out through their mail order department overnight to the radio stations. We were loving it. We'd been involved in every step of the way, and all of a sudden people were handing us sums of money. Directly to us! No

*bullshit. For us at the time, it was like, twenty G's—we probably
don't have to make a record again. That was how you look at it
while you're young.*

Because they were doing so well, they leveraged a deal with Rawkus Records
to put out one record (more on this, see Chapter 4). It elevated them to a
recognizable level in the industry. Once their record sold large numbers, it
was time for what El-P calls phase three: "Move on. Take what you need at
the time, respectfully, let everybody know up front what it's about, and take
control of yourself again." He left Rawkus and started his own label. He
had experience, name, connections, and a serious amount of weight behind
what he'd done to attract distribution with Caroline Records. El-P knows
that major labels need high six-figure sales to even crack a smile, and all
the artists on Def Jux sell at least large five figures. He adds, "We're making
a living, a killing actually!" El-P has had many label deal offers but chooses
to remain independent:

*I can't help but do it myself. I'm a controlling freak, and don't
want to convince someone else to believe in me, or the people
I believe in. I don't want to walk into an office and talk to someone
who knows less than me about music and try to explain my vision,
holding my breath, hoping that he relays that vision to whoever he
has to relay it to in order to cut a check and support what we're
trying to do. I love it. I'm proud of it. It's a lifestyle thing for
me—I know that I feel better, stronger as a grown man, knowing
that whatever is coming to all of my friends and everyone working
for me and with me is ours, truly. We've gone the right way, with
the right intentions.*

Rich Hardesty, Recording Artist

Rich Hardesty earns a six-figure income from his music. He's released eleven
independent CDs. While studying business at college in Indiana, Hardesty
wrote a song called "Never Wanna to F'n See You Again." Everybody in the
dorm requested it, and he played that trademark song at open-mic nights.
He decided to try making money from his music and began by performing
acoustically in bars. Since he was popular, they gave him a lot. He figured if
he performed three nights a week, he could work less and make more than

at a real job. Fraternities called Hardesty to play at parties. He used his college education to structure his business and recorded live shows to pass around. He learned that when they heard a live show on tape, they'd want more and would come to see him. Word about him spread. Hardesty pressed his first CD for pleasure:

> Having a CD was all I wanted. I had no idea I'd keep recording and make money from them. I wanted to have my name on a CD—my CD. I was going to be the business dude. All of a sudden I had a CD I was proud of. That was more of a success to me in my heart.

People lined up to hear Hardesty play his trademark song. It was a vehicle to invite people to shows and to sell his first CD. Hardesty realized what a large profit margin he had from selling CDs direct, and his business education took over. He runs his business in-house. Hardesty is happy with what he's created:

> I want to make money—this is my business. I do everything now. I look at being with a larger label as a way to get extra help in promoting and marketing, if it's the right deal. There's so much involved it drains me. You have to be business oriented to succeed in selling albums. I don't want to just be an artist sitting under a tree writing songs. If you want this to be your full-time job, then you have to do business. People ask why I'm not with a record label, as if that would be the greatest thing. They don't understand: I am my own record label.

Redemption Records: Ryan Kuper, Owner

When Ryan Kuper felt his performing days were waning, he wanted to stay involved in the music he loved. He used his high school graduation money to start Redemption Records in 1990 and advertised that he was accepting demos. He continued signing bands, and it grew from there. Kuper made money from his first record:

> I put out a good band with a niche and knew how to exploit that scene. I continued making money until '95—the first time I took some big financial risks and had financial losses. I had to struggle.

> *But because I took the risks, I got the most notoriety for the label and interest from other companies.*

Kuper says he tried marketing pop records, but running the label became more expensive. He says, "It's no secret that a lot of radio is still about payola, and trying to compete with that as a smaller company was an eye-opening experience for me as far as the finances of a label that size." He got radio play because of the overall marketing and money he spent. Kuper says he is solely responsible for running Redemption: "As far as people that receive payroll from Redemption Records, you're talking to him!"

Kuper has more recently been focusing on management and label consultations. Redemption will now provide management and development services to developing bands, keying in on digital, merchandise sales, and securing nontraditional partners for his releases. Efforts that used to be geared toward physical retail will be retuned. Kuper says he loves being independent:

> *It's an empowering feeling. It is an "us against them" mentality. A lot of people perceive indies as giant competitors. I pretty much reach out and ask advice and offer it to other indie labels. It's an interesting brother- and sisterhood out there. I really appreciate being part of that because you don't get that same love at the major label level. There's a credibility that will be there that will never be with major labels. I like being part of that.*

Festival Five Records: Dan Zanes, Recording Artist/Owner

Dan Zanes began his career as a member of the Del Fuegos, who were signed to several majors throughout the '80s. When his daughter was born, he searched record stores for updated versions of music he grew up with. Unhappy with what he found, he recorded his own versions of old songs and made three hundred cassettes to give to neighborhood kids. Someone passed a cassette to a record company. They asked Zanes if he wanted to put it out. He says he had already made five records, owned no masters, and got very little. He passed because "I knew I had something good. I felt protective of it." Someone suggested starting a label. Zanes began Festival Five Records in 1999. His daughter liked something to look at when she got a CD. He decided to package his music as a book with a sleeve in it, using recycled paper. Zanes says:

> I found a printer who does books and a place that manufactures CDs. We came up with a design for our board book. It's full-color, sixteen pages, and recycled paper. Many stores looked at the packaging and bought it without even listening to it. I'm so proud of it! There are no song lyrics. People go online for that. It's a better use of space if I put artwork in with text.

Zanes approached every store he found that carried kids' products, convincing most to carry his CD. He set up shows in schools and kids' venues. Word spread among parents, and his performances were packed. Zanes worked the press and a *New York Times Magazine* article put him on the map. MRI distributes Festival Five through Ryko, which handles special sales, so he's getting into museum shops and other nontraditional outlets that make sense for his music. He got the contact by networking. He also sells on CDBaby. Zanes says he's very happy being independent:

> I've spoken to all the kids' labels by now. When I say I'd like to license and retain ownership of my masters, conversations come to a screeching halt. Slow and steady is right for me. As it grows, I learn. I never wanted to know anything about the business part before. I heard that Richard Foos from Rhino Records said he was able to understand every aspect of how the business worked because he did it all himself. That's my case.

MC Records: Mark Carpentieri, President/Owner

Mark Carpentieri's band put out a CD in the early '90s. It was reviewed in blues magazines, and people liked it. Two years later, Carpentieri was doing management work. The first release on MC Records with a signed artist was in 1996. He credits going to a convention for learning the ropes.

> *We went to their convention for two years before starting our label. We had the opportunity to meet with other blues labels, see the scene and what distributors were looking for. I was running a management company. We were organized and had a good expectation of what things were. But it's all great in theory until you release the record. For our first national release, we were well organized.*

MC Records began with an artist who had a national but not huge following from another label. Carpentieri saw a need for something fresh. The artist wanted a label that would put new energy behind the record. Carpentieri says, "They thought even though we'd never released a record, I had done publicity work and management, so I was familiar with how things work." He had the business acumen and passion for music that leads to success and he likes doing it on his own. He says:

> *You can basically record what you think is good. You're not having to go through fifty million channels, and you have more flexibility to adjust to the market as you see fit, compared to bigger labels that have to go through leaps and bounds just to do the slightest change in their business practices.*

Carpentieri used lessons from releasing his own record to get airplay. He learned as much as possible by going to conferences and networking. MC Records got distribution through contacts and went on to get several Grammy nominations. Carpentieri finds tremendous satisfaction in that:

> *Having an artist nominated for a Grammy is one of the best feelings. Our first nomination was in 1999 with Odetta. It was her first nomination in fifty years in the business. I told her when we made her CD that we would do everything possible to get her a nomination. When that actually happened, it made me feel great that I did this for Odetta and that a record on my label could be honored by a nomination. Getting the second nomination was a confirmation of the path that we are on. This was also Kim Wilson's first solo nomination.*

Saddle Creek Records: Robb Nansel, Owner

Robb Nansel took over Lumberjack Records in 1996 and changed the name to Saddle Creek Records. It began with friends who played in bands. Rather than continue trying to get industry attention, they did it themselves, with guidance from friends who'd already done it. Nansel says the bands spend years touring and creating word-of-mouth buzz. Everyone works together to advance the label. They keep it casual:

> We don't have an A&R division, and nobody looks for acts. We do what we want to do, how we want to do it. We know the bands well—exactly how they want their music marketed. When you work with a larger company, they would want to market the record in ways to sell it. Our bands aren't as concerned with selling it as they are with making sure that it is presented properly.

In May 2000, Saddle Creek did an exclusive distribution deal with Southern. Nansel says, "They liked how we handled ourselves and saw our potential. We let them handle it all so we don't have to worry about it. They keep track of accounts and pay us monthly. We just send the stuff to them." As bands gained popularity, Nansel says the label had to get more structured. But they avoid the majors because Saddle Creek is artist oriented and focused on the music:

> We've been offered deals for a while. I think that majors can do good things, given the right situations. But at this point, we're still putting out a lot of records that don't need that type of push. I think it would benefit some of our artists and would sell more records. But I don't know if the end result would be a positive thing. Acts that sell more records would probably benefit more than the smaller ones—the acts we put out because we like the records and they don't have a huge audience. Those records would get lost.

Nansel says they're growing. For a long time he did everything, but now they have a staff. They've discussed what they'd do if a major label gave them lots of money, but they couldn't think of anything important. Nansel says they all work like mad and don't get paid well, but they're happy being independent:

> Music keeps most of us going. We get to come into a job we like. We get to work on music that we really love. We don't have to answer to anybody, and we don't have to do anything that we don't want to

do. So it's great. We get to meet a lot of bands, hang out, and go to shows. That makes the music fun.

Trout Records: Trout Fishing in America

Trout Records is the label for the duo Trout Fishing in America—Keith Grimwood and Ezra Idlet. They began in the late '70s. In 1980, they pressed cassettes and vinyl to sell off the stage. Dick Renko, manager for Trout Records for over twenty years, says, "We were in the first wave of the DIY releases." They released their first CD in 1990. Idlet adds, "The main thing for us at first was developing a mailing list. When we played other cities, we brought our mailing list. When we'd go back there'd be a crowd. When we release a record there's an audience ready to buy." Trout Fishing also does kid's music. Grimwood adds, "A lot of times you're not supposed to do that. This offers us the flexibility of playing different styles of music that we might not have with a record company." They alternate adult and kid releases. Renko likes their approach:

> *It's still an in-house operation. Ezra's wife runs the label. I do management and booking. Because we're small, we've felt we have to be cautious in the development of Trout Fishing in America and the Trout Records label. We've been able to keep this tight and to make the agenda our own to serve the children's outlet and stay on course with their folk-pop music as well.*

Grimwood says, "Instead of focusing on getting signed, we focused on the music." Idlet is 6' 9", and Grimwood is 5' 5", which attracts attention. Eventually they began selling through distributors. Trout Fishing in America now plays for performing arts centers, festivals, and private functions. Trout Records has had interest from labels. Renko says, "There's a chance we'd take a deal if all the elements were attractive enough." They've grown into a viable label, with a Grammy nomination under their belt. Grimwood says:

> *I thought that you were supposed to sign with a record label. Doing it this way has been the most surprising thing I have ever done in my life. I'm not this kind of person. I travel by normal channels. I am very proud of the fact that we're independent.*

CHAPTER 4

Financing Your Business

There are no easy answers for "Where do you get financing?" Depending on your circumstances, background, and the strength of your business plan, financial backing is tough. With so many people starting labels, people are wary of investing in a new record label. If you develop a great business plan, create a huge story for your artist(s), and implement an impressive marketing plan, people may take you more seriously.

Getting Money from Outside Sources

Many of you will finance your label out of your own pockets, like I did. I liked not answering to anyone. Many investors expect at least a say, if not active involvement, so be prepared for that if you get outside financing. Banks are hesitant to loan money to startup labels. If you get a loan, you'll need to put up collateral. Do you own something of value that can be taken from you if you don't pay back the loan? Without a successful track record in the record business, I've been advised that a personal bank loan is easier to get than a business loan. If you hope to get a large loan eventually, get your business started first and apply when you can show serious sales. Have a strong business plan.

Many people find private investors. Let's face it, the music industry is an exciting place and can appeal to folks with money to spare. By investing in a record label, they get a taste of the industry. I've heard of an amazing variety of types who invested in record labels. Some do it as a tax write-off—investing in a business for a loss. Some just want to get repaid with interest. Some want a percentage of profits. Some want involvement in what goes on with the label, which makes them the biggest pains in the butt if they don't understand the music industry. Some people get donations from fans or sell the CDs in advance to get the money to make them. There are websites that have systems for you to get funds from music lovers.

Where do you find investors? Look everywhere. People put ads in local papers or business journals. Talk about your plans to everyone. You never know who may love your music and want to get involved. The best kind of investor is one who gives you what's referred to as "angel capital." Ryan Kuper says, "It is funding that does not come with a heavy hand of interference, from someone who is willing to fund—like an angel—trusting you are doing the right thing." Love those angels! People laugh when I tell them to look for rich people who aren't connected to the industry for money. Rich people might get a kick out of being part of it or having a share in music they like. The money you need might be small change to them.

Announce that you're looking for investors at gigs. Talk. Talk. Talk. Someone unexpected might bite. Be prepared with a business plan and an exciting pitch. Wait until you're ready. If you're the artist and your music is appropriate, contact corporations in the fall and let them know you're available to perform at holiday parties. If you get a gig and the people seem to enjoy your music, find a subtle way to let people know you're looking for investors. Ya never know!

When you find an investor, use a lawyer to structure the agreement so you maintain control, and look over anything you may sign, even if it seems straightforward. No matter who invests, have everything in writing. Spell out exactly what the investor is putting into your company and what they'll get in return, and when. Even if a friend invests, sign a formal agreement. You can't be too careful about money.

Affiliating with a Larger Label

How do you hook up with a larger label? Folks with track records or industry relationships have it easier. If you have major success with an act, you may get taken seriously by a label. But if no one's heard of you, doors won't open easily. You may have to kick them down with independent success. It may take several successful records or acts before anyone pays attention to you.

Nobody will give a deal to someone without proven success or an act that's hot. Labels need to recognize benefits for working with you. They want to see your artist in magazines and playing to a full house. Most important, they want impressive record sales. Large numbers have the most impact. If a larger label knows you've sold many on your own, they can visualize the potential with their clout behind it. Concentrate on getting as big a buzz on your record as possible before looking to a larger label for support. The more you have to offer a label, the greater your chances of hooking up with one. El-P (Definitive Jux Records) says success can put you in the driver's seat:

> Because a lot of record labels were knocking on our door, we arrogantly designed our own contract. I said I want 50 percent of everything, complete ownership of my masters, 100 percent creative control, and I'll sign a deal for one album. We held it out in front of us like the arc of the covenant. All the infidels fell and burned away. At the end of the day, Rawkus Records were the ones standing. Once my deal was done with them, it had brought us, and Rawkus, to a pretty recognizable level in the industry.

Large labels pick up successful indies to find artists and develop them. Gregg Latterman (Aware Records) got a joint venture with Columbia Records because he'd shown he could find and market good artists. He says, "They came to me. We broke Train, Five for Fighting, John Mayer, and a bunch of new ones. I own our company, and we jointly own the stuff we do together. I think that's the best of both worlds."

Major labels like indies with successful grassroots marketing and a proven sales base. But not every indie would work with them. John Szuch (Deep Elm Records) says:

> I wouldn't get anywhere near majors. It's such a foreign idea to me to take money or use distribution of a major record label, because their motives are simply profit. They do not care about artists or records. It's solely about money. And if they're giving you money, somehow you're going to be taken advantage of when it's in their best interest.

Should you strive to hook up with a larger label? Many indies said they'd take a deal *if* the right one were offered. Yet they're still flying solo. *The Music Business Registry* (www.musicregistry.com) has great directories. Their

A&R Registry is updated every eight weeks with A&R people at most major and independent labels, including those in the UK, with direct phone/fax numbers, email addresses, and assistants' names.

Nowadays larger labels don't offer many P&D (pressing & distribution) deals. They prefer to own equity in the company. Below are common ways indies hook up with larger labels. I say "larger labels" rather than "majors" because you might want to go with a strong independent that has good distribution.

P & D (Pressing & Distribution) Deals

A P&D deal means the larger label presses records and distributes them. An indie label's responsibility is to sign the artist, produce their music, design and prepare the cover artwork, and deliver the finished master and artwork to the P&D company. The P&D company manufactures the records and gets them distributed through their distribution system. The indie label is responsible for all marketing, promotion, videos, advertising, and publicity. The P&D company deducts manufacturing costs and a fee for distribution from record sales. The indie label gets what's left, except for money that's held on reserve against returns. That's a basic P&D deal.

John Luneau, head of business affairs at Palm Pictures, says nowadays record companies are wary of doing P&D deals. They don't want to get stuck with huge returns and try to collect from a small label that may be out of business. The larger label must be convinced that the indie has the knowledge, money, and staff to market a record nationally. Without a hit record, it's unlikely anyone would want to distribute a label with no proven ability to market and promote. Luneau adds:

> *Companies only want to get involved with a small label if they believe that label is going to be savvy and make money. And be around in two years. Ideally, they should have a track record of being in the business before and having successful records under their belt—records that consistently sell what they project. If you're the smaller label, you should only consider this if you are a full-fledged label, with a marketing, radio, A&R and royalty department, because you'll be responsible for paying royalties to the artists and to the publishers.*

The P&D company administers the deal and sends the indie regular written statements. The indie has a right to audit the books. While the deal is with a label that administers it, the distributor for the larger label gets records into stores. For example, if you had a deal with Atlantic Records, Atlantic would administer it, but the distribution itself would be handled by Atlantic's distributor, WEA, which is a separate entity. They each make money on the deal. John Luneau says:

> The label that does the deal with the smaller label might charge them a percentage that would more than compensate them for what their distributor charges them. The average the larger label would take is 20 to 25 percent of gross receipts (based on wholesale price paid by record stores). The distributor's portion comes out of that. It might be more, depending on what the distributor charges the larger label.

Sometimes a P&D company will give the indie an advance on distribution to offset production costs, make a video, for promotion, etc. Luneau says, "If you're a successful smaller label, the larger label may seek ways of participating with you on a bigger basis, such as advancing money to you for marketing a record." This amount is then deducted from the indie's earnings and shown on the next statement. If the indie's act is hot, there's more bargaining leverage. Sometimes the P&D company provides a budget for various forms of promotion because it feels the indie has a better grip on where best to use it. It depends on how badly the larger label wants the deal. Luneau warns they may want a share of the profit in return.

Sometimes larger labels just distribute indie product, without doing pressing. In this case, the indie handles all manufacturing, and the larger label just gets the record out through its distribution system. In such arrangements, most of the terms are similar to those of a P&D deal, except there are no manufacturing costs involved.

Joint Venture Deals

Joint venture/equity deals have become more popular. Whereas in a P&D deal the larger label gets a set fee per record sold, a joint venture deal involves the larger label sharing the profits. The label offering a joint venture pays all operating costs and usually handles promotion, videos, etc., then it deducts all costs and a small percentage for overhead (to cover administration costs, etc.). A percentage is taken by the joint venture label's distributor, and the indie and larger label split what's left over, according to their agreement.

A joint venture deal is usually not structured as a partnership, in the legal sense of the word. One party isn't legally responsible for the other's obligations. In a partnership, the partners share everything. In a joint venture agreement, when money is collected for the sale of records, all expenses are taken out first. Then the joint venture company and the independent label split what's left. This arrangement might not be the best one for you at the beginning. Since all operating costs are deducted from the top, you could stand to make less money in a joint venture if the record doesn't sell well.

To get a joint venture deal, you need something serious going for your label. It's unlikely for someone not known in the industry to convince people at a large label to invest in his or her dreams, however good they sound. Labels do joint ventures to take advantage of the talent, know-how, and street savvy of someone they know to have strong potential. But you'll have to prove yourself before a label will want to work with you on any level.

Record Label Cooperatives

Since there's strength in numbers, musicians are joining together to share resources, and cooperative relationships have become popular. Some companies are structured to allow indie artists to have some benefits of being on a larger label. Michael Hausman, Aimee Mann's manager and managing director of United Musicians, explains:

> When I founded Aimee's company, there were lots of things about the record business that are set up for labels that have multiple artists and multiple releases per year, like distribution and hiring staff. It helps to have more than one record. I thought that there were more artists in Aimee Mann's situation, who wanted their own label but didn't necessarily want to hire a full staff, have an office, and all the infrastructure, contracts, etc. to facilitate it. I thought, why don't we start something that helps artists have their own label? It's been building ever since. United Musicians is a distribution, marketing, and promotion co-op for artist-owned labels. We're not looking for new artists—they come through friends and family—only established

ones that have the ability to produce their own records, tour, do publicity. They have their own label, and we pick up whatever activities they're not going to do on their own.

United Musicians' artists are distributed through RED. Hausman's staff helps with press, manufacturing, online sales, marketing, and promotion. They have very specific terms about what they'll do, and artists can do whatever else they want with the song or record. Artists retain all options, such as for TV/film. If they choose, they can take their copyright and go elsewhere. Hausman thinks this is a better situation for an established artist with a strong business sense or who has someone on their team with one. Musicians pool resources to hire staff and have other cost-effective advantages of a label with several artists. Hausman adds:

We don't have the overhead and make money on a much lower sales number. We make sure to cover the bases for our artists—press, club advertising in the market when an artist goes on the road—and stay on top of everything. That pays off with established artists because you know there's a fan base. We do lots of email marketing, keeping lists of fans current.

Azalea City Recordings is an artist-run cooperative record label based in the Washington, DC area, started by Grammy Award–winning mastering engineer and producer Charlie Pilzer. He wanted a label that let artists keep the rights to their work, maintain creative control, and work together to get music heard and distributed. Seth Kibel, an artist on the label, says:

Being a member of the label carries quite a bit of prestige within in the industry and especially in the Washington/Baltimore music scene. The artists on the label are some of the leading lights of the music scene in the Greater Washington area. It's a close-knit musical community, so everyone pretty much knows everyone else. We have processes and procedures in place to allow new artists to join the label, when all involved deem it to be a mutually beneficial relationship. We pool our financial resources for a number of activities, including advertising (in national magazines and elsewhere), conferences, CD samplers, our catalog, etc.

Kibel says they all have healthy fan bases of open-minded music lovers, making it beneficial for all involved to schedule multi-act shows. They've been voted "Best Washington Area Record Company" by the Washington Area Music Association (WAMA) for the past three years. Kibel says it works well for them, explaining:

> The co-op allows us to pool our resources, both financial and more, in ways that otherwise would not be possible. For example, our label has a strong presence at a number of national and regional conferences, such as the national Folk Alliance Conference. That would not be possible if we were all operating independently. Also, in this day and age, when everyone and their sisters are releasing albums independently, it gives our releases and our artists a certain amount of cache and prestige to be on a highly respected label.

Each artist is free to set up and exploit their own distribution networks and do their own promotion, in addition to what the label provides. Kibel says the label's efforts add to any individual promotional activities that individual artists generate themselves. Most of the money goes to the artists. He explains:

> Revenue generated by individual artists' albums goes entirely to the individual artists. The only revenue that goes to the label is that generated by the CD samplers, one-time payments from artists releasing new albums on the label, as well as revenue generated by occasional label showcase performances.

The coopertive also has a website and MySpace page where people can learn about its artists and buy music. Kibel says they generate good traffic. The artists also have individual websites, MySpace pages, etc. Kibel warns that a cooperative situation may not suit everyone. You should be a team player and be prepared to work hard. He adds:

> We're not a label in any traditional sense. Each artist still pays for recording and manufacturing their own individual albums. But by pooling our resources as far as promotion is concerned, we're able to be quite effective in reaching our respective audiences. It only works because everyone on the label is willing to put in the sweat equity to build a successful label. A label like ours is not a good fit for

someone who is looking for someone to pay for them to record an album or for someone who is eager to have someone else handle their business affairs. For it to be successful, each artist must work aggressively to promote both themselves and their labelmates.

If you're an artist and know others who put out a CD and seem to have a buzz, consider whether some of you can work together for each other's good. Be careful with those you don't know well. Get to know their temperaments and ambitions. This is a big commitment—only work with like-minded people. And make sure each has enough money and resources to share. You don't want to fight over such things. Create a legal agreement, drawn up by a lawyer, spelling out everything that will be done and what each artist is responsible for.

CHAPTER 5

The Nuts and Bolts of Keeping Your Label Solvent

Nuts and bolts hold things together. In this chapter, I'll share specific business functions, mindsets, and tools that can help keep your label solid. I'm presenting these here so you can keep them in mind as you plan your label. I'll provide *many* more details on marketing later, but here are some nuts and bolts for creating the strongest foundation for your label.

Learn Da Biz

> "The greatest obstacle to discovery is not ignorance—it is the illusion of knowledge."
>
> —Daniel Boorstin

Many musicians moan that they don't understand why they aren't making money. They KNOW their music is perfect and KNOW how to market it. You can't tell them anything because they're *soooooo* brilliant. Excuses for why they haven't succeeded often have as many holes as their education. They half-listen at seminars and to other advice and think it's enough. Don't let your ego hold you back! You don't know it all. Avoid the "I know what I'm doing on my own" trap. You can't learn too much! Rolando Cuellar (Roland Entertainment) says:

I read a lot on the careers of people like Russell Simmons, Tommy Mottola, Emilio Estefan, Clive Davis, L. A. Reid, Berry Gordy, and Mathew Knowles. I have the utmost of respect for them all because they took risks to become who they are. I want to be the next them, but in my on way with my own vision.

There are many books on every topic, so there's no excuse for not filling holes in your knowledge. Peruse libraries and bookstores. Take classes or pay someone who can answer all your "dumb questions." You'd be surprised how many people have them. Ignorance is normal. Not taking advantage of opportunities to learn is what's dumb! Dave Roberge (Everfine Records) advises bands to learn and understand this business to develop realistic expectations about how much they have to work for success. The guys in O.A.R. educated themselves. Roberge says that while their team focuses on the business side and the band on the creative, they know everything about the business because they handled things themselves first. They learned because they understood how important it was for their careers. Roberge himself learned as much as possible:

I had to learn a lot to be a responsible business owner and manager. You have to treat your employees well. So it was everything from applying basic HR principles to the company to developing a company handbook, to accounting and financing, to tax liability to eventual payroll, royalty payments, and spreadsheet maintenance. There's a totally unglamorous side of what we do. A lot of it is administrative in terms of number crunching, data crunching, and creating systems where we can share information internally. The accounting and finance was probably the most difficult aspect. Although I had a background as a business major, I'm not a CPA or a qualified business manager. So I learned those functions to the best of my ability until it outgrew me. You get to that breaking point, and then hire a third party.

Jesse Fergusson, product manager for Definitive Jux Records, advises those wanting to start a label to take basic accounting. Even if you get an accountant, understand the process. Or, get someone to teach you. Panos Panay (Sonicbids) says:

Information today is plentiful and everywhere. If you don't invest in understanding the business component of your craft, you don't deserve to call yourself a professional. Call it a hobby and live in the clouds if that's what you want. But if you believe you can make a living from music, then learn as much as you can.

Try to find a mentor. Don't pester that person, but ask if you can call occasionally with a question. Many people like giving advice. If you're friendly, someone may say yes. Tap into the Small Business Adminstration resources for general stuff. I do independent consulting for those who need it. Find a way to learn. If you understand the biz, you'll make wiser decisions, save money, and have the best shot at success.

Develop Your Own Infrastructure

The best way to make money is to get organized now—you and your biz. Whether you have an office or work from home, it's good to have a file cabinet to sort paperwork. Get into good habits now! Otherwise you'll waste time trying to find things. Creative people often have a hard time taking a more businesslike approach to marketing music. I do! But you must if you want to succeed!

If you have important stuff saved in your computer, get an external backup system—a site that stores all your documents, etc., remotely. It's great insurance against crashes and viruses. Even if you make backups on DVDs, one fire and it's gone. I've been using mozy.com. It downloads in the background every day, has unlimited space and is very inexpensive. They have a free service with a limit of 2 GB! There are plenty of others, so ask around.

Create an infrastructure for your business. What does that mean? A company's infrastructure is a supportive foundation and basic framework through which you operate, like the skeleton is for your body. Your infrastructure should support the goals for your label. I included Chapter 3 and tons of input from indie labels as models for you to learn from. Start small. According to Dave Roberge, "A lot of people bite off more than they can chew. For me, it was a matter of taking on as much responsibility as I could at first, until I reached a breaking point." He did everything himself in the beginning. As Everfine Records grew, he expanded the label into functioning departments and gradually hired staff. He explains how his infrastructure developed:

It made sense to have a sales function to acquire as many consignment accounts as possible. The next department was tour marketing— O.A.R. made a lot of strides through touring. For us that was having strong relationships with promoters and understanding the promoter/management relationship. Publicity was another. This band needed stories written about them to spread the word. We focused on high school papers, local magazines, all the smaller publications. I tried to look at everything from major labels with twelve departments to what I thought were the strongest and coolest independent labels with maybe four or five departments to see what departments I needed to focus on first. When I say departments, I mean that I was basically every department—a utility player. I tried to focus on the most relevant areas to this particular artist and grow them. As the band grew, so would the label. We did it step by step. For everything we saw as growth for the band, we would try to translate in terms of growth of the label and add a new function. New media was one area we focused on. I developed departments that made sense. From there we'd add and build things.

Target your artist's strongest areas and create departments that work for their needs, even if you run them all. It helps you focus on taking care of each area and highlights what needs to be done. Then, organize to handle the responsibilities within each department. I advise you to create a list—on paper—for each department it makes sense to have, either now or later when you grow and have a bigger budget. List everything necessary to develop each, including long- and short-term goals. Break each down into small tasks to tackle, one at a time, using tools provided in later chapters.

Each part of such a list would include specific steps involved to accomplish each. Once you have distribution, develop functions for working a record before its street date (more below) and working with your distributor. Brainstorm with everyone involved. When you take things one step at a time, they don't seem as overwhelming.

Label Staff/I'm Staff

Should you hire people? Many of you have no choice if your budget is your wallet. But you may have to eventually use outside people for some departments. Ezra Idlet (Trout Records) says, "You get to the point where you can't handle the business you're bringing in, and it might be enough money for someone to take the management position. It evolves slowly and according to need." Trout Fishing in America developed a business around their own music. Keith Grimwood says when it got too big for them to handle *and* they were making money, they got Dick Renco as manager:

> *We had to have somebody deal with this business stuff. We're not businessmen; we're musicians. We try to get away from the business as much as we can. We needed advice on the big business decisions and developed a team of people that work together to keep us on the road and making music.*

Even with a big budget, start small. Let your staff grow with your label, as you identify needs. Jay Woods says, "One way to get upset in a hurry is having too much staff. If you don't have revenue coming in, or deep pockets, you're going to have a hard time justifying it." Hire an outside publicist, promoter, bookkeeper, etc. if you need them. Until your label gets going, you might not need full-time people. Use street teams (more in Chapter 15) for what you can. Identify where your own strengths lie so you can compensate in the other areas when your budget allows. Jesse Fergusson advises you to always have someone available who can answer the phone and check email, all the time:

> *People email and ask for information, and if you don't get back to them right away, they don't email again. If you email them right back, suddenly you may have yourself an interview or sponsorship or all kinds of stuff. People think that if you're unresponsive and not in communication with them, or that your door is closed to questions or comments, then you're not going to get as much done. Communication is key.*

If you have an office, see if schools can get you an intern to help. Many young people would love to learn the business. Even if there's more than one of you working on the label, interns can do even more. And no matter who works for you, make sure you teach them what to do properly. If they answer phones or make calls, they're representing you and the label. So don't just take any old person you can get and put them to work. Daniel Glass (Glassnote Entertainment) agrees:

> *Our team is small, but each person here is empowered to be an expert by being heavily trained and mentored. We also have a unique*

co-op program at our company. We have students here full-time doing meaningful things. We also have interns.

Planning to Market

Be specific about your label's goals and how you want to run it. It's hard enough if you have it together. Figure out large goals and then create subgoals for achieving them. Juni Fisher (Red Geetar Records) says:

For me it was as simple as setting a few reasonable goals at a time. I started out by keeping my day job, and had an agreement with my boss that I would be out no more than a week at a time. As the gigs started working out better for me, I extended it to two weeks at a time to be gone and then set a new goal: When I could replace my day job paycheck with gigs every month, and had work lined up for at least six months in advance, I'd make the leap. Honestly, it was the goal setting that made the difference.

Before shooting for huge sales, concentrate on selling the first records. Unless your budget can support a huge marketing campaign, baby-step toward your ultimate goals. Jay Woods (New West Records) says, "We want to sell a million records, of course. But you've got to sell ten before you can sell a million. We try to stay focused on what's right in front of us." Be realistic in your plans. Master crawling before running fast. Woods adds:

We learned from labels that had done things wrong, failed in various ways, or made difficult decisions that didn't turn out well. It's really easy for an independent label to get lured into "if I just spend this money, this is going to happen." In most cases, that's an illusion. You need a real solid footing in reality; in what it actually takes to sell. It's easy to get caught up thinking, "I need to sell one hundred thousand copies of this record" when you should be focusing on selling ten, then one hundred, then one thousand. You've got to sell all those numbers before you get to one hundred thousand. You get caught in this "I've gotta hit this home run" thing. We felt confident we could sell a certain amount of Billy Joe Shaver records. We stayed on the low side and knew we'd sell "this many." We based our marketing plan on that as opposed to the other way around—looking at the high side—what you "could" do. We did what we needed to do to see if the numbers made sense. Could we sign this artist and spend this much money and still be able to pay our bills and have the artist make money?

As I said earlier, *the key to running a successful record label is to target your audience and figure out how to reach them.* Sound simple? It may be the hardest thing you do. Great music won't sell if no one hears it. Making naïve assumptions like "everyone will love our music" leads to failure. Target your most likely group of potential record buyers and put all your energy into discovering the following:

- What publications do they read that you can approach for press?
- What venues do they go to?
- What radio stations do they listen to?
- What websites does this group like?
- What alternative marketing strategies can attract potential fans?

Once you've targeted an audience and designed a marketing strategy to reach them, you have a shot at success. Create individual marketing plans for each artist (see Chapter 12 for more details). Dave Roberge agrees:

We have a blueprint we used for O.A.R., but when we take on a second and third band we'll certainly look at the big picture. We'll individually cater every marketing plan, every approach, and every expectation to each particular artist.

If you're new to the biz, trial and error may have to teach you. Be prudent so lessons don't get too expensive! Study your market first to get the strongest bang for your efforts. Expect active participation from your artists. Marketing should be a team effort. Jay Woods says they supplement what their artists do by making sure products are in the right places and the tools are there. But if the artists just sit around and wonder why they're not successful, little will happen. If they're not creating visibility by touring and using other outlets, there's only so much you can do. He adds:

> We have to have people that are on the road. That's the key element to what we do on the developing-artist side and our established-artist side. We don't bank on radio airplay. Even when we get into that game a little bit, mainly on the commercial side, which we do, we like to be calculated about it. That's the fastest way in my opinion to throw away a ton of money. You have to be really careful. "Pick your battles wisely" has been my mantra.

Promotion can be an uphill battle. Figure out your artists' strongest areas and work them. Promotion isn't a crapshoot. Brainstorm with each artist and others who know the music to choose the first steps for increasing visibility. From Chapter 12 on, I give details for specific marketing and promotion strategies. Pay attention to everything related to your music to discover the most options. Create a full picture of your artists' assets. Plan to develop them slowly if you want longevity. Dave Roberge says, "It's all about baby steps, unless you're an image-driven band that's planning to be around for just six months—one hit single and video. But my focus is on artist development and creating careers."

Money Matters

Budgets—the big B word—can make or break any biz. It's a necessary function of running a label, and many folks aren't prepared to handle it. This is where the accounting classes mentioned earlier help. I HATE the money part, unless it's handling huge profits! But, I grit my teeth and do it. Before marketing each artist, create a budget. Money is wasted when spent haphazardly. Jonatha Brooke advises:

> Set a very loose budget. Say, "I know I can sell X amount of records." How much income is that? We can spend this much on the publicist, this much on touring, this much to buy positioning in stores and on radio. Do your best. You're spending before you have any money—totally gambling. I had to learn to not freak out each time I saw how in debt we were for the last year

while we were waiting for our check from the distributor. You feel horrible knowing you can't pay them off right away, but that's how business works.

Many factors determine whether you'll make money. Like expenses! Having a great record and people to buy it doesn't spell profit. Most serious indies hire promoters/publicists, etc. Or, they have in-house staff, which requires salaries and more. You want to balance that with what you take in so you make a profit! Daniel Glass says:

Profit is not a dirty word to me. I'm very concerned and conscious about the bottom line. I think a lot of independents aren't. They're so pure and too hip. We want to make a profit here. I want our investors to feel they invested in something good. There's two investors—the ones who put their money into the company and the fans. I respect both. It's the fans that keep you going. That's who I care about. The rest of it follows.

I can't tell you specifically how much money you'll need. There are too many variables. I've had people in my classes with budgets of $1,000 to $3,000 and people with $100,000 to $500,000 or more. How much you need depends on factors such as these:

- Whether you're working records regionally, nationally, or internationally
- What genre of music you're working with
- Whether you plan to hire independent promoters or publicists
- If you plan to do a video
- Whether you'll have a staff and a separate office or work from home
- Whether you'll be pressing CDs or vinyl and what kind of packaging you'll be using

The variables go on. My recommendation for developing your budget is to itemize everything you'll need money for and add those things up, as is recommended for a business plan. Create the ideal marketing budget, and then decide which things you can afford. You may not be able to do everything you'd like. Determine what's most important. You can't jump when someone wants promotional material that's not part of your plan if your budget is limited. Jeff Price (spinART and Tunecore) advises:

> Think about cash flow. There's a big difference between cash and cash flow. You might be getting $10,000 in six months. But how do you survive between now and six months from now? It's important when you put your business together to understand how much liquid cash you can get your hands on. Make sure you always have access to a credit line. I advise people who are starting a business to get a credit card. I hate to say it because credit card companies can be extremely evil, but have at least one that you pay in full, on time, every month. Do that for a while, because your credit limit will keep being extended. I started spinART when it was making $12,000 to $14,000 a year with a Visa card that had a $55,000 credit limit. We used that to pay manufacturing bills, which we always paid on time. That credit card saved us. It's the credit line that will support you between point A and point B. When you get a windfall, it all changes. Then you have a cash flow, and it all works wonderfully. Until then, it's really hand to mouth.

Put time into creating a budget that covers everything. Allow extra for unexpected variables. Fill in all blanks for anticipated expenses. If you're starting a label with real money, I suggest you work with an accountant from the beginning, unless you're good at accounting. Mark Carpentieri (MC Records) says:

> One of the most important business functions is knowing where your money is going. What about radio? Retail? Money can just fly out— thousands and thousands of dollars in things like ads. You have to put budgets together and separate your expenses so you know where they're going. It quickly can get out of hand. When we started we did it ourselves, and now we have a bookkeeper and an accountant but still give input. I think one thing about having a label is you have to be schizophrenic—to be able to talk about this great CD and the passion of the music and why it should be listened to but on the other hand to justify expenses. Maybe you can't hire a radio promoter on

this one or just for a limited amount of time. You have to keep that in balance.

Jay Woods advises:

Keep overhead low in the beginning. Do as much as you can on your own. The way distribution is set up, everybody gets paid before you do. If you don't have extremely deep pockets and somebody with a lot of faith filling those pockets, the best advice is to look at it like it's your own money.

Expenses affect how much money you make. I spoke to a musician who sold close to 100,000 CDs but complained he barely made money after paying everyone on his team, and one who only sells CDs touring and on her website and feels very solvent after selling 3,000. She does everything herself and sells CDs at gigs, mostly for cash. Plus she's paid to perform, licenses tracks for TV, and also sells T-shirts and other merch. So a lot depends on how much goes into marketing. Dave Roberge says:

A lot of it was learning and taking baby steps to where I felt comfortable and confident in my sales forecasting that the number of units was going to outweigh the cost to get them into the marketplace. ADA worked hand in hand with us in determining which sales programs we should target. We have the same opportunity to go into Tower Records and do the national listening stations as any major label artist. It comes down to can you afford or are you willing to spend that amount of money at retail? We do a lot of sales analysis about if we spend X, what would be the return on the investment? We have to track that because of our micro-marketing strategy, almost market by market. We do a lot of analysis to see the effectiveness of the programs that we employ. It's really important to do that. You can spend a lot of money, but if you don't look back and see the results, you're certainly not helping yourself in creating the next marketing plan and budget.

If you're not solvent, create a budget around money *and* resources. While you can't compensate for everything, many things can be done without spending a fortune. You'll take longer to reach goals, but if you want to achieve them badly enough, work your way to them.

Ryan Kuper (Redemption Records) says, "The best way is to build slowly. I started with about five hundred bucks after I bought a computer that I used for both school and biz. I built up my company making baby steps." Kuper is a great example of how small steps can bring large success. Jeff Price says things can get tough financially, but developing honest relationships can help you get over the hump. To have better credit, he advises:

> Have one or two vendors—people you hire to do things for you. Pay them on time, in full, every month, because you need credit references. Then you can refer to them to tell new vendors that you're trustworthy. Having this and a credit card you pay in full every month helps you with your credit line and getting what you need from people. You're going to find yourself in situations where you can't pay everyone. The music industry is brutal. The worst thing you can do is disappear. The best thing is to pick up the phone or write a letter to the people you owe money to and explain what's happening. Be very up front and tell the truth. "I don't have the money to pay you on time, but here's what I can do. I'll pay you X dollars every week." Or "here's what I can commit to." You'll find that people will work with you and respect you for it. And when you pay off your debt, they'll be more willing to trust you because you established a relationship of trust.

In your resources budget, list all your resources as well as everyone you can call on for favors:

- Can someone do printing for you at work?
- Will a friend allow you to use her loaded computer?
- Can you park your website on someone else's domain until you can afford your own host?
- Can you send sound files instead of CDs to some people?
- Can you learn to do your own PR and book gigs?

Ask your street team (see Chapter 15) what talents and resources they have. Put all components of your marketing plan on paper, and figure out how to handle them. Prioritize what needs to be done first. Juggle what money you have with what resources you can turn to for support.

Do one thing at a time to get one step closer to success. Eric Speck (Ace Fu Records) advises:

> You have to be frugal and smart about the deals you go into. I have outlived so many labels that had so much bigger overhead and bigger budgets and bands. It's easy to spend heavy in independent music. You can always do more and hire more people. In the end, that will not guarantee that your music will be liked. Sometimes you just have to be in the groove of what will work. So spend with momentum and learn when to basically step away from a project. You may be the only one who likes the band.

Record Keeping

I hate bookkeeping and all that goes with it! It used to be traumatic for me. But I had no choice about handling money matters once I went into business for myself. If you can afford an accountant or bookkeeper, lucky you! But many of you will do your own record keeping, at least at first. Even if you don't, understand the process. It's your business and money. Taking finances one step at a time makes them less complicated.

From the get-go, create a bookkeeping system that works for you. Don't get so immersed in your label that you pile paperwork in a box. Organize your accounting regularly. If you let the accounting function go untouched, soon papers will be piled high. Anthony Orlando, CPA, recommends:

> Keep it simple. If you can use a basic check-writing or home office program to keep track of your checking account, do so. Keep receipts and a diary for other expenses. If you can't handle a computer, use a pencil and a ledger sheet to track the checks written and other expenses.

Computer software programs make bookkeeping easy. Ask for suggestions. I prefer keeping financial records in a bookkeeping ledger from an office supply store. There's no one way, but at least consult with a professional. My accountant showed me how to make columns for expenses and income. When I started my label, I also took a class on starting a business. I learned that writing checks for all business expenses makes it easier to keep track of them. If you pay cash for items, lump them together and write a check to yourself. Note what it's for. Then I list each check in my ledger, and most of the expenses are covered.

I have a column for each type of expense: manufacturing, advertising, printing, office supplies, mailing/shipping, phone, salaries, fees for independent promoters, bank fees, studios, transportation, etc. Each check number is listed in the left column, and I put the amount spent in the column it fits into. If a check covers more than one type of expense, I write each figure into the appropriate column next to the check number. Periodically I tabulate totals to compare expenses to income. At the end of the year, I total everything and give it to my accountant for taxes.

When a store or distributor pays an invoice, note the invoice number and have a column or page for each record title. If there's more than one format, separate them. Include both the amount paid and the number of units sold. When I get returns on product that's been paid for, I list them in an appropriate column and deduct them. Starting a good system of recording your expenses, money intake, and returns from the beginning prevents headaches later. Whether your business is large or small, record keeping is essential. It makes doing your taxes and paying royalties easier. It also helps determine if your income justifies your spending.

If possible, get a professional who knows the music industry to do royalty statements for your artists. Someone who knows what they're doing also knows the industry standards for deductions and base rates of payment (see Chapter 6 for more details). If you keep the books yourself, pay a professional for lessons about the basics, and then proceed. You, as the label, must figure out how many records were sold and compute what's owed after deductions.

Filing Your Taxes

I hate doing my taxes! You probably don't like them much, either, but it's an important facet of doing business. If you're starting a label to market your own music, you may not take it as seriously. You must! Being conscious of legitimate deductions can save money, especially if you still have a day job. Even if you're not making lots of money yet, deductions help. According to Mark Fox, EA, who co-runs Fox Tax (www.foxtaxservice.com), a Minneapolis-based tax firm:

By making a business out of your art and tracking all of your business expenses, you can potentially stretch your dollars by up to 40 percent or even more. Business deductions lower your income, which in turn lowers tax. Depending on which income bracket you are in, the deductions could save you 25 percent or more federal tax, 15 percent self-employment tax, and 5 to 9 percent on state tax.

Keep a record of all expenses. If your label is a corporation, you'll file a corporate tax form, separate from your personal return. If your label is registered as a DBA, you'll file a Schedule C form with your personal tax filing. If it shows a loss, it can offset taxes on other income you earned that year. New businesses can take a loss in three out of the first five years. Be vigilant for receipts that can become deductions, advises Fox:

The IRS describes as deductible any ordinary and necessary business expense. It defines an ordinary expense as anything common and accepted in your trade or business and a necessary expense as anything helpful and appropriate for your trade or business. You can track and deduct any expense that you consider helpful in advancing your career as an independent label. This includes everything from new gear to travel expenses, recording costs, practice space rental, communications (cell phone/Internet), as well as any other promotional or research expenditures you may incur. Some commonly overlooked expenses include research and development (buying CDs, magazines, and books as well as going to concerts, seminars, classes, or lessons fall into this category), meals/entertainment (jot down on the receipt who you are with and what you talked about), and local travel to practice, stores, and any other music-related activities. Basically, anything you do that can be considered music-related can probably be viewed as part of your business—there are some limits on specific things.

I keep everything in my ledger so when tax time comes, I just hand it to my accountant. Don't forget small things like blank DVDs or scotch tape. Anything you use for business can be declared an expense for tax purposes. Since everyone's situation is different and the tax code can change each year, I can't give more specifics. Call the IRS at 800-829-3676 to get its tax kit and ask any questions you may have. I highly recommend using a good accountant to do the taxes for your label. They can get complicated if you take deductions.

Preparing for Street Date

If you follow the advice in this section, you'll set yourself apart from a majority of indie labels. Indies are known for being informal and haphazard about releasing product, and a majority press CDs when they can and then release them. Some folks think that with digital marketing getting stronger, it's much less important to worry about scheduling a release date. If you're just marketing your own music and don't care about CD sales and offline marketing and promotion, this might not apply. But if you want the industry to take your label seriously, pick a street date at least three months in advance. Announce it, promote it, and then bust your butt to release the records on time. Jesse Fergusson says:

> We notify retail two and a half months prior to release. Caroline has a mailer, and then we follow up with retail calls and fax one-sheets (more in Chapter 13). One of the first things that must be done on a record is a one-sheet: full track listings, title, artist, production credits, selling points, marketing strategy—the whole nine. After that, start your promotional tools in production—you want them all ready at least four weeks before street date.

The street date is the day records hit stores. Most successful indie labels begin promoting releases months before. They ship product to stores a few days early so it's available in stores on the targeted street date. Radio, press, distributors, and stores expect that. If you want longevity as a label, make sure your releases are available on street dates! Andy Allen, president of Alternative Distribution Alliance (ADA), says:

> We have some labels that begin promoting four to five months up front. It's terrific for us. When we go out with a release that's set up that well, people know who the artist is, what they can expect from the first week's sales. The longest possible is the best setup. The press effort has the longest lead time. National monthly magazines have a two- to three-month lead time. To have articles appear at the time the record is released, you need to get on the phone two, three, four

months in advance. We found that in order to have the record featured in a high-profile area of a store, you generally have to make those commitments two to three months in advance. Otherwise, you're likely not to get them.

You're competing against those who begin early. Many labels don't, however; you'll stand out like a beacon of light if you do. Send everyone you can a one-sheet about the record. Shock people at press, radio, and retail by showing them you know how to play in the "big league," even if you are a new indie! Give yourself an edge, and plan ahead! Gregg Latterman advises:

Before you put something out, everything should be together—the album, artwork, photos, bio, and a plan of action. So many people get busy playing catch-up. But that doesn't work very well. It works better if you think ahead and have everything in place ahead of time.

Doing advance promotion shows you take your label seriously. It also gives you a better shot at getting press and radio play. Many indie releases don't get written about because they start too late. Magazines plan months in advance. When an indie sends in material early *and* it's good, they're more likely to get press. Some editors want to be notified as much as four months in advance. Including a street date helps get publications, distributors, radio stations, etc. to work with you. Mark Redfern, publisher/senior editor of *Under the Radar*, says:

If a press release doesn't list a release date then I take that as a red flag meaning that the album is already out or the label is so small that they aren't planning much of a release and have limited distribution.

Besides written material, send a sample of the band's music in advance, too. Editors want to hear the act, not just read about them. If you can get your material pressed way in advance of the street date, great. But if you can't, burn something to send, even if you have to send CD-Rs in advance. Some will listen to MP3s or visit your MySpace page. Email the editor and ask what he or she wants. I understand it's hard to get product and then sit on it for months. But find a way to get advance music into the hands of people who might promote it if you want to make money. And make sure you're prepared for your street date. Jesse Fergusson says:

The biggest complaint people have is when records are scheduled to come out and they come out late. I would stress setting the deadlines and keeping them. Make sure you know the production schedule that your manufacturer and distributor are going on and stick to them. Build in big buffers so that you get things done before they're supposed to be done, so the records come out in a timely manner. Your promotion should correspond exactly with the releasing of the record. Otherwise you just waste money. If you're wasting promotion money, then you're losing and you'll sell less records. Every record less is less to spend on the next record.

Do you need more motivation to promote in advance? Here's one word that should motivate you: *preorders,* which are orders made in advance of the release date. If you get a big enough early buzz on a record, stores may give you preorders. This means that they believe the record will sell at least X amount of copies when it's released and order accordingly. Ryan Kuper says:

Getting preorders is a normal part of sales. All companies should strive for that. I do it with every record. We all want stuff sold before it is even out. It can mean a lot of returns, but it is usually 90 percent actual sales. It makes distributors happy.

What would make stores order a record that hasn't been released from a label they don't know? Buzz—excitement in the streets about the record. Get street teams to work your strongest markets *and* get the word out online. They can give out fliers, swag, links to your MySpace page, and music samples to get people in stores and in colleges excited about your act. Book shows around your street date. Advance commitments for press from magazines are great incentives for preorders. The more you do to show a potential for sales, the greater your chance of getting them. Then make sure your product is ready with a bang on your street date. Jesse Fergusson advises, "Records ship from three to ten days before street date. We always have a party, a performance, and an in-store. A week prior, we try to have local college radio appearances."

Record stores like indies that promote their release date. Many have great success doing preorders—thirteen days prior to street. Offer extras— a free poster, key chain, stickers, a one-song CD or link to a download for a track not on the record or a live performance, etc.—to anyone who preorders the album. Advance promotion can sell large numbers the week before a record comes out and create excitement around it. Plan a show on your street date if possible and promote it on- and off-line. Try to get a school in your area to do a show around that time to get the artist's name out, even if it's done for free.

Branding Your Label and Artists

When you begin your label, choose your brand and stick with it. Don't put out a country record one week and a hip-hop record the next. Something that indies have over majors is that people are attracted to buying their records since they have an idea of what to expect from them. According to Tony Brummel:

> That is one of the key assets for an independent label—that you actually have a brand that people care about. At the majors, because they're involved in every single type of music, the brand doesn't mean anything. There are people who will go out and buy every Victory Record but not feel they need to buy everything that Warner Bros. puts out.

Nabisco is a company brand (like your label). They have varieties of cookies (like each artist). People have favorites but may try new ones that Nabisco makes, if they like Nabisco. You want people to associate your label with a certain kind of music so they'll at least check out your new releases. Ryan Kuper learned the hard way:

> Pretty much everything on my label has been some form or another of rock. But I started as a punk and hardcore label and should have started a separate label when I did more pop and rock. Really analyze your core audience and do everything you can to stay in touch with them. I'm literally retooling my label now, and it's going to take a couple of years because of poor decisions I made in the nineties. I alienated the Redemption fan base. I'm so far from who I was when I began. I didn't stay true to it, but I'm trying to get back to it.

Artists are brands, too. The best way to attract loyal fans is to be consistent so they can expect a certain level of music. Then they stay fans! Strive to make great albums with all great songs. Music lovers are sick of paying money for an album with only a few good tracks. They're more loyal to an artist with enough integrity to want fans to love every song. That attracts long-term fans! Branding begins with getting the name of the act out. Artists should work on creating their brand recognition. The Internet makes that easier. The more the artist's name is out, the more name recognition. The more name recognition, the more likely potential fans will check them out! Don't wait until your street date to spread the word. Begin NOW!

Monitoring Product

Nielsen SoundScan (www.soundscan.com) is the primary tracking system for record sales for vendors that use UPC (Universal Product Code) scanning technology. It enables the scanner to read barcodes (more in Chapter 10) and record each sale. Trudy Lartz, vice president of sales and service for Nielsen Entertainment, explains:

> SoundScan is a tracking system used at point-of-sale cash registers in retail stores across the country. A CD is scanned at the cash register, and once a week it reports those sales to us. We calculate all those figures, produce a report on each piece of product in our system that's associated with that scan, and do marketing reports based on industry numbers that come out of that conglomeration of numbers.

Billboard's retail music sales charts are based on data recorded by SoundScan. Other industry people also check the information. If you want your label taken seriously, you'll want your sales recorded. Jay Woods says:

> Be it good or bad, SoundScan is the measuring stick that we have. We know it's a fallible system—there are problems with it—but it's as accurate as we will have. It's a tool for us. It helps tell the story. We try to make the most out of it. It's the industry standard, so people want to know.

Jesse Fergusson adds:

> Charts in general build a story around a record for the corporate/ industry people. They don't help with fans that much, but if the

industry gets excited about a record, then fans will, too. Whenever I send out an update to any of our contracted publicists, promoters, and salespeople for the distributors, I use SoundScan numbers to promote. Having an idea of what you're selling is important, but you can't spend your whole day tracking retail if you're a one-man operation. You'll never get anything done.

SoundScan offers sales reports for a variety of budgets, and they have several packages. The reports enable you to see sales for the week in specific regions. Lartz adds:

It helps you to decide what cities are the important ones to do something in and which ones aren't, instead of feeling you have to canvass the whole country. There may just be pockets that are better for you and some that aren't. A basic package can help you determine that.

Using SoundScan services isn't cheap, depending on which package you get. But the information is valuable. If you're just beginning, you can purchase a one-time report on one specific album. Lartz says:

For people with a small label—only one record out—I recommend that they don't get a package and track it weekly unless they have a specific plan in place. They can purchase the one-time report every three months so they can get a handle on where they are and what they can do next.

SoundScan allows some touring bands to get credit for CD sales at venues if they're on a registered label. Lartz says, "We track venue sales, so if they open a venue sales account, they can sell their records at venues and make sure the reporting process takes place." You'd need a UPC code and must register with SoundScan. This program helps touring artists whose sales on the road were never tracked. Lartz says, "Verification is important. We do have investigative teams that verify those things every week." Unfortunately, labels with one artist don't qualify. But if you sell a lot of CDs, you can talk to them and find ways around that. Sometimes you can go through a distributor to do it or create a co-op of labels for distribution purposes only.

CHAPTER 6

Getting Your Legal
Affairs in Order

Before starting your record label, find a good lawyer. This doesn't mean laying out money in advance. But at least know who'll represent you when legal counsel is called for. NEVER make legal decisions without consulting one. And if someone tells you it's a standard agreement so you don't need a lawyer, get one even faster! Very little is standard! Signing a bad deal can keep you from making the money you should make or kill your label. Jay Cooper, Esq., entertainment lawyer in the Los Angeles law firm of Greenberg Traurig, LLP, says:

> *Find a good attorney to advise you. Don't presume you know something that you don't know. You've got to go to somebody who's been doing this for a long time, who knows what all the pitfalls are. There's no way to educate somebody who's starting a record label about the business in an hour or five hours. I once taught a class at S.C. on the record contract alone. It was a twenty-week course, three hours a night. It's a very complicated document.*

I highly recommend having two books at hand. *This Business of Music* (Billboard Books) by Sidney Shemel and M. William Krasilovsky is considered "the bible" of the music industry. Updated regularly, it's a great reference on the industry's structure and standards. *All You Need to Know About the Music Business* (Prentice-Hall) by Donald Passman provides easy reading on the business/legal end of music. Devour this book for a clear picture of how the music biz operates. Passman thoroughly illustrates specific points to understand before signing agreements. I don't want to reinvent the wheel by going into great detail about what these books explain brilliantly, but I'll emphasize points you must understand so you don't get ripped off or rip off your artists.

Choosing an Attorney

People regularly ask me for the name of a good lawyer. Sometimes they're frantic, having just heard from someone offering them a deal and want me to tell them who to use. That's not the right way to choose legal representation.

It's always counterproductive to speak for yourself on legal issues. Someone may try to schmooze you, insisting you can informally work out a deal. No way! No matter how sincere that person may seem, you'll be outmaneuvered. Larger labels know some indies are so anxious for a deal that they'll forgo a lawyer to get it. You may be offered distribution or a joint venture opportunity, or if you're an artist, an artist agreement. No matter how good it sounds or how much you want this deal, get a lawyer!

Shop for appropriate representation *before* you need it. Don't just hire the first name you're given. Just as we all have different tastes in clothes and food, we'll prefer specific things in someone representing our legal affairs. I've encountered many lawyers who made me wonder why anyone used them. They've seemed unpleasant, unethical, or just plain dumb. Yet they had clients paying competitive fees. There are lawyers for every taste, so don't rely on only one opinion.

It's imperative to use someone with a specialty in music or entertainment. Lawyers don't learn the finer points of negotiating record deals in school. They learn through experience. Many lawyers take my classes to learn the basics. If you don't have one who's experienced in music negotiations, you may get screwed, even if he or she has the best intentions, and even if that person is your father. Only insiders know music industry standards and tradeoffs.

Interview several lawyers before choosing one. Some may give a free consultation or talk with you for a few minutes on the phone. Have questions prepared to get a feel for them both as professionals and as people.

Some lawyers are friendlier than others. Some are more businesslike. Some may intimidate you. Don't use one whose personality irritates you. This is a business of relationships, so if your lawyer annoys you, how will he or she get along with those whom they're negotiating with on your behalf?

Some lawyers may be interested in your projects. Those who appreciate your music are more likely to work well with you. Music lawyers know they probably won't put their kids through college from fees paid by a new label. But, if they see your potential to be successful, they may be flexible about fees. Look for enthusiasm. My first lawyer totally believed in me. She didn't mind if I called once in a while for advice, as long as I didn't keep her on the phone for too long. I didn't get billed for those calls. She billed when I made money from a deal. It's great to have a legal person on your side!

How do you find a lawyer without calling me? Obviously, referrals from other labels or artists are good. Ask around—a lot. Network—a lot. Most legal organizations for people in the arts (listed on my site, www.idontneedarecorddeal.com) have referral lists available. If you cold-call someone whom you're thinking of using, ask for names of clients. Ask questions. There are all types of music lawyers available for all types of prices. When you do find one you like whose fees you can afford, establish that you'd like her or him to represent you when the time comes. When a deal comes your way, give this lawyer's name when you're asked who's representing you.

Never make handshake deals, not even with people you completely trust. This industry can change people. The best way to protect yourself is to have a written agreement spelling out everything that you've agreed to. Most people aren't out to screw you, but details of an agreement can get fuzzy when money is involved. Your producer may forget exactly what you agreed to. Discussing something is not the same as putting everything on paper. A written agreement clarifies details before the excitement of money factors into the situation. If you can't afford a lawyer for all business matters, write everything down in as much detail as possible. Include what you agree to give the other party and what you'll get in return. Be clear about which expenses can be reimbursed when money comes in.

Business Affairs Department

Larger labels have a department for business affairs. John Luneau, head of business affairs for Palm Pictures, explains that major corporations have an in-house legal department handling things like litigation, copyright registration, and drafting of contracts. The business affairs department, which is staffed by lawyers, negotiates record deals with the artists and artist managers. Once they reduce it to a twelve-page memo, the legal department drafts it. Smaller labels usually use one department to handle all the functions, both drafting and negotiating artist agreements.

Indie labels often don't have a business affairs department at all. If you plan to sign artists to your label, John Luneau advises forming a relationship with a lawyer in private practice who has knowledge and experience in this area, to help you develop agreements that are right for your business. He explains:

> My recommendation for a small label that wants to minimize its legal fees is to pay the lawyer to train you to do as much of the negotiating as possible. You would then use the lawyer in the wings, advising and coaching you in the negotiations and then doing the drafting. If the negotiations go for several drafts, someone at the label would call the lawyer between each draft and go over the comments that they received from the other side. In a half-hour phone conversation they can decide how to resolve those issues and what things to counter-propose to resolve them. Then the person inside the label would get on the phone and try to resolve those issues and get back to the lawyer. This would go on until there's a final signed contract. The reason it's so favorable to the label is that it's talking to the other side that takes the time. It can just suck up hours. If you pay a lawyer to do them, at four hundred dollars an hour, that can get very expensive. I represented a couple of small labels years ago on that kind of system, and it worked to everybody's benefit.

Artist Agreements

If you're opening a label to put out only your own material, relax about artist agreements. If you're signing artists, it's imperative to have a legitimate, binding artist's agreement between the artist and your label. An artist agreement should come from a lawyer. There are no standard ones. A lawyer may start with what's called a boilerplate contract, which includes all the basic clauses. But there can be many variables. For example, if an artist is the songwriter, the contract must cover publishing rights (see Chapter 7). Your lawyer will normally make the contract as much in your favor as possible. You can give up things in negotiations, but writing this agreement definitely requires a music lawyer's experience.

It's not uncommon for artists to try to break contracts with indie labels when they smell success. After all, if a larger label wants to pick them up, why should they split royalties with you? By signing directly with a larger label, the artist gets more money and controls the production budget. I've heard of many artists who ran to a lawyer when a larger label was interested in them. Some lawyers will encourage them to try to break their agreement with you. That's why you need to make sure your recording agreement is legal and binding, with no loopholes for your artists to crawl through.

Artists sometimes sign contracts without seeing a lawyer. Later, to break a contract, the artist may claim he or she had no legal representation and the agreement is unfair. I had artists swear they trusted me when I pushed them to get a lawyer while we were negotiating an agreement. Months later, when I had offers from larger labels, they tried to get out of the deal (unsuccessfully) by claiming they originally didn't have a lawyer. You can't force artists to get legal counsel, but you can try to persuade them to use a lawyer before they sign. Some labels offer an advance specifically for hiring a lawyer to negotiate the artist's contract. Many lawyers who represent the record label put a clause at the end of recording agreements saying that the label advised the artist to go to a lawyer, and the artist chose not to do so according to their own free will. My lawyer created a separate letter to that effect, which the artist had to sign.

An artist agreement should contain specific terms of longevity. Lock the artist into at least a minimum number of albums. Instead of signing for a number of years, labels get a commitment of X number of albums. This guarantees that you as the label won't get stiffed on albums if the artist stays out on tour or takes forever in the studio. Get a commitment for as many albums as possible. If the artist does well, you'll benefit from releasing more under that contract. If the artist tanks, you have no obligation to record more. You can't lose by getting a commitment for several albums. If you don't put any out, the artist will try to get released from the contract. If he or she isn't doing well, you won't care. Your lawyer can advise you.

Owning the Master Copy

The master copy is the original copy of the recording. All copies originate from it, and most record labels make its ownership a high priority. Unless an artist has a big name or other bargaining power, it's common for the label to obtain ownership of the master copy as part of the artist agreement. But there's no standard about who gets these rights. You and your lawyer must assess how important such ownership is in regard to signing an act that's playing hardball over this issue. Jay Cooper, Esq., stresses that "It's very important to own the master copy. It gives you control of what you do with it in the future. Most record companies recognize that this is an asset, and they want to own that asset."

Important Points of a Good Contract

Your contract will specify the percentage (known as points) of the retail price of records sold that the artist royalties will be based on. Royalties paid on retail average from about twelve to fourteen points, but they could go higher or lower depending on negotiations. Points paid to a producer are usually taken out of an artist's points, but there are no rules.

You can have a field day taking advantage of music industry standards that allow you to lower the royalties you pay artists. Many "customary" provisions used in recording agreements are based on outdated factors, and some are downright unfair. As a businessperson, weigh your sense of ethics against the money you'll save if you take the deductions that larger labels do. It's good to find a balance between being fair to the artist and fair to your label. Major labels still take many unfair deductions to reduce the base price on which royalties are paid. But that's changing, as artists become aware of more options and aren't as desperate for a deal.

Donald Passman's book spells out artist deductions clearly. Some that are considered standard aren't based on factors that are relevant today. Many indie labels don't even try to use them. A good laywer who represents indie labels can guide you. Besides deductions from an artist's royalties, a label has the right to pay itself back for certain expenses, which are considered recoupable. These include things like recording expenses, advances, tour support (money that you as the label spend to support an artist on tour), equipment, at least part if not the entire cost of making a video, at least part if not all the cost of hiring an independent promoter, and whatever other expenses your lawyer can get the artist to agree to as recoupable.

Most expenses related to pressing, printing, advertising, and marketing are non-recoupable.

There are many other deductions, variables, and industry standards that you can read about thoroughly in the books mentioned earlier in this chapter and in my book *The Real Deal*. Make sure you understand these issues before discussing contracts with your attorney. The artist's lawyer will try to get rid of as many deductions as possible, but unless the artist is hot, the ball is more often in your court. This is considered a business of pennies, and if you save even one penny per record, that can add up to a lot of money with a record that sells well.

Stephanie Furgang Adwar, Esq., of Furgang & Adwar, LLP, says, "These days indie labels are a little more flexible and try to make all kinds of creative agreements. There could be a situation where the label allows an artist who put in money to own part or all of their master." I recommend that you learn about different potential deductions and then decide which to keep. It can't hurt to leave them all in a contract that you initially offer your artist and use them for bargaining leverage. But don't rip an artist off!

Nowadays, some labels offer what's known as a 360 deal. Eric de Fontenay, founder/president of MusicDish and Mi2N, says that this basically turns the traditional label into an artist-development/management company. The terms have the label provide artists with support in all aspects of their careers, including merchandising, touring, and licensing, for a piece of the artist's overall revenue. De Fontenay says, "It first took shape in a deal between Robbie Williams and EMI, but has been adopted pretty broadly by independent labels." Steven Masur, Esq., managing director of MasurLaw, elaborates:

> As CD sales decrease, artists and labels are beginning to rely more on touring, merchandising, digital sales, and advertising to make money. As a result, there is a lot of talk about 360-degree recording agreements. Independent labels have always had to take an active role in trying to ensure the success of their acts, so the idea of a 360-degree deal is nothing new to them. But if they are going to invest this money and effort, labels should be sure that their contracts give them the appropriate degree of control—and reward—with regard to digital, mobile, Internet radio and advertising sales and sponsorships. Conversely, artists should have an "out" to these arrangements in case the label does not actually invest the time, effort, and money

originally promised. In the coming years, the biggest disputes between artists and labels will come from artists who are trapped in nonperforming 360-degree arrangements.

Are 360 deals fair? It depends on the terms of the agreement. De Fontenay explains:

Its fairness lies in the details. If the label is bringing major distribution as well as a real budget for marketing, radio, touring, then it can make sense for some bands. But in general, why get a plumber to do the electrical work? Does the label have experience or relationships/ partnerships to develop all aspects of an artist's career? Do they have an effective offline strategy, or is it just about getting you digital distribution and some online marketing? If they don't have a budget and major distribution, then what's the point? An alternative strategy is for the artist to build their own team that specializes in their respective sectors: PR, radio, booking, online marketing. This will of course require some budget and business plan to be developed by the artist, but this allows them to keep full control while tapping into the expertise required to succeed.

Taking everything you can get isn't fair to the artist. Since I believe that what goes around comes back to you, taking unfair advantage will not create a successful label/artist relationship. Daniel Glass (Glassnote Entertainment) agrees:

We believe that if an artist does well touring, the ancillary effects will sweep us with them. If we have a piece of that, great. If we don't, it's also okay. We're in the record business primarily but also in publishing and merchandising. In some cases we're involved more with the artist. But if we don't feel we can build the value in those areas, we shy away from it. We don't do it for the obligatory reason of just doing it. That's a mistake that entrepreneurs are making.

Some indie labels do 50/50 splits if the artist brings a lot to the table. Some that I interviewed for this book do it if the artist has a finished product, solid touring, and is willing to work very hard on the promotion end. Usually the artist has a proven track record of being a good self-promoter.

Then the label offers a variation of terms that split profits after the label has recouped agreed-on expenses. All these deals are individual to the label. Adwar says more often a 50/50 deal requires the artist to contribute half the money. She explains:

> The artists are coming in with 50 percent of the money. Indie labels do it because it makes it possible for them to work together and get things done. Since indie labels don't have [the kind of money majors have] to spend on an artist, they're willing to work out very original deals with artists, especially if they like the masters. If they think they can do more for them, they're more willing to work out a deal. There are many other factor in the equation.

The bottom line depends on your situation, the artist you want to sign, and your finances. Talk to a good entertainment lawyer to figure out what works best for your label. There's no one size that fits all. According to William Hochberg, a music business attorney primarily representing creative talent and their companies:

> Nowadays the lines are blurred between the big bad record company and the pure and innocent artist. With major labels up against the ropes, more success is coming to smaller, independent labels who are more artist-oriented. Yet you see big artists coming out of the pampered major label world now seeking deals with hip indie labels, and you are seeing role reversal, where the artist with her heavy hitter attorney is demanding concession after concession from the over-worked, under-paid and abused little label. The indie label will often have difficulty obtaining the "360" kinds of rights we hear about, such as a piece of revenue stream from the artist's live performance, endorsements, publishing, merchandising, or acting income from TV and film. It needs to be handled on a case-by-case basis, but if the indie is resurrecting a career, it should insist on at least some of these rights.

Paying Royalties

Royalties are paid twice a year. You'll have a few months after the end of a royalty period to prepare a statement of earnings for the artists. It's best to hire a bookkeeper to do this. Once royalties are computed based on all deductions allowed in the agreement, you can deduct all recoupable expenses spelled out in your agreement before paying the artists a dime. Many never see a royalty check because they don't recoup. When you record a second album for an artist, any unrecouped debts are carried over and added to what needs to be paid back for album number two—this is called cross-collateralization. But if an artist never recoups, he or she doesn't have to pay back out of pocket what's owed.

I highly recommend getting a good accountant or bookkeeper to do your royalty statements. If you want to try it yourself, pay a professional to teach you how to do it. You need to know the base price on which points are computed, along with all the deductions and recoupable expenses.

CHAPTER 7

Copyright and Publishing Decisions

After teaching classes on the music industry for many years, I've found that copyright and publishing is an area that's fuzzy for many people. Confused souls say they don't worry about copyright and publishing—it's not important to them. That's ridiculous! Since publishing is one of the most lucrative arenas of the music industry, it's absurd to give it so little importance. Songwriting royalties can surpass artist's royalties on a hit album. Far surpass!

Owning a piece of the publishing royalties of songs on your artists' records can earn you money. Even if you have a good lawyer, it's important for you to understand the basics of copyright and publishing issues. The more you manage it properly and take precautions to ensure you're getting what you're entitled to, the more potential you have for making money.

Copyright Protection

Copyright protects someone's original work. Taken literally it means, as stated by the U.S. Copyright Office, "the right to copy." The Copyright Act of 1976 establishes the right to protect all intellectual property that we create and to have exclusive use of our songs for at least a reasonable period of time.

Getting a Copyright

Do you assume that a copyright form must be filed before a song is copyrighted? Well, it's not so. Under present copyright law, any original work that's fixed on something tangible is automatically protected under the laws of copyright. "Original" means that the person claiming the copyright created the work as an original piece. A "work" involves something more concrete than just an idea in your head; it means something tangible, such as a written document or a recording on a tape. If you sing an original song to your friends, you don't have a copyright. If you sing it into a tape recorder, you do. It's that simple. Why should people formally register their copyrightable work? Because it provides written protection or proof. According to Wallace Collins, Esq.:

> *The filing of a copyright registration form with the Register of Copyrights in Washington, DC, gives you additional protection in so far as it establishes a record of the existence of such copyright and gives you the legal presumption of validity in the event of a lawsuit. Registration is also a prerequisite for a copyright-infringement lawsuit to be commenced in federal court and, under federal law, allows an award of attorneys fees to the prevailing party provided the form is filed within ninety days of when the work is first offered for sale or before the infringement occurs.*

You can download forms on the Copyrights Office's website (www. copyright.gov). Copyright claims are received and registerd—not evaluated. If five songs with the same title come in, they all get registered.

Protecting the Sound Recording

The copyright form that songwriters use most commonly to register the music and/or lyrics of a song is Form PA, which refers to works considered in the "performing arts." When music and lyrics are copyrighted, it's indicated by the symbol ©. You, as the record label owner, should register your recording of the song by using Form SR, which protects the "sound recording" of your product. You may not own the publishing of the song, but you still own your recorded version, and you should protect it. Form SR offers protection from people copying the sound recording and using it for their own purposes. When a sound recording is copyrighted, it's indicated by the symbol ® next to the title.

When selling a recording, it's important to file Form SR. Owning the copyright for the sound recording provides protection from pirates and people who might sample from it. Form SR also registers the lyrics and music. Copyright applications are sent to the Register of Copyrights with a completed form, a check for the fee for each form sent, and a copy of your song, which they refer to as a "deposit." It's not necessary to send a copy of the lyrics or music sheet if everything is on the format you send. Since registration is effective the day the Copyright Office receives your material, send it by certified mail and request a return receipt. It costs a few dollars extra, but the receipt is proof of the date the material reached them. Hold the receipt until the Copyright Office sends your registration. It can take months for it to be processed.

Compulsory Licenses

Whomever owns the copyright has the right to do the first version of the song, called the "right of first control." After it's been released publicly, others can record the song. No one can do a cover of it until the copyright owner has done a version that's been distributed to the public. The owner can give someone else permission to record and distribute it first, as long it's documented in writing.

Once a song's been released and recorded, almost anyone can record it again. You must get a license to do this, and the copyright holder must issue one, as long as the applicant applies properly. Compulsory mechanical licenses are issued to those wanting to record and release a copyrighted work. The person requesting it must give notice of the intention to use the work and pay the appropriate fee to the copyright holder. An artist on your label can do a cover of someone else's song, as long as the song has already been recorded and the recording released. Notify the copyright owner and pay all royalties to the writers and publishers of any songs you use.

To get a compulsory mechanical license, the person or label wanting to record and release the song must notify the copyright owner of the intention to release the work before it's been made available for sale. If the owner can't be found and the Copyright Office can't help you, a notice of intention can be filed with the Copyright Office. Monthly payments must be made to the owner of the copyright based on the number of records sold. The amount paid is a set fee called the statutory rate.

Copyright Infringement = Stealing

Copyright infringement means using a copyrighted song without permission from the copyright owner. Someone can be guilty of copyright infringement if they sample, rerecord a song without crediting the writer and paying appropriate royalties, use a piece of someone else's song within the framework of their own, etc. A person doing any of the above can be sued, as can most parties involved in the manufacture, sale, and performance of such work. For example, the manufacturer of the CD could be sued for manufacturing one with stolen material. If your artist uses someone's copyrighted song, you as the record label are in jeopardy. Copyright infringement is a federal offense.

Everything in a copyrighted work is protected. Not even teeny pieces of melodies, hooks, or lyrics from other songs can be used without permission. To establish copyright infringement, two things must be proven. First, it must be shown that the work is "substantially similar" to the copyrighted one. Access to the copyrighted song must also be proven. If someone writes a song that's similar to someone else's, but they've never heard the original, it's not infringement. Let's say Ruth in Dallas wrote a song similar to one written by Jim in Chicago. If she can prove she's never been near Chicago, Jim has no case, unless he can prove his song was played somewhere Ruth had been. Coincidences happen. To prove infringement, you must show that the person who produced something similar to the song that existed first had an opportunity to hear it before writing their own.

An example of obvious access would be if the original song was played on radio. Even if the writer of the second song claims he or she never heard it, if the song had played, there's a good chance of winning the case. Or if both artists recorded in the same studio or lived next door to each other, or if someone came to a show where the copyrighted song was performed, or heard a tape of it through a friend, or was in any situation where he or she could hear it, access can be proven.

The access factor is a prime reason why many record labels refuse unsolicited tapes from unknown artists/songwriters. They don't want to be sued because they have an artist singing a song that sounds similar to a song sent in by someone else. If their policy is "no unsolicited material," they're protected. There's no limit on what can be awarded in a copyright infringement case.

Should Sampling Be Allowed?

Sampling is taking the sound of a recording made by someone else and using it in your own recording. Many musicians consider it an art and like to lift beats and sounds and hooks from other people's records to incorporate into their songs. But unless you get permission to use a copyrighted sound, you run the risk of being sued. Unauthorized sampling is copyright infringement.

I'm often asked how much one can legally sample from someone else's record. The answer is: nothing. If someone can prove that a single note came from his or her record, you can be sued. Most labels have a clause in their artist contracts stating that there's nothing in the finished products that infringes on anyone's copyright. Your artists are legally responsible for not using uncleared samples. Unfortunately, as I said earlier, anyone involved in a record that infringes on someone's copyright is at risk—and guess who's the most seriously at risk, especially if your artists aren't solvent? Make sure any samples used on your product are cleared; if any are not, don't allow them to be used.

If you decide to use a sample legally, the percentage of songwriting royalties needs to be negotiated with the person who controls the copyright, and use of the sound recording has to be licensed from the record label. There's no set licensing fee. Apply for a license before releasing it. Contact the label and ask for someone who handles copyright clearances and ask for permission. Or you can go to a music clearance company. If you don't want to pay a licensing fee, get your artist to reproduce the sound in the studio and sample from that instead. Then at least the label isn't involved. You'll still have to work out a percentage of royalties with the owner of the copyright.

Understanding Publishing

It's not uncommon for a label to include publishing in the recording agreement. I said earlier that publishing/songwriting royalties can be good sources of income. That's why you as the owner of a record label should consider getting at least a piece of the publishing rights assigned to you. I will emphasize, however, that if you're not prepared to work hard to do what a real publisher does, you should think twice about how much, if any, publishing you take.

Co-publishing Agreements

Many folks confuse the total songwriter's royalties with the publisher's share. Let me explain this. The diagram below represents the total songwriting royalties, which come from three sources. A precedent was set years ago whereby the songwriter, who created the product to be sold, and the publisher, whose responsibility was to market the product and make sure all songwriting royalties were paid, split the royalties 50/50. Publisher's share refers to 50 percent of the total copyright revenues. The other half is referred to as the writer's share, which goes to the writer of the song.

A publisher deals with all business-related details regarding the songs in its catalog, since many songwriters can't effectively handle their business. Publishers usually have the copyrights of the songs assigned to them. The publisher's responsibilities include issuing licenses for use of the songs, finding other artists/producers to record them, and making sure royalties are paid. Real publishers are knowledgeable about different sources of songwriting royalties and the best ways to license songs. Since they take care of the business side, they get 50 percent of the total royalties. None of this is set in stone, and agreements can be structured with different percentages, as long as everything is in writing.

Many independent record labels take 50 percent of the publisher's share. referred to as a co-publishing deal. It means that at least two people are sharing the publishing royalties earned by the song. A co-publishing deal doesn't have to be a 50/50 split. The publisher's share can be divided into whatever percentages are agreed to in writing. The songwriter, however, is entitled to the full writer's share of the royalties. It's unethical for a label to take any of it. In the diagram, the publisher's royalties are split 50/50 between publisher and label. As you can see, the songwriter, in addition to the 50-percent writer's share of the royalties, also gets 50 percent of the publisher's share, for a total of 75 percent of the royalties. The label gets 50 percent of the publisher's share, which is 25 percent of the total royalties.

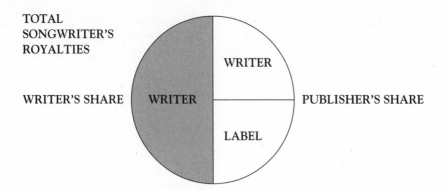

TOTAL
SONGWRITER'S
ROYALTIES

WRITER'S SHARE

PUBLISHER'S SHARE

If you go after a co-publishing deal, it's your responsibility to market the songs. That means trying to get them licensed in a variety of avenues (see Chapter 15) and finding other ways to exploit them to earn an income. Many indies do the legwork and accomplish this. If you intend to, by all means get a fair share. But if you're just taking it to grab more rights to potential income, think twice. Your lawyer should be able to advise you about what's fair. Stephanie Furgang Adwar, Esq., says:

> A lot of my indie labels aren't taking the publishing. It's too much for them. They won't be able to satisfy their artists. Indie agreements tend to be a little fairer than the big label agreements. They're usually smaller and shorter, too. Until an indie has some kind of distribution, they're slowed down in what they can ask for.

Songwriter Royalties

There are several sources of songwriting income that get divided between the songwriter and publisher. One is mechanical royalties, which are paid by the record label for the right to manufacture (i.e., to mechanically reproduce) and sell a writer's songs. A mechanical license is issued by the publisher holding the copyright on any songs recorded and sold by your label. It gives your label permission to manufacture and distribute records for each song. Your label must pay mechanical royalties to the songwriter(s) for each record sold. John Luneau, head of business affairs for Palm Pictures, says:

> Lots of indie labels forget that as a record label, they owe mechanical royalties to publishers for the music on their albums and that they need to secure mechanical licenses for each song. If the songwriter is always their artist, the mechanical license can be built into the

recording agreement. They would pay a separate royalty along with the artist royalty. But if the artist records songs that they don't write, or their own songs are owned by a third-party publisher, you can get into serious trouble releasing records without mechanical licenses in place. A lot of indie labels learn the hard way that you have to pay mechanical royalties. They might get audited by Harry Fox and get slapped with an invoice for unpaid mechanical licenses. If they don't pay, they get slapped with a copyright infringement lawsuit in federal court.

If you hold the rights, you technically issue yourself a license. Some labels cross-collateralize this royalty—use money an artist earns as a songwriter to recoup expenses in the way artist royalties are used. It isn't illegal if it's in the contract, and it can save you money. It is, however, unfair. A second potential source of income is performance royalties, collected by the performing rights societies ASCAP, BMI, or SESAC. They issue licenses for use of music written or published by their members when it's played or performed in public venues including clubs or on radio and TV. They charge fees appropriate to the particular venue and distribute royalties to the writers and publishers. A third source of income is synchronization royalties, which are paid for use of a song on TV shows, in commercials, in movies, etc. Payment for a "synch" license depends on the project and what you as the owner of the music rights will accept versus what the user is willing to pay. The publisher has to work out a reasonable licensing fee.

All this income comprises the total songwriter royalties earned. A 50/50 co-publishing agreement between you and your artists/songwriters would give you 25 percent of all earned royalties. If a larger label picks you up, you'll probably have to give up some of your publisher's share rights. But keeping even a small piece could make a nice chunk of change if the album hits big. Larger labels give an advance on their share of the publishing. Smaller indies often don't. John Luneau says:

> *Many indie labels neglect to realize how immensely profitable owning publishing can be. They neglect to make offers to their own artists to acquire their publishing. If you have a roster of artists whose sales are pretty predictable, you can predict how many mechanical royalties are going to be due to the songwriters and base your advances on those projections so that you never overpay. If you never overpay for your publishing rights, at the end of the day, not only will you break*

even, but you'll earn your share of the mechanical royalties, which can be very lucrative.

Opening Your Own Publishing Company

To collect the publisher's share of royalties, you must open a publishing company. Songwriters collect the songwriter's portion of the royalties directly but also must open a publishing company to collect their share of the publisher's royalties, which won't be paid to you directly. Even if you only hold a piece of the publishing rights, you need a company to collect royalties.

Opening a publishing company means submitting three potential company names to either ASCAP, BMI, or SESAC. Pick the society your songwriters are affiliated with. If you have songwriters affiliated with all three, you'll need to establish a separate publishing company with each one. The society checks to see that the name you've submitted isn't already in use. Try not to choose too common a name since it's more likely to have already been registered by someone else. A publishing company is a business, so treat it as one. You're required to register it legally as a business. It must have a street mailing address (as opposed to a P.O. box). You can start by either incorporating or getting a business certificate. Once you have established it as a business, you can open up a bank account for when royalty checks arrive.

Controlled Composition Clause

Record labels can be discriminatory toward singers who write their own songs, since they supposedly earn artist royalties. They feel that since artist royalties are paid, songwriter royalties should take a cut. This is unfair! Songwriting is separate from being an artist. Many folks in the music industry consider the controlled composition clause unethical, but many labels use it. According to attorney Wallace Collins:

> *Under U.S. copyright law, Congress established a statutory mechanical royalty rate for songwriters and their publishers based on an upward-sliding scale tied to a cost-of-living index on a per-song, per-record basis. However, one of the many royalty reducing provisions in any record contract is known as the "controlled composition clause," which contractually reduces the mechanical rate for a songwriter/recording artist and the publisher on songs written or*

otherwise "controlled" by the artist. Most such clauses also place a limit on the total number of songs on which payment will be made and may fix the point in time at which the calculation will be done (thereby circumventing the cost-of-living index increase). For example, let's assume a typical clause, which might say that the songwriter/artist will receive three-quarters of the minimum statutory mechanical rate payable on a maximum of ten songs per LP. The mechanical royalty on the artist's entire LP has a cap so that even if the songwriter/artist writes twelve songs for his or her own album, the artist's publishing, which should be worth about eighty-three cents an album at the full rate, is only allocated fifty-two cents under this clause. To further illustrate, assume the twelve-song album has six songs written by the artist and six songs from outside publishers. The outside publishers are not subject to the artist's three-quarters rate. So the six outside songs get the full rate and are entitled to a total of about forty-one cents. Since the mechanical royalty on the entire LP has a contractual cap of about fifty-two cents, the recording artist's publisher is limited to applying the remaining eleven cents to the artist's six songs, so that the artist's publishing royalty is worth less than two cents per song. The most treacherous dilemma for the songwriter/artist is that, even if the record company does not expressly acquire the artist's publishing rights in its contract, the value of the artist's publishing may so greatly be reduced by the controlled composition clause that the artist may find it difficult to get a publishing deal elsewhere. This is particularly true if the mechanical royalties are cross-collateralized with the artist royalties, which means that, until the artist royalties are recouped, no mechanical royalties are payable on the recording artist's publishing rights.

Just as your decisions about artist royalties require the weighing of ethics and economics, the same applies to contracts with artists who write their own songs. There are no laws about what you can or can't do regarding songwriting royalties. Industry standards are designed to put more money in the label's pocket. Almost anything is legal if it's in writing and signed by both parties. It's up to you to discuss these issues with your lawyer and decide what standards to follow. Let a combination of your conscience and your lawyer be your guide.

CHAPTER 8

Signing Artists to Your Label

I was always my favorite artist when I ran Revenge Records. Why? Because that assured the artist would be on time to the studio, wouldn't complain when royalties weren't supporting a high lifestyle, and, in general, would not be a big pain in the butt! Dealing with an artist's ego, problems, temperament, overblown expectations, and more was often the main source of aggravation when I ran my label. If you're putting out your own music, be grateful not to have to worry about the issues that come up with artists. If you're looking to sign other acts, read on.

What to Look for in an Artist

If you find an artist who you think is fantastic talent, should you rush to sign her or him? No. Many other factors should be considered. It's easier to make money if you sign someone with more than one asset. There are many factors to keep in mind. Mark Redfern, publisher/senior editor of *Under the Radar* magazine, advises:

> Sign good and interesting artists! Most of what I listen to from smaller labels is pretty dull and derivative. Most bands all sound like rip-offs of better bands, and there isn't much originality. And then sometimes bands try too hard to be original and interesting and end up making

unlistenable experimental music that's supposed to be hip and cool but really isn't any good.

An artist who performs well live will sell more records. Some sound great in a studio but may tank on stage, and live appearances are great promotion. A good live act has more potential for achieving a high public profile, and the bigger their following, the more sales from the get-go. Fans who come to an artist's gigs will likely be first to buy the artist's release on your label. I know many A&R people at both major and independent labels who won't touch an act that doesn't have a decent-sized following. Ryan Kuper (Redemption Records) says:

> *I need a band that has a stable lineup and is not tied down by huge commitments, like a salaried day job. They must have a desire to get on the road and tour in support of a record. If they won't tour, it makes it so much harder for a publicist, distributor, salespeople. If they're not available for a regional interview or in-store performance, it makes it tough.*

Another factor to consider before signing an act is their material. Does the artist write great songs or have access to someone who does? It saves you from having to find material, and you might earn money from owning a piece of the publishing. How is the artist's musicianship? Artists who are pros in the studio are a blessing. The recording process goes more smoothly when an artist has a professional attitude and great skills.

An artist's image is important. These days, a good sense of style is more important than good looks. Different genres have unique styles and nuances. The artist needs to fit in. One who works this angle well has the best chance of finding support from the tastemakers in their genre. A personable artist is more marketable. Friendly ones who are good with people get along better with everyone they work with, including the press. Personality enhances an artist's image. Beauty isn't always a top priority, but an artist who radiates personality has a better "look." Personality comes across in photos and during live shows and should also reflect in the music. Eric Speck (Ace Fu Records) says:

> *You want a band to speak to you in one way that makes them remarkable and unique. There's a personality or charisma they should*

*have. Be captivating or have charisma lyrically or vocally. For me the
most important thing is the vocals—the ability to be unique.*

Artists who educate themselves about the industry are often more realistic
about money expectations and what it takes to succeed. That includes a
greater understanding of how much they should do to promote their records.
Do they have a press kit and local radio play? Have they been working it hard
on their own? Jesse Fergusson (Definitive Jux Records) says that after talent
and skill, he'd look for:

*Flexibility and a willingness to work hard. It's not just about getting
a deal and rapping. The artists at this label that I see succeeding are
the ones that will work their asses off, before and after the record is
out; who will do what it takes to further their own career, which is all
we're asking them to do.*

I preferred signing artists with finished recordings. It obviously saves
money on studio expenses, but that wasn't my main concern. If the
material was at least close to its final state, I knew the artist could actually
follow through in the studio. I don't like gambling. Those of you with
larger budgets might feel fine about investing in a good producer who
might make an act sound great on a recording. I liked knowing that the
artist's material was great before we signed. Some acts can't bring what
sounds killer on stage into the studio if the energy from an audience
isn't there. I've heard too many flat recordings from artists who sound
great live. John Szuch (Deep Elm Records) looks for:

*Anything I am passionate about and think is great. We have a series,
the Emo Diaries. We just put out the eleventh chapter. There's been
147 we've worked with on that series, including Jimmy Eat World,
who have done fabulous for themselves with their hard work and
dedication to making really great records. I want the music to move
me. I know I love a record when I have it in my car for weeks on
end. We don't listen to CDs online or take MySpace submissions.
If the song and music are there, that's always the most important
thing for me. We like bands that are touring, doing hard work,
out promoting themselves, keeping their website and MySpace
page updated. We eventually look at that to see if this band is a
self-sufficient machine that really understands there's a lot of*

work to do. There's even more to do when you sign with a label. We have a function. They have a function. We look to see if they have a manager and who books them.

Be VERY careful about signing artists with a penchant for drugs and/or excessive drinking. Even if they seem under control during performances, in the long run it can lead to trouble! Artists who overindulge in drugs and alcohol are often unreliable. Although the music industry is known for the partying lifestyle, more labels are bypassing artists who appear to have addictions. If you need help dealing with a substance abuse problem, contact MusicCares (www.grammy.com/musicares). They have many good services. As a label owner, an artist is your commodity, and excessive alcohol and drug abuse can damage that commodity.

Make sure that anyone you sign has at least a few key qualities that will help him or her succeed. The more they have, the more you have to work with. That translates into record sales. BUT don't allow your business sense to smother your passion. Sometimes you hear an artist and just know you have to work with them. Szuch says, "Eventually you need to meet them. Look in their eyes, talk to them, and see what their passions are. When you see them play a live show, I think you can really tell."

Checking Your Artist's Attitude

The last artist on my label was my favorite artist by far. Besides having a great set of chops, his main goal in life was to do music for music's sake. He was pleasant, polite, on time, and professional. If I needed him for a promotional gig, he was happy to do it because he loved performing. Period. He wasn't moody, temperamental, or thinking about how much money he should have been making. He practiced so much before going into the studio that he was able to do his vocal track in one take! He focused on getting out and performing music, in whatever way possible. He was my dream artist!

Regardless of how much talent an artist has, it's often not worth going the distance with an act that gives you a hard time on a regular basis. Unless you have resources for a large staff, you'll be living in some ways with your artists. Many take their problems into the studio, to gigs, etc. If they don't have managers, you may be the babysitter. I've had calls from artists during the night who'd lost a wallet and needed money, or had a fight with a band member. I've bailed an artist out of jail the night before a gig. Once you invest money and time, an artist's problems can become yours. You may have to deal with them or lose the artist—and your time and money. I can say from experience that it can be very unpleasant. Be selective about artists you choose to work with; make sure you can work in peace with them.

Some artists have bigger egos than others. Try to get a read on how self-absorbed an artist is. Of course you want your artists to be confident. That's attractive. But when they think that because they have talent the world owes them success, that having a large following or getting good reviews gives them license to do as they please, they'll eventually look ugly to you. An artist with a bad attitude can affect work relationships on many levels, including those with producers, engineers, record store people, and other artists if they vie to be top banana. Difficult artists develop reputations that might keep some folks away. Unless they become very famous, few promoters want prima donnas on tour. Journalists won't want to interview them.

I prefer artists who are at least somewhat flexible about their music. An "I want my music my way because I know it all" attitude isn't uncommon, but it's a real problem. When everyone tells an artist he or she is terrific, the artist often thinks he or she knows it all and won't consider suggestions. An artist should be able to work with a producer who may want changes in the original song or arrangement and show respect for the whole recording team. If an artist seems surly before being signed to your label, watch out. The situation only gets worse later.

I highly recommend signing artists who have some visible means of support. Too many artists have no financial security. You want them to be flexible for touring, but if nothing is going on at first, they'll look to you for income. As I said earlier, many artists make little from royalties. Decent-paying gigs may be scarce before an artist is established. Earning very little money in the beginning is a hard reality for many artists. When they see their music selling and receive adulation from fans, they may feel entitled to serious bucks and get surly when money expectations aren't met. Or, friends and fans who expect them to be spending money freely may pressure them. These problems are especially common among young artists, who often have a hard time accepting a lack of money when they've achieved a certain level of success.

An artist who is realistic in his or her expectations is easier and more pleasant to work with. Be objective in deciding which artists to sign. Even if you're dying to sign an artist because you love the music, weigh the pros against possible cons. Interview potential artists about their expectations of being recording artists just as you'd interview candidates for jobs at your label. Make sure you're on the same page. Dave Roberge (Everfine Records) advises, "You have to take the time to understand them and ask, 'What do you want? What are your expectations?' If you don't hold that as a preliminary conversation, you're doing an injustice to that artist."

Ask artists where they see themselves in a year and how much money they expect to make when their records are released. Clue them in to reality before they sign. Evaluate the artist's temperament, at least a little, to avoid anyone with serious attitude problems. You've been warned!

Where to Find Artists

There's a lot of unsigned talent around. It's not hard to find good artists, if you make an effort. Some labels go to clubs where their genre is performed. You'll find a variety of artists performing live every night in most cities, playing everything from rock to jazz to hip-hop to standards and everything in between. Go regularly. If you see performers you like, talk to them or their managers after the gigs. Network your butt off at live venues, and ask for recommendations of acts that are looking for a label to put them out. Ask the people who work in clubs if they've seen any unsigned artists lately that made a great impression. Find out where they're playing live, and check them out a few times.

The Internet offers an unlimited resource. Nowadays, with all the social networking sites, it's much easier than ever to find artists. Most artists have their music posted, along with their touring schedules, bios, press, etc. Look around and see what you find. You can get most of what you need without ever contacting the artist. Then check them out live, too, and get to know them in person. Daniel Glass (Glassnote Entertainment) found Secondhand Serenade on MySpace. Then he checked him out in real life. He explains:

> We went to see him perform live. What sealed the deal was going to San Francisco and seeing him at his house. He and his wife, with two babies crawling on the floor, were sealing envelopes, sending out

T-shirts, CDs, and letters. And before we went to dinner they had to go on MySpace to speak to some fans. That's indie! That's the kind of guy I want to do business with. He still does most of that, but we distribute the CDs and T-shirts. He must speak to at least one to two hundred people online, which is why his fan base is so strong. He communicates, and that's a great artist!

Word of mouth is a good way to find artists. Put yourself into the music scene regularly, and keep your ears open for news of acts people are raving about that as yet have no record deals. Let everyone you meet know you're looking for talent. Ask in clubs if anyone's seen an act worth signing. Talk to people in music organizations. Go to music showcases. Songwriters' organizations often showcase songs written by their members, who are often the artists performing those songs as well. Become friendly with people who run recording studios, as they often record talented acts.

No matter where you find artists, make sure they have no commitments on the side that you don't know about. Ask questions. Have they signed deals with producers or had other indie label deals before? Do they have a management or publishing deal you should be aware of? After investing time and money in an act, you don't want someone coming out of the woodwork with a contract that's been forgotten or ignored. Sometimes an artist signs an agreement that doesn't work out and walks away, thinking it becomes invalid by that action alone. But if an artist becomes known on your label, a contract he or she signed earlier with someone else may surface. Be careful. Ask lots of questions to find out where the artist's been in the years prior to your meeting, to make sure the person has no signed commitment with anyone else. If the artist tells you an old contract is over, ask to see it and show it to your lawyer.

Signing Someone under Eighteen

I once signed an artist who was under eighteen years of age, the daughter of a woman I was friendly with who had heard a song I'd written. She asked me to give her daughter a chance to sing it. She was terrific, but my lawyer gave me a major argument. In most states, a contract signed by someone under eighteen doesn't mean diddly. And if a parent signs it, the diddly doesn't get more valuable. Often you must go through the courts to protect yourself legally when signing someone underage.

The laws were set up in many states to protect kids from being exploited by their parents. Depending on the legal jurisdiction, contracts offered to minors need to be validated in court. The court sets itself up as the custodian for the minor. The contract is reviewed, and it's determined whether its provisions are in the minor's best interest. If it's deemed that they are, the court validates the contract. From the standpoint of the minor, this is a safeguard. From your standpoint, it's a process that's costly, incurs legal expenses, and the time it takes may delay your project. And never forget: You should absolutely not invest one dime in an artist until you have a legal contract.

The mother of the artist I signed did use her daughter's age to screw me. She swore that she'd honor the contract that she and her daughter signed. My lawyer started the court procedure. I put the record out and it did well, attracting a deal with a great label. But just before we signed that deal, the head of the label called my lawyer saying the artist's mother came to him behind my back to sign a deal directly with his label, saying that since our contract wasn't valid yet, she could break it. The label head didn't want to work with an artist whose mother was so unethical, so he nixed the deal and we all lost. My lawyer had to bite her tongue to keep from saying, "I told you so."

All this is to warn you: Be very careful if you consider signing someone underage in states with strict laws. Check with a lawyer in the state where the underage artist lives to see if there are laws governing what makes a contract with a minor valid. You may luck out and discover someone living in a state where that doesn't require going to court. But if your lawyer tells you that a parent's signature on the contract isn't enough, you may want to consider looking for another artist.

Advances

It's good to give an artist a reasonable advance on royalties if you can afford it. My budget didn't allow for it most of the time. When I offered a contract to an artist, I put it to them straight. I couldn't give them money up front, but I'd do everything I could to promote the record well. Most artists were willing to take those terms. There are artists who'll agree to signing without much of an advance just to get their material out. I covered all expenses for anything related to their records and gave them immediate advances when I started getting money from record sales. Daniel Glass says, "The only way the playing field is not leveled is for advances. We give less money up front. But artists get paid quicker here, and they get an honest shake. The majors give a bigger up-front check."

Labels with real budgets either give their artists a fixed recording budget with a built-in advance or what's referred to as an "all in" deal. A recording fund is allocated to pay for all of the recording costs. The artist isn't given this money directly. You as the label owner monitor how the money is used and pay recording expenses out of this fund. Whatever money isn't spent on the recording goes to the artist as an advance. If you do all-in deals, it's good to remind your artists to be careful about choosing a studio and people they hire to work on the album. You don't want them to cut corners on quality, but they shouldn't get carried away. Point out that any cost savings means more cash in their pockets at the end.

If you can afford to give an advance, it's the fair thing to do. How much is your call. Speak to your lawyer to decide on common ground between what's fair and what you can afford. Remember, since it's an advance on royalties, it's recoupable. If you believe in the record, you'll also feel more confident that you'll recoup the advance. I always gave producers advances. If you have a different type of royalty structure for your artists that offers them more of the profit, your situation merits individual consideration. Discuss this with your lawyer and your accountant before making any decisions.

CHAPTER 9

Creating Your Product

Technology has changed the face of recording. Before stepping into a studio, put serious thought into planning the creation of your product. Make sure you end up with as good a recording as possible, before releasing anything. Settling for an okay recording won't sell it. If you don't believe in your product 1,000 percent, it's hard to push it with enthusiasm: Don't cut too many corners in the studio. A killer sound makes more fans want to buy it and will earn more respect from industry people. There's a lot more you can do for a lot less money. Marc Urselli, three-time Grammy Award–winning engineer, producer, mixer, composer, and sound designer, says:

> *The wide range of new recording software and hardware available to today's indie musician has cut down the cost of recording and has drastically altered the recording process. Like anything else, there are pros and cons to this. Everything got cheaper and is now in reach, but there has also been a decrease in the overall quality of recordings, mostly due to the fact that a lot of indie artists don't necessarily have much experience as recording engineers or producers. One advantage of recording at home is that you can play it until you get it right, and you can experiment with the sounds for as long as you want, without looking at the ticking clock on the recording studio wall; however, with unlimited possibilities and time come other issues. Often things are overproduced because it's easy to get distracted by the technology and the many possibilities. Also artists have come to greatly rely and even depend on technology,*

which made many of them lazy and less focused on their playing and on the importance of rehearsals and so on and so forth. Obviously the greatest advantage is that now an artist can make a record for very little money.

Choosing the First Release

Put thought into what would be best for your first release. If you're the artist, think carefully about which songs to include from a marketing standpoint, rather than from a personal one. If you're signing acts, make sure your first release is as strong as possible to give your label the best chance of getting noticed. Research helps. Study the markets for your genre. Devour trade publications and get a feel for what's selling around the country and the world. Go to stores that carry music magazines, and look through those publications. Learn about what trends are coming and going. The more educated you are, the better your judgment will be when it comes to making creative decisions.

Keep your ego in check. Just because you love the material you intend to release doesn't mean it's as marketable as it can be. No one knows everything. Play your rough mix for people who aren't friends. Get objective feedback from those in the thick of the music business, such as people working in record stores, DJs who play music, and even kids on the street who buy it. Don't tell them you're the artist, songwriter, or producer or mention your personal involvement. You'll get a more objective view if potential critiquers aren't concerned with hurting your feelings or insulting your taste. For Revenge Records, I considered folks on the street my A&R staff and played material I considered releasing on my boombox for them, without sharing my relationship to it.

Get input from those who know what's selling in your genre. Ask for suggestions about making your product more marketable. Learn by keeping an open mind. Don't take all negative comments seriously, but if a number of folks make the same suggestion, give it serious thought, without taking criticism personally. Not everyone will like your music, and negative comments don't mean it's no good. That's why a wide range of feedback helps determine if the product needs work. Don't ignore anything that might make your recording stronger.

Choosing a Recording Studio

Choosing a studio takes research. Word of mouth is best, but if you can't get recommendations, learn all you can. To make better decisions, read a book about or take a class on the basics of working in a studio. Studios vary in what they offer. You may not need the fancy toys offered by some. Ask what advantages each studio has. Arty Skye, owner of SkyeLab Sound Studio in New York City and a producer and engineer with thirteen platinum and gold records, advises:

> *For an artist with little experience in the studio, the first thing to look at is, are you comfortable in the environment? Did you meet the engineer you'd be working with, and do you like him? If you feel nervous, uncomfortable, or intimidated, chances are you will not achieve your goals in the studio and will end up wasting money. If you're more experienced, the equipment becomes the number-one priority. Do they have what you need? Will you be compatible with other studios, or is their format so out-of-date or unique that no one else is using it? This could put you in a bind if you decide to remix or continue your project at another studio. Who is their regular clientele? Look at their client list and ask to hear samples of work that was done in the style of music that you're doing. The equipment necessary for one style of music may be totally irrelevant for another style. Make sure you have a match.*

When choosing a studio, price is a consideration. It doesn't matter how great a studio is if you can't afford it. But don't sacrifice too much quality. Many studios give better deals for using their facilities at odd hours. I recorded during what's known as "graveyard" hours. I hated beginning late and working until early morning, but I got to use better studios for prices within my budget. No matter what you're told, try to negotiate a better price. Some studios give better rates if you book a block of time.

Technology has driven down the cost of recording dramatically. Today you can make a record with Pro Tools or other digital systems for a fraction of what it might have cost just a few years ago. This helps level the playing for indies!

Choosing a Recording Team

Unless you or your band has good studio skills, you'll need competent people working with you. Don't count on a person who comes with the studio for everything. Just because someone has a great studio does not mean he or she is proficient as an engineer or producer. Anyone can buy equipment, but it takes an experienced professional to do the best recording possible. Choose your recording team carefully. Putting the right players together can mean the difference between a mediocre and a great recording.

Getting the Right Recording Engineer

An engineer works the board in the studio and controls the flow of a session. Engineers can be pains in the butt or the key to a great recording. I've had engineers who argued with artists, which wasn't productive. You should trust your engineer, since he or she is an integral part of the decisions. It's important to use one whom you respect, as well as one who works well with a team. An engineer executes the ideas of the producer. Be careful about whom you entrust this job to. Arty Skye says:

> Engineers are the ones responsible for the sonic quality of a recording. They record and mix the music and handle all the equipment and technical aspects within the studio. While being a technical wizard is a prerequisite for the job, a strong musical background and a creative mind are necessary as well. A potential hit song with a lousy mix will not have much success, while a simple song with an exciting mix might have more of a shot. A bad engineer can wipe your master tape (or discs), run up time in the studio, erase stuff they shouldn't, create tension, and basically destroy your session! Since the engineer is driving the session while recording, one who is fast will save time and money. A good engineer becomes the copilot to the producer and often has a say in the artistic quality of the music. A great engineer keeps everything running smoothly and makes your music sound better than you dreamed possible.

Some engineers act like producers, whether you want them to or not. They may try to direct the way the songs are recorded based on what they themselves think rather than on what you want. I've had engineers try to stick their two cents in when I didn't want it, which wasted time. There are loads of great engineers. Ask around. I've used house engineers who did a great job. But however you go about it, make sure you have the right engineer for your project.

Using a Producer

Many people don't hire a separate producer, which can be a mistake. A producer orchestrates the flow of your recording, like the director of a movie orchestrates the action on a set, and makes critical decisions about your recording. A producer takes a song to the final level, makes sure the tracks are put down properly, and decides when it's finished. How can you entrust this job to someone who may not have producing skills, or allow artists to produce their own material when they may find it hard to see beyond their own vision of what the material should sound like? A producer has a very specific role, according to Arty Skye:

> From an artist point of view in most styles of music, a producer's role is to understand the artist's vision and have the technical and musical ability to not only make it a reality but also to make it shine. A producer should keep the sessions running smoothly, anticipate any problems beforehand, and get the best out of everyone from the artist to the engineer. The producer is responsible for everything while in the studio, and their experience in the studio can save massive amounts of trial and error, thus saving time and money. A great producer should be able to take something ordinary and make it extraordinary, or to take something terrible and make it acceptable. But don't expect a producer to be able to turn a turd into gold!

A producer helps to maintain good relationships between the engineer and others on the team. He or she needs a great ear and a sense of what's current in today's music market. A good producer can take a song that isn't working and make it fly by using the right beats and sounds. It's hard to be objective about your own music. Producers get better by doing their jobs regularly. It's hard for a musician to have the seasoning a working producer has. Marc Urselli explains:

> First and foremost a producer offers experience, but he/she also offers a different (new) set of ears and a fresh take on things. Often bands

have been working on their songs for months and might have a hard
time getting some perspective or being able to listen to their songs
from a distance. They are too involved. The fact that a producer
(which, mind you, is not just somebody that owns a computer and
a recording software!) has worked with many artists allows him/her
to bring all of those experiences to the table and to put his knowledge
and background to the client's use. The producer can shape the sound
of a band in many ways and facilitate the process of making a great
record. Obviously trust is pivotal, but as long as you pick the right
producer, you can really bring it all together!

How do you find a good producer? Word of mouth is best. Ask people in the studio you plan to use, other musicians, and even music lawyers, who often represent good producers. Look on records you like, and see who produced them. Arty Skye advises:

In choosing a producer, there are several things to consider, because
anyone can call themselves a producer. First, do you like them and trust
their judgment? If not, walk away. If you don't like them, you won't
enjoy being in the studio working on your music, and if you don't
trust them, you're not letting them do the job you're paying them for.
Next, what is the level of their experience? Ask to see a discography
of records they've worked on and to hear some of their work. Do they
produce part-time and have regular day jobs, or are they pros with
countless years in the industry? Will you be working in a real studio or
in someone's apartment? Will they be hiring an experienced engineer
or doing it themselves? Basically, you're looking for producers with
credentials and experience, or you might as well do it yourself.

Can you use one person to engineer and produce? It depends on the individual. Some engineers are good producers. If you find such a person, consider yourself lucky to have someone to do both jobs. Many engineers can't produce but would love to direct the recording session. Without a producer, an engineer can make whatever musical decisions he or she chooses, but it may not be right for your music. It's a producer's job to direct the engineer, and sometimes keep them in check. Check the credentials of engineers/producers on both levels before committing yourself to someone who may be great at one job but not so great at the other. And keep in mind that having a separate producer and engineer means there are two sets of ears to listen for trouble or to come up with ideas or solutions to problems.

In the Studio

The studio is where your product is born, so treat it as an important aspect of your label. Success hinges on getting a great recording. Opening a record label means little if the recording itself isn't up to par. Plan for your project as much as possible to ensure the best quality.

Preproduction Planning

Preproduction planning saves money. Preparing before entering the studio saves on the time it takes to choose a direction and order of production. It's good to have a meeting with the songwriter, producer, artist, and any others involved before the studio work. The producer orchestrates the planning.

Plans should be mapped out in detail prior to paid studio time. Decide the order of laying your tracks down. What kind of sounds do you want? Are you using samples? Have they been chosen? When will you bring in session players? Do you need the artist or whole band for every session? Sometimes it's easier to have the musicians come in only when they're needed, rather than sitting around for too long and getting restless.

Your act should rehearse like crazy before reaching the studio. Sloppy playing wastes time and money. Encourage the singer to rehearse in front of a mic that's in a fixed position. In the studio, they'll have to stand in the same spot and try to stay still. Let them get used to that a bit before they're on paid studio time. Practicing saves time, which saves money.

Working in the Studio

I knew nothing when I first went into a studio, so I sat by the engineer watching everything that was turned, tweaked, and plugged, asking many questions. It's good to know what's going on. Don't feel funny asking about anything you don't understand.

Set rules about studio behavior. Will you allow friends to hang? Have limits on fooling around. One person should be in charge—the producer. You as the executive producer investing the money have the right to make sure the job's being done properly and your money isn't wasted. Discuss your role with the producer in advance to eliminate problems when you're on the clock.

It's your call whether to allow the use of drugs or alcohol. But when players get high, they slow down and get sloppy on your dollar. Some won't work without beer. But watch their behavior if you allow that. I recommend staying sober yourself to control things. If the session is long, refreshments will keep the energy level up. Keeping your team happy helps get a good recording.

Getting the Right Mix

Don't cut corners during a mix, which can take ages. Sometimes folks rush it when time gets tight. It's not worth it to invest in a record that's not done to your total satisfaction. I've worked on a song for over twelve hours. Some mixes go longer. With a good team, it can flow smoothly and quickly.

Let the engineer start by doing a rough mix on his or her own. Engineers usually have a feel for how a recording should be mixed. Starting with mix levels close to where they should be can save time. Once the engineer's done with this, the producer can adjust and fine-tune it all. A producer with good ears should work without interruption with the engineer. Once the producer is happy, the rest of the team can listen to determine if anything can be improved.

When the mix is done, listen to it on several systems before you leave. Keep the board set up as your ears clear. Hearing music over and over at high volume for hours can desensitize your ears to subtleties of the music that might bug you later. Listen carefully to make sure the mix is exactly how you want it. Bring a walkman, a boom box, etc., to play a copy of the mix on several types of playback equipment. Does it sound as good as everything else you play on each system? If it doesn't, do another pass and make sure you're satisfied before the engineer shuts down the mixing board. Marc Urselli says there are many factors overlooked during the mix, especially now that everyone is mixing records, some without prior experience. He advises:

> Less is more! Often these days mixes are cluttered and overproduced or too busy with tracks that are not necessarily needed. Ultimately it is all about the song! If a song is a great song, it should stand the test. Another often overlooked thing is the sound of the room (or the lack thereof). You can use it to your advantage, and if the room is dead-sounding you can create ambience with reverb, but you have

to do it with knowledge and make sure not to overdo it! Yet another important thing to remember is that you can't just make everything louder. Balance is key. Volume, pan, and frequencies can all help you with that. Often you can make "room" for, say, a third guitar, by simply EQ-ing the first two guitars differently. Mixing is an art, and it takes a bit of time to master it, just like any other art.

Are the vocals up enough? Play the song for someone who doesn't know the words to see if they understand them. If the vocals are low, do another pass making them louder. Take precautions to ensure the mix is done to your satisfaction before leaving the studio. Don't assume that if it sounded good when you were mixing it that it actually is good. An engineer can tweak the high-tech system and make it sound better than it really is if he or she wants you out of the studio! That's why it's important to hear copies in systems providing a more realistic sound. It's heartbreaking to get home after a long night in the studio and realize that some levels aren't where they should be. Then you must decide if you can afford to do it over or if you have to put out a recording that you're not completely happy with, which is lose/lose.

Home Recording

With costs dropping and studio equipment becoming portable and less expensive, many more people are recording at home. But buying all the toys and recording gear available is no insurance that you'll use it properly. Should you invest in buying equipment to use at home? Marc Urselli advises:

> *Those who are "technologically challenged" or who don't want to have anything to deal with on the technical side of things are probably better off not trying and should keep focusing on the right side of their brain. My advice is, if you do it at home, understand that it takes a lot of work and a lot of time to get it right. And understand that the limitations of the equipment and of your experience as an engineer/producer will probably prevent you from getting the same type of mixes and sounds professionals get. Being one such professional myself, people might think that I am afraid of losing clients to technology, but that's really not my case; in fact, I work with a lot of artists whose recordings are*

a mixture of home sessions and studio sessions. Don't take my word for it; if you are inclined to do it all yourself and to deal with all the technical things that come bundled with it, go out and try it. Just don't assume that it will be easy and effortless. Once you get the hang of it, it can be fun, but you have to be able to make time for everything, and you have to LOVE doing it!

If you decide to take the plunge, carefully figure out what you actually need to record your genre. Talk to people at several stores to see if there are some common threads in their advice. What's the minimum equipment necessary for someone on a budget who wants to record at home? Urselli recommends:

It all depends on what you want to record. If you are an electronic music artist and you already (likely) own a computer, all you need is a music software. Depending on which you go for (Reason, Live, Pro Tools, Logic, Digital Performer, Garage Band) you can spend as little as $0 and upward of $500. If you need to record live instruments it gets more complicated, and pricey. Microphones and preamps become important choices, and you'll get the sound you pay for. If you are a singer-songwriter (say, guitar and vocals) you can probably get away with a two-inputs recording interface with built in preamps ($150–$450) and a couple of mics (depending on type, brand, and quality, anywhere from a couple hundred dollars and up). However, if you want to record drums then obviously you will need more microphones, more inputs, more preamps, and so on and so forth. Fast computers, fast external hard drives, lots of RAM memory, and many other factors will play an important role in the performance, the number of tracks you can record, and the amount of money you have to spend. Get a Mac! They're the best for recording.

CHAPTER 10

The Manufacturing Process

A high-quality CD can make people want to play your product. Nice packaging makes it more appealing to consumers. When choosing a manufacturer, don't assume that all of them will do the same job. If the sound quality isn't up to par, your music will get less play. If your artwork is lame, people may assume that the label is lame. In trying to build a market for your label, put your best foot forward in terms of manufacturing your product.

Getting Started

Manufacturing product isn't as simple as it sounds. I hear people say that they're starting a label and will make a CD as if it just takes a call to order them. The best way to learn about manufacturing is to ask questions. I'm not wild about technical stuff, but I managed to understand the process. Find someone who can answer your questions. People working at technical jobs often enjoy showing the ropes to techno-infants like I once was. At least develop a working vocabulary about the manufacturing process to communicate on the subject without feeling totally ignorant about it. The minimum you need to know can be made clear through the explanation of a kind-hearted expert. Tony van Veen, president at Disc Makers, America's largest CD and cassette manufacturer for independents, warns:

Don't confuse value with economy. It's a common mistake to try to cut corners in manufacturing. While price is important, you get what you pay for. The cost of buying the best (as opposed to getting stuck with the worst) is extremely small when compared to the overall cost of recording, manufacturing, and promotion. This is your label's music that we're talking about, and it's got to compete with the majors on retail shelves and in the eyes of the buying public. Don't sabotage your chances of success just to save a few bucks.

A good pressing plant can usually handle all the steps to a finished product. It'll arrange to get your product mastered and to have labels, inserts, jackets, and imprints taken care of. If your time is limited, using such a plant is convenient. Some manufacturers farm out some components of their orders to other companies. Some manufacturers have in-house printing, for labels and packaging; some don't. Some manufacturers have mastering facilities; some don't. Loads of folks like one-stop shopping and are very satisfied with going to one manufacturing source for everything, especially if most of the steps are done in-house. I've been told there's not much difference in the price. The most important thing is developing a good relationship with the person who's orchestrating the process.

Mastering

After mixing your recording, it should be mastered (sometimes called postproduction), which fine-tunes the product. Mastering enhances the mix by further equalizing sound levels. You're selling your recording short if you choose not to master it. Doing so can perfect the quality by resequencing songs, adding or limiting compression to raise the level of the music, and using basic EQ to add to the lows, mids, and highs of a program. Arty Skye (SkyeLab Sound Studio) explains:

Mastering is the process of taking the completed mix and sculpting it with compression, limiting, EQ, and more, so that it has the best possible sound quality for the specific style of music. A rock record and a rap record are mastered much differently. The levels will be pushed to their limits so that the music comes screaming off of the CD at a much louder volume. EQ and levels will be matched between the various songs and put in the order required, with the proper spacing between the tracks. Great mastering can do wonders for an okay mix. Nothing sounds quite finished until it's mastered.

Use a mastering engineer with a good reputation because he or she will know what music for specific genres should sound like as well as what's needed to make a good mix sound great. Mastering makes all the songs on an album work and flow together. Some may have been recorded in different studios or with different engineers. There are subtle differences and tones that an engineer will recognize and adjust to make your songs work as one recording. Don't skimp on mastering—it can make or break the final sound.

Packaging

Your product should look nice. You can have great music, but if the presentation on the package doesn't reflect creativity and quality, people may not be motivated to buy it. Even digital downloads come with artwork. Why spend money preparing a quality recording and not package it with the same respect? Remember what I said about putting your best foot forward. An indie needs to pay attention to the appearance of its products. If your packaging isn't attractive and professional, your label won't get taken seriously. Do I sound like a broken record? There's a reason!

Many fans will buy a CD if the packaging is special. Eye-catching artwork makes people notice your product. It can create curiosity about an act and motivate someone to at least listen to the music. This is especially true of music that caters to markets in which the audience is young people who are particularly conscious of image. If a package shows the artist looking exceptionally attractive, cool, or trendy, kids are more likely to buy the music. If they like two artists equally, they're more likely to buy the one whose music has nicer packaging.

You're competing against a gazillion labels. Visuals make your product stand out. It's human nature to be attracted to what looks good. Stores may display an interesting or clever-looking CD. A cover that looks like a lot of money went into its design might make a reviewer want to give it a listen. An A&R person at a label you're trying to get distribution from may give you the time of day if he or she sees you took yourself seriously enough to put a lot of work into how your product looks. Industry professionals get hundreds of new products a week. They can't check out everything. Do what you can to make sure they want to check out your product.

Designing the Artwork

Get your packaging together while preparing the recording. Printing takes time, so allow enough to do it right. It's good to have a graphic designer do your artwork. If you don't have a talented friend, ask around at art schools or put up an ad. Your printer or the sales rep at your manufacturer may have recommendations. There are good, young graphic artists around trying to start up their careers. Try to find one who'd like the opportunity to have the design of a CD cover for their portfolio. According to Jim Pettid, owner of Media Services (www.mediaomaha.com), a CD and DVD manufacturer with a full graphics department:

> I think the biggest problem we see when artwork arrives is the quality and format. Everyone designing for a release should remember that their print can only be as good as their work. We see too many jobs designed in RGB format, which is great for the web and for bubble-jet printers, but it's not possible to use a real printing press in that format. Printing presses are CMYK format, and 300 dpi. The DPI for the web is only 72. Resolution can never be increased, so it's best to save everything at 300 dpi—that includes all your digital pictures, scanned images, etc. Last, designers have to remember that for the best quality of print on the disc itself, simple is better. The discs are still mostly silkscreened, so complex shading and imagery really don't work well. All manufacturers should be willing to walk your designers through the finer points and of course should have a graphics department that can do the work for you if you are unable.

If you can't find someone to design your cover but have some visual creativity yourself, take a stab at doing your own simple design. Photos are effective for artists who look great, but they aren't used much these days. Be careful. A photo can turn people off before they hear the music. It's more important for the name of the act to be in large type that is clear enough to read, preferably with great, eye-catching artwork. Don't use artwork that won't stand up to the quality of other CDs.

Choosing the Copy

There's no set formula for what copy should be on your cover. Look at products in stores with music similar to yours for ideas. The front cover of a record in any format should show the name of the artist and the record title. The back cover usually lists the individual songs. What you include on the cover depends on whether you're putting out a CD accompanied by a booklet, which may contain other info. Include a copyright symbol (©) followed by the year of copyright, along with a statement that unauthorized duplication of your recording is a violation of the law. Many labels are choosing to put less on their covers these days, but it's your decision. However, don't forget to include the name of your label and your logo!

Designers must take into account information for the spine (side) of the product. It should show the name of the artist, the title of the record, the name of the label, your logo if you have one, and your catalog number. A catalog number is the number you assign to each product. Choose it however you like. When I started, I was told to take a few letters from the name of my label (I chose REV) and add five numbers (REV00001). Each product after the first is then assigned the next highest number (REV00002, REV00003, etc.). But there are no set rules. Some people begin with a higher number than 1 so it doesn't look like they're just starting out. It's your call.

While it's obvious that the packaging should include the artist's name and the title of the record, I've been told people have forgotten them. The logo and name of the record label should also be visible. Information on CDs varies from simply listing the artist's name and the title of the CD to listing the names of individual songs, the catalog number, song publisher, and more. Again, it's your call. Look at other recordings within your genre. There's no wrong information to include.

Do you want a booklet to accompany your CD? It's always nice to have one, but can you afford it? Adding a booklet with more information about the music and artist makes the CD look better, but don't skimp on more important components (such as the basic artwork) in order to include one. Include a contact phone number, fax number, email address, and website on your copy so people buying your product can get in touch with you.

Getting Materials Printed

Save money by giving the printer "camera-ready art," which means art that is ready to be photographed exactly as it is. Talk to the printer before you prepare your artwork so you know exactly what needs to be done. Even if you hire someone else to prepare it, understand the basics so you can keep track of the process. Having your artwork prepared correctly avoids problems and extra expenses later on.

Have the printer supply proofs once everything's ready for the press run. Before okaying the printing, go over the proofs carefully and show them to your designer. Make sure everything looks and reads exactly as it should. If you're using mixed colors, get a proof of the colors, too. Make sure you check samples of the paper on which the material will be printed. Keep a tight rein at every step to prevent problems in the finished product. Then, if your printing doesn't turn out as you ordered, you have a reference for what it should have been and recourse for demanding that the job be done over again correctly.

I recommend ordering enough printed material to cover a second run of records. Since it's considerably cheaper per unit to print up more at once, it's cost-effective if you expect to manufacture another batch. The major cost of a print run is the setup. At the actual printing stage, it may not cost much extra to produce a larger quantity. You don't want to waste time waiting for your packaging to be printed a second time when you have orders on hold. Many record manufacturers won't schedule your order until all the components—including the printed labels, booklets, etc.—are in their hands.

Bar Codes

A bar code is that rectangular series of horizontal lines with numbers under it found on most products sold in stores. Each bar code involves a series of twelve numbers called a Universal Product Code (UPC). The first six is the manufacturer's (your) ID number. Scanners used at cash registers are used to record sales, and many stores use SoundScan, which I discussed in Chapter 5.

To get bar codes for your products, you need to apply for a manufacturer's ID number through the Uniform Code Council (www.uc-council.org) in

Dayton, Ohio. There are forms to fill out and a fee. The ID number is specific to your record label. I'm told there are computer programs that allow you to make bar codes yourself, once you're registered. But there are a number of companies that can make up the codes and bar code films, and they don't cost much. You'll need a separate bar code for each format. Otherwise store scanners won't be able to distinguish a CD from a 12-inch.

Should you get bar codes? If you plan to sell your product mainly at gigs, by mail, or by consignment in local stores, and you don't care about being tracked by SoundScan, bar codes may not be necessary. But if you're starting a label that you plan to sustain, you'll definitely want them. Many distributors won't touch a record without a bar code because most stores want them. If you want to show sales, get one. If you put out a product without a bar code and it takes off big-time, register your company and make bar code stickers as a temporary measure until the next pressing. It takes a while to get your number from the Uniform Code Council, so allow enough time. They charge more for a rush job.

The Manufacturer

When choosing a manufacturer, shop around. Call for catalogs, ask for references, get samples. Look for both price and quality. Talk to people at several companies. Do they seem willing to work with you? Will they put what they promise in writing? Don't just take the cheapest offer. If the quality isn't good, your label will lose credibility. If a cheaper plant takes much longer to produce, you may lose more than you save. What's their approximate turnaround time for a second run? What guarantees in terms of timing and quality do they offer? Base your choice on a combination of factors. I would never use a manufacturer that didn't show potential for a good working relationship. Jim Pettid advises:

> Find someone you are comfortable with. You'll always be able to find someone cheaper or who claims to be faster or who will tell you all the great projects they've done. Just remember, at the end of the day, the way they treat you and your project means more than any of that. This is why a personal referral from a friend

who has already used a company is one of the best ways to find a manufacturer.

Manufacturing Costs

There can be a big difference in price between manufacturers. Some offer package deals for different varieties of one format, such as CDs with and without booklets, or packaging in jewel boxes or cardboard. Some itemize for each specific expense. There are many variables. If you get a package deal, find out exactly what it includes.

Packaging has an impact on the total cost. Jewel boxes are the most popular type of packaging for CDs. Another choice is a cardboard box that looks like a book, similar to a record album jacket. These can be more expensive than a jewel box if they have plastic CD holders inside. A cheaper version allows you to slip the CDs inside a slit, like a record sleeve. For promotional copies, you can save money by using even cheaper versions. Personally, I prefer cardboard. It doesn't crack like plastic, it's better in terms of ecology, it's usually cheaper to mail, and it requires no assembly.

I'm not going to discuss manufacturing costs in terms of specific dollar amounts here. Prices change too frequently, and there are too many variables involved. Call a variety of manufacturers and ask for their catalogs or check online. Compare prices and talk to reps at several manufacturers before making a decision.

Working with Your Manufacturer

It's imperative that you develop a good rapport with everyone at your manufacturer. They have many clients. If they get to know and like you, you may receive better service and support. Be courteous and friendly, even when things go wrong. They'll love you for it! You also may get more realistic input concerning manufacturing decisions, rather than answers based on what they want to sell.

Before committing to a manufacturer, try getting a specific time commitment for the project to be completed. My manufacturers got to know me as someone who wouldn't let up until my order was filled. For a while, I used a small company with few machines. If one went down, work backed up fast. I understood that stuff does happen, but I still needed my product on time. I was nice but persistent in my need for results. I think they pushed my order through just to appease me, which was fine.

One way I maintained good relationships with my suppliers was by paying my bills on time. Many folks don't. Manufacturers have to pay for materials to make your product, so they need prompt payment. I'd always arrive with my full payment. That's an endearing quality in a customer! All the companies I worked with always cooperated when I needed something in a rush, at least partly because they knew they'd get paid right away, no sob stories, no excuses, no bounced checks.

CHAPTER 11

How Record Distributors Operate

Many labels still consider good distribution a necessity somewhere down the road if your goal is to maintain a viable record label. While sales of CDs have dropped substantially, they're still selling. Daniel Glass (Glassnote Entertainment) says, "We are probably a 50/50 business—digital and retail." Most labels I spoke to have given similar percentages of CD sales. Glass adds:

> We believe in strong distribution. We rely on great partners. I'd rather pay two extra points but have great distribution. The last thing I want to worry about when my artist is in a city is if the record is in stores.

Do You Need Physical Distribution?

If you're putting out a record just to attract a deal, you may not care much about distribution. If you tour a lot and have a huge following, you may be happy making much more per unit selling fewer CDs directly to fans and rely only on digital distribution. The level of distribution you need depends on your long-term goals. John Robinson (Shaman Work Recordings) believes that CDs are good for two things—touring and to distribute to top key selling markets. He explains:

> *CDs are great for touring. In the current climate of the industry, CDs definitely sell more at shows than on retails shelves. The importance of distribution to retail stores truly depends on the caliber of marketing and promotion that will be done. Larger companies with more marketing dollars are able to exploit their products extremely quickly in all the major markets; therefore, distribution is more beneficial.*

Many musicians and small indie labels are choosing to skip CDs altogether and just market music digitally. Others are selling CDs only at their artists' shows and online. But if you want to sell on a broader scale, stores are still considered a good direction. Kelly Vandergriff (Five Times August) says, "It's becoming less important with everything going digital, but there will always be people who want to hold it. We wanted to get Five Times August's CDs in stores." Eric Speck (Ace Fu Records) says CDs are still viable for now, and he continues working with a distributor. He explains:

> *The reality is that CDs will slowly be faded out. Kids have replaced the record sleeve with the website. They see what they used to look for on a record sleeve on the website—photos, videos, and whatever else is posted, and let their imaginations run wild. The secondary content to the music used to be in the packaging, and now it's online. So I do think CDs are becoming less and less relevant and convenient for people. I definitely think it's still important to get into stores. At least right now there's still something magical about going to a record store and seeing the energy and new releases with cool artwork. There's still something there that won't go away soon, but it's becoming more niche.*

On the other hand, John Szuch has been runnning Deep Elm Records since the mid-1990s. While he understands that his bands need some CDs for touring, he's phasing them out and has only digital distribution. He explains:

> *We haven't gotten CDs into stores in a couple of years. On our new releases, we put out a limited pressing of maybe one thousand CDs, making it special for fans. It gives the band the ability to bring CDs out on tour. But when we burn through those thousand, it's off to the digital world.*

How Distributors Operate

A distributor is a wholesaler of CDs, records, and tapes. It stocks product from record labels and gets it into retail stores. Some distributors handle videos, merchandise, etc. in addition to recorded material. A good distributor gets your products into stores so they're available when your promotion kicks in. A not-so-good distributor might not get products where they need to be and will return them all in six months.

People ask why they need a distributor. Why not sell to stores directly? If you get what you're striving for—a record that sells well—you won't want to worry about getting product into stores. At first it's fine to go straight to retailers. But once steady orders come in, you'll have enough to do without servicing stores regularly. When sales get strong and more stores want your product, using a distributor enables you to run your label efficiently. The few national independent distributors—ADA, RED, Caroline, and Koch—distribute many established indies and some major label products. But you must create a national demand for your product before one works with your label.

Independent Distributors

Independent distributors have good relationships with independent stores and chains that support indie music. They also get records to one-stops (see below). Independent distributors are often more knowledgeable than majors about specific genres, and they can act quicker. Independents can hit appropriate markets when a buzz is created much faster than majors. They may give indie labels more personal attention, especially for records with good promotion.

Andy Allen, president of Alternative Distribution Alliance (ADA), qualified that while they're solely owned by the Warner Music Group, ADA was created in 1993 by Warner and a couple of indie labels to create a national distribution system, since there were none. Warner Music Group wanted to create a distribution system to serve independent labels and be involved with acts that were touring but didn't have a big hit record yet. They wanted a more artist-friendly distribution system. ADA distributes indie labels and selected projects for the Warner Music Group.

National independent distributors want labels with a proven ability to market product. Some will guide you in marketing. But it's not their responsibility. A national distributor wants to see a national demand for your product. It also wants you to have the money and knowledge to promote a record nationally. A national independent distributor needs more product than a regional one, since they service more outlets.

Nowadays, independent distributors give P&D deals to many of their labels. They pay for pressing and recoup it out of the label's earnings. Jesse Fergusson (Definitive Jux Records) says, "Our distributor fronts the money for pressing. It comes out of the back-end accounting. They'll also front money for marketing and advertising." Labels with this arrangement say the distributor usually gets better prices on manufacturing because they do a higher volume. Andy Allen says:

> We manufacture about 70 percent of what we distribute. It's a service to the labels as a courtesy. The label can choose to use us as a manufacturer. We have a built-in advance for manufacturing in the way we deduct. The manufacturing charge is delayed until you ship the record, and then it's deducted from the revenue the record would generate. We take a distribution fee. The labels own their music here, and we're their selling agent. When we sell the record we report to them via statement what was sold and at what price.

Walter Zelnick, with City Hall Records, an independent distributor, says they'll consider giving a P&D deal under the right circumstances:

> They must be something we believe in strongly and think we can move the amount we invest in the pressing. We put marketing money into those programs, too. There are a few ways to do those deals. One is to base it on a royalty. Another would be very similar to a distribution deal, but we'd put a fee on top of our pressing as an administration fee for handling the pressing and keeping the paperwork. If we believe in it enough, we'll give an advance.

One downside of using a large distributor is potentially large returns. No matter how many are ordered, there's no guarantee of sales. If a distributor sends product to many stores and one-stops, each account could return a substantial amount. You have little control over how many units the distributor sends to one-stops or large chains, where records can sit in a warehouse. My first record sat in the warehouse of a large chain store while my students fumed about no stock at the local chain outlet. The store manager swore he ordered it. The main warehouse gave me excuses. No one knew why it got held up, but it took two months of calls to get a batch into the store, which sold out immediately. The reorder took almost as long.

Whatever a store doesn't sell gets returned to you. It's nice to get a distributor who cooperates by being more conservative about how many pieces they ship at one time. Some don't care because they can return them whenever they want. In the end, it's not the distributors who lose money if product comes back. They just return it to you for credit against what they owe for the order! A good relationship with your distributor might mean they'll be more prudent about how many CDs they distribute at once.

One-Stops

One-stops carry every title and charge more for catering to what are referred to as mom-and-pop stores, often small neighborhood record shops. Mom-and-pops can create a buzz on a record and break one with a local grassroots buzz faster than a chain store can. Chains do well with records that have high visibility. Fans come into those stores knowing what they want. Mom-and-pop stores get the word out on records their customers *should* know about.

Mom-and-pops don't need large numbers of every record title. Only a few kids in the neighborhood may like a certain artist. They can't afford a whole box of a title if only a small number of units will sell. Larger distributors don't want to break up boxes to sell a few units of a single title to a store. One-stops buy records in realistic quantities and sell mom-and-pops the quantity they want. They're better to deal with when you begin. If you get a one-stop in the region where your market is, you only need to give them enough product for the market.

It's easier to control the quantity that one-stops order, and that can mean a lot fewer returns. Not many records came back from my one-stops, since they ordered small numbers and reordered when they needed more instead of ordering extra, just in case they were needed. The better the relationships I developed with one-stops, the more they worked with me to order realistic numbers and contacted me when they needed more. Often it's also easier to get paid (more in Chapter 13) by one-stops.

What Distributors Look For

Should you be concerned from the start about getting distribution? No! Focus on marketing your music. You need a distributor to sell records. Distribution isn't the end-all, cure-all. You can ship two thousand pieces and get them all back if you don't promote to your target audience. Distributors get records into stores, period. Finding one is easier when there's a good buzz on your artist; otherwise, why have them sit in a warehouse?

Andy Allen (ADA) says, "Distribution is a warehousing function, a sales-and-solicitation function, a processing-returns function, and a collecting-the-money function." That's it! You do the rest. Records sell when people know the artist. Before carrying yours, distributors need to see that there's a large fan base to buy them. You and distributors have the same goal—selling records. Creating a demand achieves that. I'll repeat this over and over like a broken record—you must focus on creating that demand.

The best way to get a distributor is to put all your energy into marketing and promotion. Don't worry about getting distribution at first. When you create a demand for your product, distributors pay attention. Do your groundwork first. Be patient, and create a foundation to sell from. Until you identify your potential market and develop strategies for promoting to it, having distribution won't sell CDs. Distributors don't care how good the music is if nobody knows about it. Allen explains:

> You have to create demand for your artist. In most cases, if you've successfully created demand, people are going to want to work with you. From a distributor's standpoint, the label that is successfully creating demand for an artist is the one that a distributor wants to work with.

I asked distributors what they look for in a record label. They consistently answered that they're looking for records that already have a market, with a label behind them that's working its butt off to promote them.

Michael Bull, vice president of label relations at Caroline Distribution, says, "Very basically, we like labels with great records and the knowledge, desire, and means to market and sell them effectively." Michael Koch, president of Koch International Corporation, says he wants a label with financing behind it. His decision to carry an indie label is based on how much funding the label has, its artist roster, and its management. Allen says:

> We look for somebody who we think is going to consistently come out with great acts and will know what to do with them when they do. It's helpful if they've shown national sales. On occasion we've done a deal with a startup, but not very often. I want to make sure that from a size or billing standpoint it fits in with the rest of the labels we're working with so they don't overwhelm the small labels.

You'll hear a lot about "developing a story." That's what everyone, from the media to stores to radio to distributors, looks for in an artist. A story doesn't mean a tale about the artist. Rather, it means the progressive growth and development of the artist as a marketable entity. A story refers to how much touring the artist is doing, how much radio play the record is getting, how much the press is writing about them, how many CDs they've sold. Distributors want to hear the buzz get louder as each page of the story unfolds. Nowadays, a reasonable budget for promotion is a big consideration. Walter Zelnick says:

> Right now we're looking for labels that hopefully have a marketing budget. In the old days, things could sell well on word of mouth. Now it's taking a lot more work and money. If someone comes to us with a really great record but no money and nothing to market it with, it's going to be tough.

It would be lovely if only the music were important, but marketing music is a business. Sales potential outweighs the importance of artistic ability. Sending a well-produced, beautifully performed album to a distributor won't get you distribution if you have no fan base, media coverage, radio play, or promotion behind it. Alan Becker, vice president of product development for RED Distribution, a national music-software distributor and an affiliated subsidiary of Sony Music, says that while "the music speaks the loudest at the end of the day," distributors aren't A&R people. He explains:

We look to work with people who are determined to be successful and have the wherewithal or experience in addition to the money to achieve success in a marketplace that's dominated by the major record companies. We have to be convinced that we're working with people who understand those factors and what it takes to overcome them. We look for aggressive people who are used to working at a very grassroots level and have the patience to stay with a project over a long period of time versus a company that has a pressure to have success quickly; people who have a very clear artistic A&R vision— trendsetters versus followers. We look for creative people who, in addition to the music, can create clever advertising opportunities for us and create clever concepts that have not been tried before.

With so many indies competing, single yourself out by getting your act together before approaching a distributor. Don't bring them your dreams. They've heard them all. Put together a marketing and promotional strategy and implement it, no matter how long it takes. Use the tools in the upcoming chapters to develop your own business into a reality. Make a distributor want to carry your product by offering a product that has an audience to buy it.

Who Pays Distributors?

Distributors usually take product on a consignment-type basis, although smaller ones might buy some if they already have orders for it. When the product sells, they're paid by stores and in turn pay the label a price per unit. If a product doesn't sell, it's returned to the label for credit against the amount the distributor owes for the order.

Larger distributors mainly work on a fee-per-record-sold basis. Returns, discounts, advertising, and a reserve for returns are taken into consideration when they pay you. Most distributors allow the label to set the retail price. Some distributors offer the label a price for each unit sold, and the label bills the distributor. Walter Zelnick explains:

Some people think it's a fee. We don't work like that. The label decides the retail price. We tell them what we pay for that price range, and then they bill us whatever it is, and the standard invoice is 150 to 180 days. We tell them if we think they're not priced competitively.

Negotiate terms with your distributor. "Terms" refers to the amount of time the distributor has to pay the invoice. When payment is due, the distributor can return unsold product to you for a credit against its balance owed. Distributors don't always pay indies promptly, especially at first. Exercise patience. Until you establish yourself as a serious label, you probably won't be a priority.

Returns are an ongoing problem. After spending so much on manufacturing, records come back if they don't sell. Record stores return them to a distributor for a refund with few restrictions. Labels get stuck eating the returns in the end.

CHAPTER 12

Creating a Marketing Plan

I t's imperative to develop a plan of action to get your artist known to the public. If you don't promote the heck out of your product, there may be no market for it. Find ways to create a marketing plan that will get your artist enough exposure to sell records and attract good distribution.

Creating Your Foundation

Develop marketing and promotional strategies with incremental baby steps toward getting more visibility, well before street date. As each component is added, the buzz on your artist can increase. Don't wait until product is piled in your office or living room to consider how to market them. A strong foundation gives you the best chance for reaching your goals.

How can you strengthen your foundation? Start by living and breathing your music! Immerse yourself in the genre you're marketing. Learn all you can. When I marketed hip-hop, I listened to every rap radio show, went to hip-hop clubs, and read all the hip-hop magazines. When I marketed dance music, I was in clubs regularly studying how DJs mixed it, counting beats per minute (BPMs), and getting friendly with DJs. Associate your label with whatever music scene it fits into.

Learning all you can about your genre gives you an edge. If you're not part of the culture of your music, you'll miss the marketing boat. If you're not familiar with magazines that cover it, how can you know which ones to send material to? If you don't know the radio stations and DJs playing it, how can you get airplay? If you don't know what club DJs set trends, whom can you approach? If you don't network in appropriate music venues, how can you make contacts? Educate yourself NOW!

Gather resources. Talk to as many folks as possible to get marketing recommendations. Read trade magazines like *Billboard* to keep abreast of what's happening in the industry and consumer magazines to stay abreast of what's popular. Check the Internet for appropriate websites and resources for your genre. Get busy on social networking sites! I can't emphasize enough the importance of absorbing as much as possible about your genre of music—the foundation for marketing and promotion.

Networking

Create the best chance for making a go of your record label by getting out, making industry friends, and developing as many "people resources" as possible. Networking is available to everyone. A friendly smile can get great mileage. Showing appreciation for people's help attracts more support. This industry is built on relationships.

Networking means creating and maintaining a network of people whom you know on a variety of levels. To accomplish this, go to as many places as possible where you can meet music industry folks and begin the necessary interactions to build working relationships. Creating a network of people gives you more possibilities for support with your label and increases your mailing list. As you collect business cards, note relevant facts about each person on the back. Include the date and where you met as a reference, so you don't have a pile of cards that mean nothing to you later.

Begin networking immediately. The more folks you know, the more potential recommendations for services, avenues of promotion, and resources you have. Someone may know a good photographer or a DJ at a radio station. Developing good relationships by networking can get your artist a good promotional gig. You never know whom you might meet or where contacts can lead you. A note to anyone who's helped you or whom you want to keep in touch with can solidify relationships. Many folks are don't say thank you. We're saturated with emails. A real note, sent by mail, will make you stand out to someone you appreciate or want to stay connected to.

When people like you, opportunities manifest themselves. Each contact is a stepping stone to another. A reference can get a distributor or club promoter to take you seriously. Building relationships with industry folks means developing a level of respect and comfort between you. Once that's established, they're more likely to take your call. A musician or indie label can be a source of mutual support and sharing of resources. Never be a snob and judge whether someone can help you. Everyone can be a good ally. You never know who'll help with your website or bring a crowd to a gig. Jesse Fergusson (Definitive Jux Records) says:

> I wouldn't recommend anyone start a label before spending time to get to know people in the industry. So much of this is about who you know and the connections you are able to make. I can't stress this enough, especially for artists trying to do it on their own. Try to get out and meet people. You never know who you'll meet who could be a down-the-road person. I've had that happen many times.

People resources cost nothing. I talked earlier about the resources of people working in record shops. They're often involved in the creative end of music, as producers, DJs, etc. and/or work in stores because they love music. They know what's going on, which distributors are better, and other helpful info. Get friendly with them. And don't forget to offer a sincere thank-you. My friends in stores guided me every step of the way in starting and running my label, for which I was always grateful!

Get out to clubs, industry events, and live performances of acts similar to yours. If you like an act, invite them to your artist's gigs. Indies support each other, and clubs are a good place to meet them. Music conferences are big and impersonal, but they bring together many folks to network with. There are music industry conferences all year long. Subscribe to the indie-music.com newsletter for a good calendar of events. South by Southwest (SXSW), held every March in Austin, Texas, is considered the biggest conference. I like more specialized ones. For example, the CMJ Music Marathon (see Chapter 17), oriented to college radio, targets the college market. Be friendly to everyone you meet, and keep in touch when possible. The Internet makes this easier.

Marketing and Promoting Options

Techniques for marketing and promoting vary with the music and what your artists have generated on their own. Do they have press, a following, and regular live shows booked? Create a marketing plan around what the artist started. Study available resources—what they cost and the potential for sales by using them. Then realistically determine what you can afford. There are many options. You, or you and your team if you have one, must choose the best avenues for creating a buzz around each artist. One may have a stronger touring base. Another might have strong name recognition on the Internet. Weigh it all, along with budgetary allowances and constraints.

Be flexible, pay attention, and prepare to roll with situations. Jay Woods (New West Records) says, "It's a reacting sort of business. You can be proactive to a degree, but you've got to be ready. If you catch a break, be ready to jump on it. Maximize it and exploit it in whatever way you can." If your artist gets press, use it to get more. If a radio station gives it good airplay, work it with other stations. Make sure stores are stocked. Don't spend money too freely, but create a marketing plan with breathing room. Ryan Kuper (Redemption Records) says:

> I like a loose, fluctuating way. Some people fail because they lock themselves into an ultimately rigid system: "On this day we go for adds on radio; this day it's available in stores." You can't do that. The coolest thing about indies is that we're flexible. Today we can pick up and run or close down. If we're spending too much money on something, we stop the bleeding. That makes us different from majors. I've seen people who've worked at majors think they can operate an indie like that on a smaller basis. That's not the case.

Artist development requires artist visibility. People need to hear it, read about it, and see it performed live. To avoid wasting time, decide your direction for marketing way in advance. How will you make the artist's presence known? Prepare press kits (more in Chapter 16). Compile a list of radio stations that might play the music (see Chapter 17). Book gigs. Target club DJs (more in Chapter 18). Plan how to saturate the digital world with your artist's name and music (more in Chapters 19–21). Most important, solidify relationships with industry people so you have support when the release date arrives. Mark Carpentieri (MC Records) says:

> *Every artist is a little different. We decide if we're going to use an outside publicist or radio person or do everything in-house. That's going to affect what we do. We go through the artist and their touring schedule; decide what we think is unique about them, whether it's their age or something that they do that no one else does, or a former claim to fame. So besides the great music, we can make it an interesting story as well. Great music is always objective, but a story is a story.*

Videos

Is a video worth the investment? A good one that gets viewed often can increase record sales, but it depends on on your audience. Are they likely to be where videos are played or posted? Nowadays, technology allows videos to be made cheaper than ever, and online sites offer unlimited places to post videos for free. That's made videos a better promotional vehicle than before. Eric Speck says:

> *Now is the time to make a video. You can promote it online. It can be seen without a giant video budget. It's still hard to get your video on a TV show, but at least now you have the recourse of getting it online, on AOL—get MySpace or Pure Volume. There are a lot of sites where you can get a video seen and start an organic interest in it. The OK Go video is a good example. I don't think the band was even close to a priority for their label. They may have been close to being dropped. But they made a very compelling and cool video. It got out there and people got excited about it. Now the band has a good fan base from it.*

Part of the cost of videos used to be in duplicating and mailing them. Now, sending a video is often just a click to upload it to a site. Indies don't go after television coverage as much. Some cities have good cable shows that air videos and are worth pursuing. But the main video exposure now is online (more in Chapter 21). Sometimes you can get a store, club, or roller rink to play it. Ellyn Solis, founder of Vermillion Media, adds:

*Offline, you should always service your video to lifestyle outlets such
as coffee houses, boutiques, privately owned indie film theaters, etc.
in your local market. They are always looking to help "their own,"
and it is money well spent to distribute your video that way.*

If you consider making a video, figure out your goals. How will your audience
see it? Can you promote it online? Have you found alternative venues to play
it? Jeff Price (Tunecore) says the playing field for videos has changed greatly
for indie videos from when he began SpinArt Records:

*You'd need a label to deliver it to MTV. Now, anyone can broadcast
themselves on YouTube. The cost of making a video can be nothing.
You can use your cell phone to film something on the street, and if it's
interesting, people will view it.*

If you have access to equipment for shooting even a homegrown video,
it's worth trying. Rich Hardesty sometimes has someone follow him
around with a video camera, and his fans love the films. He says, "I've
always made fun videos. I may put them together and give them away
to fans." If your artist has a good live performance, consider making an
inexpensive video for your website. Dave Roberge (Everfine Records)
finds this useful:

*I'm a big believer of having a video in an electronic press kit, so
whether you're trying to acquire college gigs or something else, it's
there when they need a very short, three- to five-minute snapshot of
what the band is.*

Many factors should be taken into account before deciding to film a video.
What's your budget? A video has to be able to compete with many others.
A creative young director can do a killer video for a fraction of what major
labels pay, but you must find the right one. Freelance video director Steve
Penta of White Light Productions has made videos for major label artists,
including the Killers, and for many indies. He says:

*I'm a big believer in vibe. When you meet someone who gets your
artistic vision, you know. It's something in your gut that feels good
about working with that person. Don't get someone who comes up
with a crazy idea that doesn't feel right and do something you're*

half hearted about, and get a finished product that's not what you wanted. You should feel confident that the person gets your music. At the same time, if you're on a really low budget, and someone offers to do it for free or a couple a hundred bucks, sometimes it's worth the risk.

Creativity is the key to a video that gets attention. And that doesn't have to cost big money. Often the artist can come up with a better concept than an outside party. While you may not have much of a budget, film something that looks professional and worthy of your music. Jennifer Nielsen, marketing manager at YouTube, reassures:

You don't need a slick and expensive music video to have success on YouTube. All you need is a little creativity and a camera to create something truly original. YouTube is about connecting with people and showing your personality through video. Bands should pick up a camera and start filming their day-to-day lives, what makes them original, and why people should watch and listen to them. This is the best way to connect with a new audience on YouTube.

A video gives you a platform for your music that can reach people around the world. It brings your music to life. Be vigilant about the life you give it. Plenty of artists make videos shot almost for free, but people forward them to others at a very fast rate, and before you know it, they have a huge following for the music, too. Having made several videos, I've learned that it's the concept, not the production value, that can ultimately catch people's eyes. Nielsen adds:

Videos that make you laugh out loud or that are bizarre or simply brilliant get the most attention on YouTube. There is no real formula for a video to go viral, but original content and opinions are popular as well as videos that express emotion and tell it like it is. Check out our most popular users in the Channels area of the site. This is where the most popular content is and the users who have the largest audiences.

Get ideas from other videos. Then find the best way to bring your music to life on camera. New technology makes it much cheaper. Penta believes it's important to focus on not just getting the means to create one video but that you accumulate the means for creation, so you can make videos yourself. He says having a half-decent camcorder and laptop you can cut video on is much better if you intend to continue your label long term. He says, "Being a true artist means being able to create every facet of your art—from the digital to videos to live shows. Then you drive your career yourself." He believes many indies don't understand how much they can do on their own, if you get the equipment, and advises:

> If you have the means, and the money, try to buy the equipment yourself. Home editing software isn't hard to get your hands on. I use Final Cut. Rather than hire a low-budget director, get the means to create your own stuff. If you take the time to learn it, it's a good investment in your career. Panasonic is where it's at right now as for cameras. The Panasonic DX-100 is the standard issue, kind of like the Les Paul of camcorders. Most reality videos are shot on it. It makes any content you do for YouTube look awesome and gives it a quality that people can't put their finger on but know when they see it. People watch so much reality TV that it's a format they're comfortable with. It doesn't look cheap. For most of our videos now I use the Panasonic DX-200. It shoots in HD. On the technical side, have a good synch-playback system. If you're shooting slow motion, make sure the playback is set to that speed, especially if you're synching with mouths. A lot of professional directors get very anal about lining up the synch to the performance. A bad lip-synch makes your video look cheap, so make sure that's dead on. When I'm in Final Cut, I've gotten really good at learning how to synch video up with very, very specific moments in the audio, so that any kind of shifting or thing that's off isn't noticed.

You can make a good video on the cheap! Penta has been known to make good videos for as little as three hundred dollars. Low budget doesn't mean poor quality. Penta says what's really key to shooting lo-fi videos is coming up with concepts that fit the budget and the equipment you have. It's also important to be realistic about what you can do with it. Some things just don't work on a tiny budget. He explains:

> A lot of young directors take a camcorder and try to shoot an epic masterpiece. It always winds up looking super-cheap. I see

150

that a lot in hip-hop. You want the crazy, glossy video but just have a five-thousand-dollar budget. It never works right if you're shooting on a camcorder. Figure out how to make what you have work right. To save money, I've found that doing a video in a band's hometown is almost always the best way. A band in their hometown can pull in many more favors than anywhere else. If you don't have money for lighting, get those bright orange work lights from Home Depot. They substitute really well for lighting on a budget. You can buy five of those lights for twenty bucks each, and they're up to par. Real lighting is insanely expensive.

If you have a budget to hire someone, ask indie labels for recommendations for directors who can make a quality video. One way to save money is to find a college film student who can use his or her school's resources. Post a notice in colleges that you're looking for someone to film your video. But if you go this route, you may not have as much input as you'd like, since students may see it as their own project. Before shooting one, watch lots of music videos. Get a feel for what works in your genre so you know what styles and effects to go after. Talk to your producer. It's your money—don't be afraid to give input. If something doesn't feel right, address it fast. Penta advises:

It's not technical as much as it is passionate. The one problem I have with artists is they get uncomfortable on camera. The most important thing is to let yourself go, and go all the way with it. If you think about the biggest video, it must have felt insanely foolish the first time they came out doing whatever it was. Sometimes those things translate best on the video.

If all of this sounds too overwhelming or your budget is too tight to consider a video, there are *very* inexpensive alternatives cropping up each day as technology goes crazy. Check out Animoto, which has software that allows you to make videos from digital photos. Its CEO and cofounder, Brad Jefferson, explains:

Animoto is a simple concept where a user uploads pictures, uploads their own songs if it's a musician, and a few minutes later they get a video with high production value in it. We're trying to mimic the creative process that's done in the post production room for film and television.

When they put things together, there are certain things they do that are kind of repeatable. We patented something called Cinematic Artificial Intelligence, which is algorithms that mimic the post production process to put imagery together with music in a way that's compelling and looks like the images go together with the music perfectly. They can be from thirty seconds to ten minutes. Our business model is that it's free to create a thirty-second video. If you want to create a larger video, it's three bucks per video, or thirty bucks a year for as many as you want.

Their website calls it "technology that thinks like an actual director and editor." Jefferson says a thirty-second video is typically ten to fifteen photos. Their algorithms analyze the music, by beat, tempo, the energy, and by climactic elements, like a cymbals crash. Then it maps in the imagery with the appropriate motion design based on that song. Often the movement that's put into them makes people ask, "How did you animate my picture?" Since you can make thirty-second videos for free, it's an online promotional tool that you can take advantage of if you have access to a digital camera. Jefferson says:

We've noticed that it's mostly independent artists that create them and put them on their MySpace pages. Some artists change their video with every tour. The best thing about Animoto is that at the end of every concert, if you have pictures from it, you can upload those pictures with a song, and a few minutes later you have a video from that show. It allows fans to stay current with the band and experience a concert at nearly real time.

Include photos of the audience too, so they'll send friends to watch them. What can you do with these photo videos? Jefferson says at the end of your video there are buttons at the bottom. The first is a remix button that allows you to click, and a few minutes later a totally different video comes back. The next is for email. Put in people's email addresses and it sends them an email with a URL link to the video. The third allows you to post the video to your Facebook or MySpace page, blog, website, etc. They also give you code to embed it anywhere and recently created a button that allows you to synchronize it with your iPhone or most mobile devices. The next button gets it on YouTube. Animoto is also developing a program that allows indie artist to submit music for non-musicians to use in their videos. Jefferson explains:

Since most of our team is musicians, we wanted to promote music on the site. Each song in our music lounge has been hand selected by us. It's music we really like and think will work well with Animoto. We have a new music submissions program. Artists can upload songs to us on a monthly basis. We pick the top ones we like that month and introduce them into our collection. Based on how well they perform, the top ones will be added permanently to the collection.

That can give your music exposure by being on other people's videos. If you do several videos, you can put out a DVD with all of them. If you have several artists with videos, have a label compilation to promote them all. Some fans buy them. DVDs are inexpensive to make, so it can be worthwhile to invest in one for promotion. Pay good attention to the packaging, as advised with CDs. Jim Pettid (Media Services) says:

DVDs' most popular packaging is still the Amaray case. This is that standard case you see every time you buy a movie. We try to remind people, the options for CDs apply just as easily to DVDs. Unique and interesting packaging is limited only by what you can imagine.

Charts

There are many types of music charts in a variety of publications. They indicate radio play, retail sales, and club play for overall national rankings, geographical regions, and genres of music. There are charts for different levels of commercial and noncommercial radio and charts for video play. Some are more influential than others. Having a record on the charts for commercial radio stations in major markets will increase sales more than charting on college radio. Because of its longevity and the accuracy of its information-gathering systems, charts in *Billboard* have the highest recognition, according to Geoff Mayfield, director of charts for *Billboard*. He says:

Billboard's been charting music for more than fifty years. Part of the reason that we have stayed ahead of the pack is that we have, during this decade, embraced new technologies that weren't available to us before, so that we can do what we do in a much more scientific manner. The universe of sales that we can use to project our national charts is more than 75 percent of the U.S. retail marketplace. When you consider that [famous polls such as Gallup] make handsome livings dealing with a fraction of 1 percent [of the populations they are surveying], you can imagine the luxury of having a sample that large on either the radio side or the sales side. We have it on both sides. On the radio side there's a division of our company called Broadcast Data Systems (BDS). It actually does, from a scientific point of view, the same thing for us on the radio side that SoundScan does for us on the sales side. It has listening posts in more than one hundred markets. It measures 85 percent or more of the radio listeners in the United States.

Mayfield says the system listens to the radio twenty-four hours a day, seven days a week. It can get very specific data, such as the number of times a record was played or the audience size. There's lots of information indies can get, according to Mayfield:

The companies that provide us with our chart information can offer detailed information to the labels that's even more significant than what the national charts can tell you. They give you local information. You'll be able to see which radio stations actually impact sales. There are a lot of meaningful things that you can get out of looking at the detailed data that these companies provide that is of equal if not greater significance to the importance of the national charts.

Only *Billboard* uses SoundScan and BDS. Charts in other publications are usually compiled from a panel of reporting stores, DJs, radio stations, etc. Charts are based on playlists/sales figures from these reporters. Radio stations and club DJs put their playlists together and send them in.

Indies have a much harder time getting on the most significant charts. It takes much work/resources to promote to reporting stations and stores on a national level. In order to chart, you must get serious play and sales in the right markets simultaneously, which is hard to coordinate. Promoters have relationships with the players. However, studying the charts provides info that can be useful in determining what markets might be right for your artist.

Finding Promoters

If you don't have radio, retail, club, video, and digital/new media promoters on staff, hiring a professional who has relationships in the area in which you need to work your product is one way to go. Promoters are expensive. Some give indies lower rates than larger labels, but often you get what you pay for. Promoters logically put more energy into those paying more, but if you find a good one, they can be a big asset to your label.

Be careful not to waste money on someone who can't provide what you expect. Promoters can get only so many records or videos played. If you decide to hire one, check their track record. Ask for references and information on what chart positions he or she achieved for other labels. The best way to find a good promoter is through recommendations from other indie labels. Otherwise, talk to the people in the music industry you're trying to reach—music directors at radio stations, club DJs, etc. Ask if they can recommend a promoter they like dealing with.

Planning a Marketing Strategy

Many new labels are opting to just promote and market digitally. I agree that online opportunities are unlimited, with a huge reach. But not all potential fans or music buyers are on all the sites or will see your act. If your resources are limited, concentrate on the digital areas that will get you the most bang for few bucks. But, many labels still feel that offline promotion and marketing is still viable and very helpful. If you can create strong street teams (See Chapter 15), those fans can work the physical world, at least in regions where your acts tour or have a buzz.

Decide what regions to hit first. Without deep pockets, it's more prudent to work a small area initially and grow from there. Working your product nationally means you'll need to manufacture a lot more. However small your first run is, you can get more as you work your way to other regions. Baby-step from region to region. Be patient and you'll create a much larger market. Dave Roberge successfully used a micro-marketing strategy with O.A.R. He explains:

> When that band first started to create a buzz, it was in specific areas
> of the country—South Carolina, Arizona, and Ohio. When we

first tried to acquire consignment accounts, we looked at it as a micro-marketing strategy. It made sense for us to spend ad dollars on a region-by-region level. With that approach, we kind of look at it almost like a spider web. You start in the center somewhere and go part by part and build it, almost like a web. If an artist's strength is in the Carolinas, we're going to employ a micro-marketing strategy that focuses on the Carolinas. We'll develop the Carolinas before we move into Atlanta and as far north as Virginia. It's about mastering that one market and creating a presence in that market, because without that one market, you're not going to be able to get to that second and then the third market. A lot of stores we spoke to in the beginning were only impressed when they heard about that second store carrying the product, and so on. A lot of it is going out there and proving yourself. We started small, with baby steps. You're not going to go from X to 4X overnight. You have to start somewhere and go from X to Y to Z. We weren't in a position at that time to spend $2 million at radio to push a single to make the band go from Columbus, Ohio, to a national phenomenon. It had to take time.

If you market regionally, start in cities that you have access to, where the artist tours, or those with the best potential for selling your music. Choosing a region can depend on the music. Your hometown might not be a good market for your music. If your artist has a story building in a specific region or is playing live there, that's where to start. If your record doesn't work in one region, try others.

If you already have distribution, get input from the distributor for a retail strategy. If you need to attract distribution, create a base of stores you can sell to directly. I identified as many stores as possible that sold my style of music in regions I planned to work first. The Internet makes it easier. There are directories and lists online. Talk to people in stores, DJs, and people at other indie labels. Pick their brains for the locations of stores that may help you. Also check trade magazines specializing in your genre.

Reaching Your Audience

Your marketing plan must reflect a combo of working your artist's strengths and your budget. What is your artist prepared to do? What can you afford?

What are the most realistic areas in which to invest? Budget your energy, too. I ran myself ragged at first, jumping whenever someone called for a promo package or an idea for me to try. It got exhausting and scattered me so thinly that I wasn't as effective as I could have been at anything. Plan what you can realistically do yourself. PR? Radio promotion? Street marketing campaigns? Budget your energy so you have enough for what's essential. Ryan Kuper says:

> It's different for every act. I base it on what I think I can get from the band—can I get them on the road for months? If so, will I go heavier on street team promotion or a publicist? Or am I going to just put this out with print ads and hope the band gets some love? Sometimes I tag-team releases with another label. We say, "This is what I do best and can bring to the table. This is what you do best and can bring to the table. This is what we can do together."

Tony Brummel says that some artists can potentially reach other demographics and fan bases. People who like X, Y, and Z artists might be into yours if they knew about them. He adds, "You might sticker the product with a clever press quote that might allude to an artist that people might be aware of." Do what you can to reach the fans of artists who are similar to yours. The Internet is another vehicle for reaching them (see Chapter 21). Street teams (see Chapter 15) can get the word out.

Make postcards to advertise your artists. Put an album cover or photo on the front and contact info, quotes if you have them, and your website address on the back. They can be used like flyers and handed out. David M. Bailey says, "For every new album, I get five thousand postcards printed. I may or may not mail them. I hand them out like water at shows." For new indies, the micro-marketing strategy works best. To the best of your ability, get your artist's name out one market at a time. Jesse Fergusson suggests choosing whatever number of markets you're going to work. He's found cost-effective ways to increase awareness:

> Pick a key market and concentrate on awareness through affordable print advertising. A lot of distributors will offer multi-cut advertising. They take out an ad and charge [10 percent for each of ten cuts that will be used in the ad]. So you pick your key markets. If you're a hip-hop artist, make sure you're in all the hip-hop magazines.

If you have great music, you'll find a way to market it successfully by working hard. Don't look to the bigger publications or clubs at first. Start small. Have a multitiered marketing plan. Concentrate on ways to sell your first one hundred records. Then work up to larger numbers. If you have great music, online opportunities can allow others to know about it. Focus on one market or one social network or one neighborhood at a time! If you get fans talking about your music, others will hear about it!

CHAPTER 13

Getting Product into Stores

Getting distribution isn't as easy as just wanting it. Unless you have an act buzzing loudly, it takes time. Distributors want labels that appear to be striving for longevity. You must convince them they'll make money with your label. Relationships developed in retail stores help with initial sales, and as your product sells, your artist's story increases.

Getting into Stores

Record stores are closing. Indie labels are selling more music digitally. Are stores really necessary? That depends on your model, which I talked about earlier. You don't have to go after national distribution or even use distributors at all if you feel retail sales will be limited. But, if your acts are touring, getting CDs into stores in those regions can sell more CDs. You can often do that yourself. So, do you still need physical distribution in the world of digital? Jeff Price, founder of Tunecore, an online digital distribution company (more in Chapter 20), says yes:

> There's still an advantage to manufacturing physical product. You don't have to. Many people don't and do just fine. But it has to fit you. If you have an active touring band, there's something to be said for having physical product. But there are much higher risks in doing physical distribution. There's an outlay of cash to manufacture product and the cost to move it to retail stores, hoping it sells through and having to give pieces of the pie to others along the way. If the

inventory doesn't sell through, it all gets returned for a refund and you're stuck with it. Physical sales are decreasing. Distributors are getting more picky about who they let in. It costs them a lot of money to warehouse and try to get the stuff on shelves. If you're going to go into the physical distribution world, be prepared to outlay a huge amount of money up front.

If you want to get some retail sales, start in regions with a buzz for your artist. Developing relationships with retail folks provides great allies. If a store thinks the record can sell, they'll take some. Even chains take CDs on consignment. So much depends on your attitude. People in record stores respond to friendliness and enthusiasm. If they feel your love for the music, it can get their attention enough to listen. Having great music and at least somewhat of a story can give you a shot. John T. Kunz, owner of Waterloo Records, an indie-friendly store in Austin, Texas, warns, "It's as much work for us to stock someone who sold one or two CDs as someone who sold a few thousand. Artists need to understand this." Show appreciation for stores that support your music. They don't have to!

When leaving records on consignment, give the store a copy of the invoice. Whether you bring them in person to a store or to a distributor, write "received" at the bottom of the invoice. Have whoever accepts them sign that they were received. Otherwise there's no proof. If you ship them, save the receipt. A signature ensures that when it's time to get paid stores can't deny having received them. Make a good impression on folks in record stores. Be courteous. If they like you, they may push your product harder. Smaller stores can get people interested in buying something. Choose your retail price beforehand. John Kunz says, "Some people want to price their merchandise so cheaply it makes people wonder what's wrong with them. They need to have a developing artist price." He also wants bar codes, explaining, "Otherwise it's more work for us."

Show you have your act together and have business sense. Ask for help when you don't know something. Figure out how to fill out an invoice. Kunz recommends you come up with a package that has things retailers want. For example, "Make sure their name is very legible at the top 30 percent of the cover, not at the bottom." Kelly Vandergriff (Five Times August) says they got into Walmart by using persistence without annoyance:

We Googled Walmart executives and just started sorting through the thousands of result pages, reading articles, press releases, etc.

Through that, we found names, then email addresses. We actually did this with Best Buy and Target also. We started emailing and calling people we thought might be in charge of music. Two years go by (in this time I would every now and then send a "checking in" email). One day we get an email from someone at Walmart with the subject line: How can we get your CD? We never heard anything from Best Buy and Target on the first album, though the new record is in those and most other retailers.

When I released my first record, I went to every store within driving distance and established relationships with record buyers. After meeting in person, I'd follow up by phone. I found stores in other states, too. Call the store, ask for the buyer, introduce yourself, and ask if he or she would like a promo copy with a one-sheet (see below). Send it and call back in a week. Start with markets where people will be aware of the artist, because of radio play or the artist does live shows regularly. Be realistic. No one will carry your record if they've never heard of the artist and there's no promotion. Dave Roberge (Everfine Records) says they sparked interest from distributors because they were making an impact at retail on their own:

The first way to do it is by making champions of retail stores and entering into consignment accounts—proving you can move product off the store's shelf. Retail is becoming more and more competitive. You can have major label distribution, but it doesn't mean your product will be on store shelves. It's become very tight. So our focus was independent stores first and making an impact with the people that we really felt understand and care about music.

Getting Started with a Distributor

Your records are beginning to sell in stores. The story on your label is building. You're tired of sending product when stores run out. You want distribution in place, thinking you'll be set. Not true. Don't for a second think that a distributor will make your label run smoothly. Put all your energy into creating demand for your product! Even if you convince a distributor to take some, they won't market them. That leads to returns. Instead, go slowly, one market at a time as you create a buzz that drives people to stores. Also focus on building relationships that can help you in retail down the road.

Finding a distributor that gets product into stores efficiently can be rough. It's frustrating to arrive in a town for a well-promoted gig and discover that stores have no product because the distributor didn't ship them. Some actively alert stores to your product. Others just fill orders if stores request it. Finding a good distributor requires patience and shopping around. Persist in building a big enough demand to attract a good one. There are no surefire methods. Start with a great product, an identified audience and a way of reaching it. If distributors believe your material will sell, they'll work with you more. Depending on the genre and demand, it's better to start with several small ones in markets you can promote in than one that covers a larger region.

If you want national distribution, you need a solid marketing campaign on a national level. Why manufacture and ship product that may not sell because you haven't done enough marketing? Don't let your ego push you to pursue distribution you're not ready for. Start small and work your way up. Keep in regular touch with stores. If they say the record is selling, ask if they need more. When your reorders are steady, contact local or regional distributors. Explain where product is selling. Have promotion in place at this point. Be confident. Find ways to market the record yourself until a distributor accepts your label. The more sales you show, the easier it is to attract one. Michael Bull (Caroline) elaborates:

> We look for labels with an excellent roster of artists that fit more or less into our strongest genres, a clearly defined aesthetic vision, some history of prior success (as a label, and/or among its artists and key staff), good connections, an understanding of the distribution side of the business and what a label's responsibilities are in relation to that, good catalog, a strong and consistent release schedule, an understanding of consumer and retail marketing, and adequate financing. Of course, labels with all of these qualities are relatively rare, and exceptional strength in one area can offset weakness in another.

One-Sheets

A one-sheet is a sheet of paper that describes your product with details that tell the artist's story. It's a concise summary of pertinent information including specifics about individual members of a group, a short description of the music, reviews and other press, where the artist is touring, radio play, and any other promotional information that will create excitement about the artist. All this should fit succinctly on one page. Walter Zelnick (City Hall) explains:

> A one-sheet is important. That's what a lot of customers want to see. Even though they're getting a new release book from us, they want a one-sheet. It's a tool that's very handy for some customers. A well-laid-out black-and-white one-sheet—a simple sheet with all the information—is more important than a beautiful glossy that leaves stuff off.

A one-sheet should include the label's name, the artist, the name of the release, the release's UPC, its catalog number, the release date, and the suggested retail price. Andy Allen says a one-sheet is what sets the record up in all the data systems throughout the industry:

> It's what initially communicates info about the act and that particular project to the buyers. In the case of a brand new band, it may be the only thing you have to introduce the music. It should be accurate and easy to understand. Most buyers have asked us to have a one-sheet that's clear and concise, with the information presented in a way that can be easily digested.

Ask stores or distributors for samples of good one-sheets from other labels to see how they're organized. Some are done in a more high-tech way than others. Most include a copy of the album cover. Some are in color on glossy paper, but distributors and retailers assure me that the content is much more important than fancy presentation and that plain black-and-white faxes better. Stores find good one-sheets very helpful. Distributors prefer working with labels that provide them with enough sheets for the retail stores they service. Providing them shows you're serious.

Finding Distribution

When you begin, using local distributors gets people familiar with your label in your targeted market(s). As you develop a track record with sales and promotion, shop for larger distributors. Start in one region and expand from there. Work it! When you feel ready for national distribution, Michael Bull advises, "Do your homework. Identifying which distributors are strongest with the type of music and type of label you've got *before* soliciting will save time in the long run." Be prepared with a marketing plan and a picture of your finances. Andy Allen says, "We have to make sure that they're in a position to market the records effectively. We ask probing questions about the financial stability of the label, where their money comes from, and whether they're adequately prepared to market things." Call and ask how to approach them. Bull says:

> We're approached in about as many different ways as humans can communicate, but the best is: first, a simple introductory email sketching the label's general concept, roster, key past, current, and upcoming releases, and sales history and expectations. It will often be readily apparent to the distributor whether the label might be a good fit for them, in which case the conversation can become more detailed.

How do you find distributors? Get suggestions from buyers in stores. If a store uses more than one distributor, ask which one they think is best. Those working in stores often know which distributors indie labels like or which they hear other labels complain about. Pick everyone's brains. Alan Becker of RED Distribution says:

> There are many ways to find distribution. If you're looking for a national distributor, you better have the ability to create the activity that can keep the attention of a national distributor. You better have an act that has the ability to get on the radio, have a tour that's going to run from California to New York . . . to create that kind of national profile. Otherwise, it might be best to work on a more local or regional basis. On a local level, you could be a local phenomenon at your college or in a vicinity that could support you without having to take it in a more regional or national basis. So build up a local following that can then be leveraged to a regional distributor, then on up to a national distributor to make that entry a little bit smoother. I think in looking for a national distributor, it's best to start out locally, build up a following, create some results. Create some activity that you can bring to a larger distributor so that you're not put at the mercy of being one of the few starter,

not-very-well-looked-after labels. In any distribution system, the distributor can't do everything for everyone. They spend a lot of time with the labels who are creating the most activity. I think it's better to start out at a more manageable level, at a less high-maintenance type of distribution company until you're able to create the kind of activity that can keep a national or regional distributor focusing on what you're trying to accomplish.

Call buyers at local distributors and send a one-sheet and the product. It's good if someone at a store lets you use his or her name as an introduction. Some distributors want to receive a business plan, samples of product, release schedule, and financial prospects. Dave Roberge says that after he talked to ADA, he met with Andy Allen:

I went to New York with my business plan, my catalog, sales figures for the band, every piece of press, anything you could think of to sell him on the fact that we were a legitimate, one-artist label, and that we had pieces in place to maximize that relationship. Based on that meeting, he was impressed enough to give us that shot. At the time it was a unique deal in that the record label was one artist with three pieces.

Roberge had proven that O.A.R. could sell records, and he had his act together for marketing. Creating demand attracts distribution. If you get a reasonable buzz going on your act, however local, write a letter to distributors. Include pertinent information about your artist's story on a one-sheet. Hard facts are most important. Ask if the distributor would be interested in receiving the music and promotional material. If you've created a market, it isn't that hard to get a small distributor to stock at least a minimal amount of your product. Once the distributor sells some, they'll order more.

Working with Your Distributor

You can have more than one local or regional distributor in different locations. Choose several that complement each other in terms of regions and specific stores covered. Go to as few as it takes to cover the necessary ground. National ones want exclusive rights to distribute your product. An agreement should include specific payment terms.

Send invoices with all shipments to distributors. List exactly what you're shipping, the unit price of each item, the terms of payment, the number of cartons being shipped, and the purchase order (PO) number that was supplied when it was ordered from you. Most invoice forms have sections clearly marked for each of these items. The invoice is placed in an envelope marked "Invoice Enclosed" and taped to the outside of a carton containing your shipment or mailed directly to the accounts payable department of the distributor. You can buy invoices in an office supply store. You can also buy "Invoice Enclosed" envelopes.

Some invoices have a packing slip—a list of what's being shipped, without the price—as the last page. A packing slip includes the number of cartons sent, number of units, and a PO number. It goes to the shipping office. If your invoices don't have packing slips, make your own. Either cover the area where prices would be on the last page of your invoice so the carbon doesn't go through, or on business letterhead write "Packing Slip" and list what you sent. Just as with your invoice, put a copy of the packing slip into an envelope marked "Packing Slip Enclosed" and tape it to the outside of a carton in your shipment. Don't put the invoice and packing slip in the same envelope. They go to separate departments when the shipment arrives.

Once you have distribution, develop relationships with the sales reps. Call or visit them. Ask if they want promotional copies. It shows you're actively trying to market the record. Call regularly to see how your product is doing. Distributors carry a lot of product by many labels, and yours can get lost. By developing relationships with reps, your product may be one they push. Ryan Kuper says:

> A lot of labels have distribution, and they whine a lot. They say, "My records don't sell," but they're not doing anything proactively to get those records sold. Sometimes I'm on my distributor saying, "Hey, you've got to give me more love. When you make your sales calls, I want to make sure that you're pitching that product, because this is what I've done. The band's on tour with a national act. I placed print ads in magazines. These are the reviews we're getting back. Interviews are happening. Radio is going on." You have to stay on it. A lot of people expect a distributor to do everything.

Keep in touch with stores. Let them know which distributor has your product and thank them for pushing it in their stores. Notify a sales rep at the distributor about any stores showing interest in carrying your product. Michael Bull says:

> Understand your role in the label/distributor relationship, and make the distributor aware of how you will make their job—putting the right quantity of records in the right stores for each release—as easy and productive as possible.

If a store expressed interest in my music, I'd call my distributor and tell the sales rep whom I spoke with in that store. Distributors like a label that works its product. It earns you respect and possibly greater priority in how hard the distributor works with you. Walter Zelnick advises:

> Keep supplying us with important information: Is your artist touring, getting airplay? Give us copies of important press and anything we can use as a tool to give to our sales reps so they have a story to tell buyers. With email, update us weekly if there's new information. We send out weekly messages to our reps about increased airplay, charting information, and other stuff.

Let the distributor know if you're working radio and where your artist is playing live. Send them any press write-ups. All such information can help the company move your product into sales outlets. Build good relationships. Andy Allen says:

> Most of it is about communication—letting us know about the artist, the setup of the project, and the continuing update about what's happening so that we can pass that information to our sales force, and they can pass it through to the buyers of the accounts.

Release Dates

There are certain times that can be advantageous to release new product. Labels tend not to release anything during Christmas season, although I released my biggest-selling dance track then and had less competition with club DJs. Andy Allen says:

> From a seasonality standpoint, there's no good or bad time anymore. We've found that our indie labels tend not to release things in the

fourth quarter because programs are a little more expensive, and the onslaught of the major artist's releases tends to come out in the fourth quarter. Any other time of the year can work fine.

Labels traditionally release records on a Tuesday. Once you have distribution, they can direct you. Many send material to stores way in advance of the street date. Talk to your distributor for guidance on your schedule so it works with their mailings. It can help attract preorders. Walter Zelnick explains:

We like a label to give us two months notice and work with us in our release book. We've cut it back to once a month. They get at least two months of publicity in our book. For example, in December we send out the February new release book. The customers will have all of January and the beginning of February to order.

Getting Paid

It's said that the only way to get paid by a distributor is to follow your first record with a second. That's because distributors will pay for the first release when they have another record on which money is owed. Then they can credit any returns from the first release against what's owed on the second. This is true to an extent, but a record label can get paid more frequently.

Distributors Aren't Bad Guys

Distributors don't have the best image in the music industry, especially in regard to paying. This reputation comes with the role of being middlemen. Distributors aren't trying to cheat labels, but they must protect themselves from a lousy system. If they don't get paid, neither do you. Record stores don't always pay bills on time, so a distributor can't always pay quickly.

Returns can come back long after a record's been shipped. A distributor then gives the store credit and gets credit from the label. Therefore, they must be prudent about paying, especially with newer labels. Distributors like keeping an open invoice (one that hasn't been paid yet) as a safety against returns. Why? For example, if a new label is paid in full, and fifty pieces are returned a year later, it could be hard getting money back from the label on those returns. Indies often change distributors or go out of business. Would you give a distributor back money if you closed your label and then got returns? Most wouldn't. Therefore, distributors always want to owe you something. An open invoice ensures they can get credit for late returns.

Maximizing Your Chances of Getting Paid

Give yourself the best possible shot at getting paid. If you use regional distributors, don't spread yourself too thin. The more companies you use, the more you'll have to collect money from, and the more from which you can get returns. Don't get carried away with orders. Memorize my motto: *Orders don't pay bills; sales pay bills.*

Too often, we get caught up in the thrill of getting large orders. Trust me, the thrill disintegrates quickly as returns arrive. It's exciting when people agree to carry your product. You may work hard to convince lots of stores and smaller distributors to do it. But orders that you push for don't mean you'll see a dime later. Don't leave large numbers of product on consignment with anyone who'll take them. Be as selective as possible about which distributors and stores you place product with. Use as few as needed to cover the greatest area of stores and distributors in regions where you have promotion in place. And leave as few units as is necessary. You can always send more.

Distributors pay faster if they take a label seriously. As you get established and release more records, your label becomes more appealing to work. Getting paid gets easier when the artist's demand grows and you seem more likely to stay in business. Your leverage increases as sales do. Don't despair if it's slow initially; they get better—as good as you make your label! The best way to get paid is to release records that sell.

The terms (length of time) of payments from distributors can vary. Get them in writing. It doesn't mean you'll get paid, but does give you proof on paper if you must go to court to to collect what's owed to you. Sometimes larger distributors wait longer, unless your product sells through fast. They handle larger amounts of product and get returns from stores, chains, and one-stops. If you know the product sold well in retail stores, ask your distributor to return any stock and credit them on the invoice. Then ask for at least a partial payment on what they owe. If they pay 75 percent of that amount, they can keep the 25 percent open until you send more product.

Much of how you're paid depends on your relationship with your distributor and how much the distributor respects your label. Distributors do need indie labels, so they're not looking to screw you over. But the system forces them to be cautious about paying too soon. Walter Zelnick advises:

> Make sure you've got something that sells. We'll even pay people early if we're sure it's selling, to take advantage of early discounts. The main thing is we don't want to pay for things that aren't selling. Hopefully distributors order what they need. Go for small orders and look for reorders instead of loading people up. That's better in the long run.

Smaller distributors can work with you by taking less at a time. I've had local distributors take as few as twenty-five units. Stifle the impulse to convince them to take more. *Orders don't pay bills; sales pay bills.* If they sell out, they'll reorder. Some local ones will pay from order to order. If you ask, they'll pay the last invoice as a new one arrives. At the initial meeting, ask that the terms be made invoice to invoice. With a smaller one that's out of town, try to arrange for COD orders only. If they won't pay up front and you want them to carry the product, send the minimum number of units they'll accept. When they reorder, insist on sending the shipment COD for payment of the first invoice, plus shipping. If there's a market for the product, they'll work with you. If there isn't, you don't need the distributor.

When I ran my label, I tried not to give any distributor too much product at once. When I'd get a big order, I'd ask if they'd take less, since *orders don't pay bills.* Distributors sometimes order more than they need, to be certain they have enough since they can return what doesn't sell. As you establish relationships and they learn to trust that you won't run out of product when it's needed, they'll be more flexible. I'd assure them that if they reordered, they'd receive product fast. Often they agreed to cut orders. A small order sells through faster, leading to reorders. Then you can ask to be paid for the first invoice. If you have product a distributor wants, refuse to ship more until the previous invoice is paid. Alan Becker (RED) advises:

> In our business fortunes change, so when we're hot, we're getting paid very regularly by our customers, and when we're not, it's a little bit more difficult to get paid. Therefore it's harder to pay all of our

distributed labels. Enter into a deal—have a written contract—and still at the end of the day, unfortunately in this business, sometimes you have to sue to get the money that's normally due you. If you have a contract and you're working with a stable company, you're going to get paid. My advice on getting paid: Have a contract. Have a good lawyer.

If you have trouble collecting, small claims court is an option. You have a right, when the terms are due, to demand either payment or return of your product. The catch is that if you cause too much trouble, you may not get distribution for your next record. I limited distributors that weren't close enough to take to court. Those far away from you know chances are you'll never come and sue if they don't pay.

If a distributor comes to you, you can get more of your terms met. My rule of thumb was that if a local or regional distributor called, we did it my way, which usually meant COD shipments. When distributors want your product, it's usually because they have a demand for it. Sometimes it's an overseas order. I used to insist on COD—paid right away. They often agreed, since overseas orders have few returns. When distributors call, there's leverage for getting paid.

The picture I painted may discourage you, but it's reality. If you're serious, get motivated to get paid by putting your energy into selling records. That's why I advised you concentrate on developing a demand. You CAN do it, if you have an act with great music and persist in working it. So get focused and develop those skills! You CAN achieve success.

CHAPTER 14

The International Market

Do you want your product out overseas? Do you think American music flies out of the box once it gets there? The overseas market has an alluring reputation. Let me fill you in on what could indeed be a lucrative market if you understand it.

Breaking Down the Overseas Markets

Where is overseas? People refer to "overseas" like it's one big place, which is ridiculous. The overseas market comprises all the countries in the world that are across an ocean. Yet we lump them together when referring to foreign markets. Do that and your music will probably drown trying to cross the ocean. Tom Ferguson, international editor of *Billboard* magazine, explains:

> That there's no such thing as the "European market." Don't be fooled into thinking that because a number of European countries now have a shared currency, it's suddenly become one country. There are huge differences in economics and culture—not to mention language—between the individual countries in Europe. Sometimes there are even differences in culture and language within the same country, like Belgium, for example. Likewise, there are real differences in working practices from country to country. And we might have various directives from the European Union being put into place in our individual countries' national legislation, but the legal systems

172

in the various countries within the EU are still wildly different. In particular, remember that copyright law in much of Eastern Europe is, to put it mildly, not strictly enforced! Overall, do your homework, talk to other U.S. indies who have experience of Europe, and rely on the guidance of a good local distributor. IMPALA (see below) is also definitely worth contacting.

Each country has distinctive likes and dislikes in music, just as there are regional preferences in the U.S. Ferguson adds, "Bear in mind that Europe is such a diverse group of markets, that what's popular in the UK might go down like a lead balloon in Germany or France."

Philippe Kern is founder of the Independent Music Companies Association (known as IMPALA) (www.impalasite.org), a nonprofit organization based in Brussels that aims at promoting the interests of the independent music industry with governments, international organizations (WTO/WIPO), and European institutions (European Union, Council of Europe); and also founder and managing director of KEA European Affairs. He says, "The European marketplace is very diverse. Trading in Germany is different than trading in the UK or Spain. Each market has is own specificities and should be taken as one—there is no such thing as one single European market." Having an accurate perception of foreign markets helps you make realistic promotional decisions. Tom Ferguson says:

Obviously, a lot of major American acts are just as successful in Europe as they are in the States, although certain styles of U.S. rock in particular just don't seem to travel. The John Mellencamp school of "mainstream" roots rock, or the blander rock acts like Matchbox Twenty and Dave Matthews, just don't seem to strike much of a chord in Europe. The more mainstream country acts also don't tend to do so well here, for example, but we do like the real mavericks—Lyle Lovett or Steve Earle can tour and pull sizeable crowds, although their albums aren't likely to trouble the upper echelons of the charts. And obviously, a lot of hip-hop won't play too well in non-English language markets, unless you're Eminem, of course.

Many folks have the misconception that people in foreign countries love all American music. No way! There's only a market for your music in a specific country if it conforms to their musical tastes. Susan Rush, head of label management for Pinnacle Records, the biggest distributor for independent labels in the UK, says, "It's not an easy time at the moment, but there have always been niche markets in the UK for U.S. artists, especially in alternative, punk, metal, hip-hop, and urban genres." Ferguson adds:

> It's impossible to generalize about "indie American artists" in Europe, unfortunately. There's a long tradition of acts that couldn't get arrested back in the States yet that can sell tickets and shift a decent number of albums in Europe. Currently, acts mining the "Americana" scene are doing pretty well on the indie scene in Europe. There's always going to be some interest in the latest flavors to come out of New York as well.

How do you approach international markets? Ask your distributor(s) for advice about which countries might be good markets for your label. Read music magazines and trades with charts from other countries that are potential markets for your music. Check magazine stores with foreign publications. Reviews include specifics that can provide insight into what folks there like or dislike in music. Know your own music well enough to recognize similar acts to get clues about which markets might welcome your product.

Peter Thompson, managing director of Vital Distribution, an independent sales, marketing, and distribution company, says, "The Irish tend to like American music. France is very insular. They tend to promote French music." Tom Ferguson points out:

> Rather than genre shifts, the main movement in Europe over recent years has been towards domestic repertoire over "international" (i.e., the U.S.). France in particular has strict quotas limiting the amount of non-French music being played on radio, so U.S. acts face tougher competition than before in getting airplay. Otherwise, there's been a swing toward pop music in most European markets, but there's still a big market for rock in Germany, and metal goes down well in the Scandinavian markets. The UK is probably the most "trend"-oriented market in Europe, but it's currently heavily weighted in favor of straight pop acts.

Philippe Kern adds:

> Nordic countries are more receptive to metal and country music, but it is difficult to generalize—the trend in Europe is the success of

local repertoire over international repertoire—classical is having a hard time, but it is much stronger than in the U.S. Jazz is popular in Denmark and Nordic countries in general.

Holland and Belgium have always been receptive to American music. Kern says that the market concentration in radio, retail, and distribution make it difficult to break new artists, just like in the U.S. So you need to be prepared to market there like you do here.

Getting Distribution in International Markets

Getting distribution in foreign markets is similar to getting it in the U.S. You also need to create a demand or strong story for your record before foreign distributors carry it. There are distributors that work within individual countries, and regions referred to as "territories," and larger ones that distribute in several territories or across all of Europe. Peter Thompson says:

The European markets are saturated. There are a lot of labels out there, and I think people are focusing on the key labels. It's hard to get new labels distribution everywhere. But there are territorial differences. We have a lot of contacts throughout Europe—companies we can use—and we try to find the best possible ones for labels that give us the rights to do so.

Most American independent distributors don't distribute overseas. Some one-stops do. When I ran my label, some sent product to countries where they might sell. Most distributors with access to foreign markets are limited in how many outlets they can get product into. They usually send a few copies to their account in potential countries to test interest. Dance music is still the easiest to sell in many international markets through one-stops. Just like in this country, DJs all over the world love new music. It's a big job to pursue distribution and work music in foreign markets. Susan Rush says:

Whether it's UK or U.S. based, we need to see them build their profiles either through smaller distributors or our main competitors. The market at the moment is not conducive to labels putting records out just to "see what happens." There are too many labels and too many releases, and the consumer has too much choice, so retailers are expecting labels to deliver more, as they do not want to take risks.

It's difficult to attract distribution if your record is cold. Peter Thompson says, "It helps if we're familiar with the label or artist. In a swamped marketplace, we question whether to take them on. If we're familiar with the artist, we try to find a way to make it work." If your artist is doing well here, it might not matter to foreign markets if they're not known there. Tom Ferguson says, "It's vital to come to the European markets in person. If a U.S. act isn't prepared to show its face over here, do press, and tour, then forget it." Just like here! Susan Rush adds, "If they don't, there are fewer options to get promotional coverage and therefore less profile. Making key appearances should consolidate what your promotions people are hopefully beginning to build."

Distributors want to see a story behind the artist and how it relates to their market. Your artist must establish a presence in those you target. Touring can work, but it takes time. Peter Thompson says, "If they come over once, they would make a few inroads. After two or three times, they'd probably start getting a lot more interest." If the artist is good! If you want to make money in a territory, promote there! Susan Rush says:

> *Having a demand for your releases in the UK is important, so we look to see if labels are building up their profile via imports or whether they already license to UK-based labels and might be considering doing it themselves. If that's happening, we would expect a label to set up UK-based promotion and marketing partners. Ideally, you would also have someone in the UK managing the day-to-day distribution activities, but if that's not possible, you certainly need someone who is contact-able every day and understands what's required for the UK market. Email makes things much easier, but it means things move quicker, and everyone expects faster responses.*

As Rush says, the best way to market a record in a foreign territory is to hire a representative for your label in that territory. Thompson agrees:

> *From our perspective, having somebody we can regularly speak to in the UK, during business hours, is key. It may not be so bad for*

a New York label, but it would be very difficult to communicate properly with the West Coast because of the time difference. Things can move very quickly in the UK, so you need to be able to react very quickly. We like to feel that a label we're working with is serious about what it's doing and investing in that by having someone in our territory, on the ground, who understands our territory and how it works, and the frustrating nature of what we do. Often the biggest problem is trying to explain to somebody thousands of miles away why they haven't sold as many records as they think they should because they're selling a lot in America. They're not selling any records in the UK because no one's heard of them. I don't want to spend all my time on the phone explaining the basics of the marketplace. It's easier if we can speak face-to-face with people and build up a proper rapport. Then we work together to achieve our aims. It's building up a relationship.

If you have someone based in the territory, that person should know the marketplace well. It's expensive, but it's something to consider if you want to work foreign territories. Perhaps you can find other indies in the same situation and hire one person together in a cooperative arrangement. John Robinson says:

Shaman Work has made plenty of prosperous movements in the international markets. Our music is available all through out Europe, Japan, Australia, and South Africa. We have also had artist and representatives from Shaman Work travel abroad as well. The best way to get into the international markets are via press with both online and print publications across seas. Definitely know that when things are in place, the international markets are usually more healthy and supportive than here in the U.S.

The press in some countries can be generous with American acts that they like. I got quite a bit of media coverage in the UK for myself as the "rappin' teach" and for my other acts as well by going there and developing relationships. Networking can put you in touch with radio stations that might play your record and magazines might review it, if you send a copy. Juni Fisher (Red Geetar Records) uses www.radiosubmit.com, a company that gets roots music to radio stations, to get her music on radio in overseas markets:

I use radiosubmit.com for radio submissions, to keep from having to mail an expensive package overseas to DJs who are asking for western music, but when you see their playlists, they are playing country. So they can download a song or two for free; they are happy, and I have not wasted money sending a CD that will likely not result in sales or bookings.

Thompson says, "There are more nationwide specialty shows in the UK, and many are very supportive of American acts at the moment. But things change quickly." John Szuch (Deep Elm Records) says his artists have done well in oversease markets:

The overseas market is still very good to U.S. bands. We've never had trouble getting a tour organized overseas. You just need to be careful about your bookings and who you deal with. It's like a vacation, too—phenomenal to drive through Europe playing shows, in all kinds of different countries. Our bands always bring CDs to sell at shows. We do have distribution deals. Sometimes we send a band over because someone licensed the release in that territory. Your distributor's job isn't to make people aware of your tour; it's to get records into stores. Your job as a label is to help get people into those stores. Fans of the bands have helped us get over there.

The Internet definitely makes it easier to connect with potential fans in other courntries who might join your street team and help artists come over. Visiting a potential market can solidify those all-important relationships, which you can later maintain with phone, fax, or email. I got my records on radio in Europe when I went to the DJs. The press is also friendlier in person. Write-ups in foreign magazines establish a foundation for your market. Once people got to know me, I sent my later releases and followed up from home. Jonatha Brooke says she's made inroads in Europe:

It's really daunting to do it yourself there. You have to go territory by territory and have a separate deal with each territory. We decided to hit the countries that love singer/songwriters: Denmark, Belgium, and Ireland. We've actually built a little audience over there. We do short tours and keep pounding away at the press. We've got one distributor in Denmark and a different one in Ireland. We're just hooking up with a German distributor. I started in Denmark and went from record store to record store asking them if they'd buy some on consignment. I had a couple of gigs set up. My first gig was through the conservatory. I did a songwriting workshop and performed at the end. In a year's time we went from an audience of fifty to one thousand, the second time back. I sell a ton at gigs in Europe. They don't know if they'll find it again, so they buy it then.

It *is* possible to work directly with a foreign distributor, if you identify an audience in specific countries and find ways to reach it to get the story started. Get your artist touring in those markets. Go online to find contacts. If your market increases, Susan Rush advises, "Consider manufacturing in Europe and shipping from a European base. But I would only do it if it's obvious there is a growing demand for the labels, rather than pushing just to feel like it's ticking distribution boxes in each territory."

How do distributors pay? Peter Thompson says, "We take a percentage of the dealer price of the record and try to set the price as a UK dealer price. We [support our labels/artists]—advise them on everything from how to format the record, how to price it, to what stores to pitch it to." He says that major labels come to him, too, because they have their marketing down so well. The programs for foreign distributors are similar to those here. Rush says:

Certainly the UK market is similar to the U.S. market in that retailers have the power, and sales to the chains are generally sale or return. Labels also pay for retail marketing (racking, co-op ads, etc.), and returns can be heavy. This means manufacturing and shipping can be very expensive, so the label needs to make sure it has a viable business for it to work. Otherwise it should just sell on import.

Choose a distributor with care. Sometimes just one for all of Western Europe won't work, and sometimes it will. If a distributor doesn't have separate marketing people in each country, product may not have the sales it should. One can't treat all parts of the international market with one big strategy and hope for success. Respect each market with an individual plan.

Overseas Royalties

Artists don't get the same royalty rate for foreign sales as for sales in the U.S. For acts signed to American labels, the overseas rates are lower than here, which your lawyer should detail in your artist agreement. Many of those reductions are considered industry standards, like the clauses in artist agreements I mentioned earlier in the book. They all favor the record label, of course. Your lawyer can help with this.

A nice aspect of marketing music in other countries is they pay higher rates on publishing. While in the U.S. a flat rate is paid for the mechanical license, in most other countries the rate is based on a percentage of the price paid to dealer (PPD). This can end up being considerably more than what would be earned here for the same sales. Artists get credit for use of songs they perform in each venue. Publishing is much more valuable. Philippe Kern explains:

> *Licensing fees for songwriters and music publishers are much higher in Europe than in the U.S. This is mainly due to the droit d'auteur tradition that put authors in a stronger bargaining position than on the other side of the Atlantic. Performance royalties and mechanicals are higher than in the U.S.*

Licensing to Other Labels

An easier way to get product into foreign markets is to license it to a foreign record label. Licensing gives the foreign label the right to manufacture the record on its own label instead of just buying it from your company for distribution. When independent labels license to foreign companies, they often give them the right to manufacture and sell records in all parts of the world where the independent labels have limited or no distribution.

A licensing agreement can cover a small territory such as one country, several territories together, a larger territory such as all of Europe, or the whole world except for the U.S. Indies lacking good distribution outside the U.S. often do a worldwide deal, excluding the U.S., since they'd have trouble doing it on their own. Attorney Wallace Collins warns:

> *You must make sure your agreement with the recording artist (or with the owner of the masters if you are purchasing a master*

*recording) provides for a worldwide right of distribution and sale
and permits you to use licensees to exploit this right. Otherwise,
the artist or the owner of the masters has the right to do the foreign
licensing deals directly.*

When a single or album you've licensed is released, your label is acknowledged
on it. The label with the license should give you an advance. In some ways,
a licensing agreement is similar to one signed between a record label and
artist. When expenses and the advance are recouped from royalties earned,
you receive royalties. Depending on the terms of your own artist agreement,
your artist shares that money. Collins adds:

> *As for your royalty rate, in foreign deals it is often a percentage
> of the published PPD. This is usually something between the retail
> price and the wholesale price, depending on how PPD is defined in
> your agreement. You must be very careful because percentages can
> be deceiving. It really depends on what number your percentage is
> applied to—and the definition of PPD is often a heavily negotiated
> issue in any deal. I always try to get the royalty percentage applied
> to the highest number possible. I also make the licensee state the
> actual dealer price or PPD dollar amount so I can do a "penny
> count" and know exactly how much my client receives per record
> sold. Also, I always make sure that my client, the indie label, gets a
> piece of any flat fee or third-party license made by the licensee.*

Sometimes if a foreign distributor wants to carry an American label's
product, it helps arrange a licensing deal for that label with one it already
distributes in their territories. Rather than relying on the U.S. label to get
a story going for an artist, foreign distributors prefer involving a local label
that knows how to market and promote.

Warning: Don't even think about licensing a record without using a
lawyer. While what you earn from licensing may seem like found money,
don't sell your label short by not getting all you should. An indie label
owner with an offer from an English label came to me for consulting,
insisting he believed their story about being too small to give much of an
advance. He was dying for a deal. The English label knew it and pushed
him to sign quickly. Just as quickly, I insisted he get a lawyer. A month later
he sent me a gift. The lawyer negotiated him a much better contract with
a lot more money.

Be careful dealing with businesses in foreign countries. They know it's unlikely you'll come over to audit their books or take them to court over royalties owed. Make sure you get a reasonable advance—it may be the only money you get. Check them out thoroughly before signing. A lawyer experienced in foreign markets can help.

If you do a licensing agreement, you'll probably be offered a publishing deal for the songs. I always got an advance on publishing royalties when licensing a record. Usually the licensing record label has it's own publishing company and prefers you use it. You don't have to. It's easier, but you might get a better deal from another. As I said, these royalties can be lucrative. Use a publisher that will earn you the most money! Your lawyer should handle this, too, and be knowledgeable enough about international biz to advise you properly.

International Conferences

When I asked industry folks for the best way of hooking up with international companies for a distribution or licensing deal, they all advised going to MIDEM (www.midem.com), an international music licensing/publishing/distribution conference held every January in Cannes, France, and the largest gathering of international music industry folks. Tom Ferguson says:

> The big European markets, Popkomm and MIDEM, are very indie oriented, and deals are done at both of them. So it's worth attending if you can afford it, but probably not essential. At least they give indie labels a chance to meet overseas distributors face-to-face.

Music publishers, distributors, record labels, etc. come from all over to attend, and MIDEM is considered the most important music industry conference in the world. It provides the opportunities to get lots of business accomplished, and indie labels say that the business you can generate can keep you busy long after. According to Panos Panay, founder of Sonicbids:

> Every year I do to MIDEM and come back stimulated. The business is changing a lot. It's the only place I go to that gives me an insight into what's happening. You have video game companies, cell phone manufacturers, and advertising agencies, who all go to MIDEM

to talk about this business. These companies are major stakeholder in what's happening in the music business of tomorrow. So invest money in going there.

Attendees plan meetings months in advance to best take advantage of all the professionals that attend from around the world. I attended MIDEM and experienced the frenetic business energy in every corner of the conference center and way beyond. People meet in hotels, restaurants, clubs, and on the street. Wallace Collins says, "MIDEM is four long days of meeting and greeting and miles of running around deal making and bread breaking. 'Schmoozing' is too gentle a word for it!" It's an incredible networking opportunity! It's also incredibly expensive, so don't go unless your music has a decent chance to sell internationally.

The most valuable thing you may get from MIDEM is relationships. People take you more seriously in that environment than they would if you were just another indie label sending an unsolicited package. Once they're in place, these relationships can be worked for later releases. You might not get a deal initially, but you'll get in doors later. If you make the investment, plan way ahead to make the most of it. Register months in advance and take advance of the discounts offered. Once you register, you'll have access to the directory of people attending. Contact them to set up appointments. Many book up before January. I highly recommend renting an international cell phone. You'll rarely be in your room, and a phone helps you meet up with people.

Another European opportunity is Popkomm (www.popkomm.de), a communications trade fair held every fall in Berlin. It involves a trade fair, congress, and festival and offers a presentation platform for the international pop music industry. Popkomm represents the largest concert event in the world. It includes public concerts in clubs and on outdoor stages. The concerts offer music that spans genres. Popkomm is more informal than MIDEM. It's one of the largest meeting places for the international community. If you want to break into international markets, look into attending one of the European conferences to get entrée to people you'd need to do business with. Meeting in person builds stronger relationships. Tony Brummel (Victory Records) says:

Foreign sales is about 25 percent of our business. Over the years, I've gone to Popkomm and MIDEM. It's very worthwhile if you get your packages to people and follow up with faxes and emails. Secure the meetings. It boils down to relationships. I know that I've done deals with people over the years because I've hit it off with them personally. And they believed in what my company was doing. That goodwill on their end turned into a lot of business for them as well. To an extent, this is still a people business, and there are a lot of people out there who will do business with you because they believe in music and will believe in your vision if you have a vision that's worth investing in. All of our artists tour internationally.

There are also other events going on in different countries, such as UK Music Week. The festival circuit in European markets is a great way to get exposure for your artists, if they fit. There are many, in every country. Some are open to having foreign acts. Networking and the Internet can put you in touch with them. Japan has great opportunities for music, but it's a harder market to crack because English isn't spoken as much as in European countries. Japanese directories and resources are in Japanese. But, if you can find someone who speaks Japanese to help you, or make a few contacts in Japan, it can expand into a lucrative opportunity. People from the Japanese music industry attend large conferences like MIDEM and Popkomm, and also SXSW [South by Southwest]. Go to Japanese music showcases and make friends. Many artists get over to Japan and sell lots of music there. Find your way in!

CHAPTER 15

Marketing and Promoting Outside the Box

This chapter discusses creative, alternative ways to brand your music through grassroots promotion and marketing and discusses finding outlets that pay to use music. Many labels survive in this supposedly tough market by finding ways to beat the traditional system by breaking rules and being creative. Many indies live by grassroots marketing. Below are suggestions to get started.

Finding Alternative Markets

Alternative marketing means finding places to sell your product beyond record stores. Study your market. Selling outside the box can increase sales. Depending on the music, some indies target nontraditional outlets to sell product, such as clothing stores, bookstores, health stores, and gift shops. Dan Zanes (Festival Five Records) found a great market for his children's CD in kid-related stores that sold clothing, books, toys, and even furniture. Zanes explored any venue aimed at kids. He explains:

> My CD looks different, more handmade, so it fits into places. I put on a clean shirt and went from store to store. Word of mouth got the CD outside of town. I'd get emails from other parts of the country. I believe in playing live to spread the word. I've done a lot of performing since this came out. In the beginning, if I knew

someone at a school, I offered to do it for free if we could sell CDs.
That was the starting point. I performed for families at fundraisers on
weekends. The school kept the door. We'd sell CDs.

Zanes's market keeps expanding. His unique packaging makes his CD a
special gift item for any store with kids' products. Trout Fishing in America
also does some children's music. Manager Dick Renco says:

> *We do a lot of work with libraries. Trout Fishing in America did a*
> *workshop for 150 school librarians, showing them how they write*
> *poems. Part of our mission is to make art accessible. These guys*
> *prove that art comes from everyday lives. Libraries called them.*
> *They did a public service spot advertising libraries and reading*
> *programs and do workshops with kids.*

Keep your eyes open. Be creative by thinking outside the box about what
kinds of stores and other outlets could be tapped to sell your CDs. Your
packaging could make your CD stand out as special. In the next chapters,
pros emphasize how great packaging gets you through doors. If people don't
open your package, the music isn't heard. Zanes said some stores bought
his CD without listening to it. That's marketing! Would you buy cereal
in a plain white box with generic black lettering? We're attracted to nice
packages. If you think about yours from a marketing standpoint, it might
increase your chance of success.

Besides working the Internet, have postcards to give out at gigs. I'm
still a believer in offline marketing, too. Leave postcards in an assortment
of stores, at coffee houses, and other places where people who might like
your music might be. I get subscribers to my blog by giving out postcards
and leaving a few wherever I go. With most people slammed by email
promotions, a real postcard might be held onto and checked out.

Alternative Venues

Find venues that offer opportunities to perform, get paid, and sell CDs.
Once again, think outside the box. Watch for places to cultivate gigs that
aren't clubs and concert halls. Rich Hardesty has created an empire in
the college market. Besides targeting traditional clubs and frat parties, he
creates opportunities. Since so many college kids are underage and can't

go to bars, Hardesty goes to them. Sometimes he plays private parties for excellent money. He explains:

> I tell them to charge ten to fifteen dollars a head. I can make anywhere from eight hundred to three thousand dollars. They have it in private houses at college campuses. I always sell CDs. And you entertain a market of underage kids who will support you as they turn twenty-one. The kids sign your mailing list, want your autograph, and you're creating a fan for life. I think underage kids are an untapped market. I hear from them all the time that they want to see me but can't come to a bar.

When David M. Bailey resumed songwriting and performing, he looked for places to perform and expose people to his music. He says:

> It sounds cliché, but you just gotta get out there. I played at our local church, at our campus support group, at a pottery shop. I scouted places to play and dropped off press kits with a recording. It's hard to create a draw. I looked for opportunities to play where people were gathered for another reason.

Bailey discovered that conferences offer opportunities to perform in front of large audiences, sell CDs, and get paid. He reminded me that there's a whole industry of people who manufacture things that have annual conferences. Bailey says, "Everyone knows somebody that goes to these. Get a business card, a decent recording, a photo, and a bio." Bailey has something to say that people like. In many cases, he pitches himself as an inspirational speaker with a guitar. He began with church conferences because he had contacts and worked his way out. He says:

> You do one concert for a group of one thousand people and they actually represent forty-nine different churches. Over the next six months, invitations from all these places trickle in. This worked for me well in the church arena, but I think it's true in any sector—one really good concert in front of a group of people from all over creates not just word of mouth but actual invitations to their own places.

Organizations hire entertainment for conferences, usually pay well, and attract interesting fans. Some artists support their label by working fairs and festivals, doing house concerts, performing at outdoor events, etc. I have a whole chapter on venues in *I Don't Need a Record Deal!* With appropriate music, there's good money, CD sales, and increased mailing lists. Stay vigilant for opportunities. Schools, churches, organizations for kids, and a gazillion other places can provide exposure if you ask. Don't be afraid to ask somebody if they need live music for an event your music would fit.

Record Release Parties

If you have record release parties, choose a venue with a good sound system. Try to cut a deal with the club. If they think you'll bring a large crowd, you may get perks you don't pay for. Record release parties are usually scheduled to last two hours. It's easier to get a club's cooperation if you hold it in the early evening. Sometimes the artist performs for the public later. Some labels have an open bar for an hour, but that's costly. If the artist has a large following, the club may cut a deal for him or her to do a free public performance at the venue in exchange for a party open bar. Some labels get a liquor sponsor and a cash bar for other drinks. Some clubs allow you to bring food; others provide some. The artist usually performs. Eric Speck (Ace Fu Records) advises:

> *Record release parties are only effective if there's a genuine buzz on a band and a lot of industry contacts are interested in coming down to hear the new stuff and getting a copy as an incentive. Then it makes sense. Otherwise it's just another show.*

Send special invitations to the media, radio people, agents, managers, retailers, and anybody in the music industry that might help your artist. Invite loyal fans and players who helped get the record out. Don't plan a release party if you aren't sure you'll have a crowd. It'll do more harm than good if a few industry pros hang out in an empty room. To avoid that, call everyone you invite to confirm they're attending.

Free Music

While I don't advocate giving away too much music, it's good to give people a taste. Remember, you're selling your artist and name recognition. Major labels just want to sell records. Indies want to create fans who'll support the act by buying the album, joining the street team, and coming to gigs. When you brand your label by letting potential fans hear your music, they buy other releases in the future. Rich Hardesty has gotten far by giving away lots of music. He explains:

> I have about thirty-eight live CDs, recorded at shows. I mostly give them away for free because it's a fan that will keep coming to shows. Fans pass them around. They end up on the Internet. It's live, and I'm not worried about it being passed around because it creates new fans. That's the bottom line.

Tape every gig that you can, and make some of the good tracks available on your site for free download. Fans still buy the studio version. Fans look for indies with integrity that are known for having a full album of good songs. When fans know you do, they appreciate it and buy it. Dave Roberge (Everfine Records) agrees:

> I think people have been duped. They'll hear a song on the radio, buy the record, go home and play it, and it's nothing like the song they heard on the radio. After the second and third time they're spending sixteen to twenty dollars to get duped. So they're going to the Internet, getting their one song, and the band is relevant for that one song. As an independent, I believe we need to go back to making great records that people want to buy.

Eric Speck says, "I'd give away a few songs." When you make great records, fans support you by buying them. If you give them a taste, they'll want the whole thing. Rich Hardesty heard from a high school girl in Portland, Oregon. He sent her free music and now everyone at her school is a fan. Giving away samples creates demand in places you've never been. Hardesty adds:

> Who else would turn a high school in Portland on to my music? A marketing team for a record label has all that money, but I did it for free. Now she's doing artwork for me and created a bunch of fans. I do that with many high schools. If I get a fan letter, I ask if they'd like free music. I send a live show, hoping they'll copy it and give it to everyone they know.

Nowadays, you can have free music downloads on your website, at no cost to you. Why would fans buy a CD if they get music free? Hardesty gives away live shows and sells the studio CD. Roberge says fans want the artwork that comes with an album. "We've focused on delivering innovative packaging, delivering the product in a way that somebody has to go out and own it. You've got to spend money on the packaging." Consider putting some songs on MP3 files and sending them to potential fans. If you believe in your music and give people a taste, you can create fans who'll buy many of your albums down the road. Jason Feinberg, president of On Target Media Group (www.otmg.net), says he encourage most of his clients to give something away for free online. He explains:

> A free track (or video) is about the best marketing tool in your arsenal. With such limited real estate on influential sites, an artist has to offer something compelling to get coverage. Sites love to give their readers something for free, and quite often an artist can get heightened placement from offering a track. I don't think it is wise to give everything away for free, although for some artists this is starting to make sense. Use the music purely as a marketing tool, and then drive the attention it generates a specific direction such as live shows, merchandise, and licensing. If you have a huge name and well-established career, the value of giving music away decreases quickly. In some cases it's actually a bad idea. But for the other 98 percent of artists out there, give fans something they'll love, and they'll come back for more.

Word of Mouth

Word of mouth is still the most powerful marketing tool. When you get five fans, they can tell more, who tell more, and so on. You need to find those first bits of exposure and then use them to get more. Eric Speck adds, "The mouth is still very effective, especially nowadays when it's in a state of hyperactivity through IMs and emails and everything else. If the word gets out it can ricochet around the communities."

Great music can find an audience for it to speak to, one step at a time! Be patient. It takes time to create a buzz, but if the music is there, you'll develop one. Major labels' big machines can't maneuver the streets as easily. Hip-hop artist K. Banger (the Dirt Department) uses a tool available to everyone to reach an audience. He explains:

Independent artists must never underestimate the marketing power of word of mouth! It can be very frustrating to talented artists when they do not have capital to invest in the necessary components to be heard and seen on a broad scale. But once we understand that marketing stirs up word of mouth, we can rely on our creative side to market ourselves at low cost. Word of mouth attracts people to assist in expanding your business venture from a financial point of view. When my prospects saw the streets were talking, they knew the Dirt Department was worth getting into.

Look how fast rumors can spread! When you get people talking, awareness begins. Indie labels are known for their ability to create awareness through grassroots efforts. K. Banger's word-of-mouth campaign began with family and friends. He explains:

They let their people know about my CD. One friend told an acquaintance with a slot on a Rutgers, New Jersey, station. The radio-show host played it. Although the station doesn't have strong signals, it was a turning point in my local market. The host warmed listeners to me, buzzing the website URL. I did promo rhymes to promote their show and sponsored it since they were giving me so much burn. Next thing you know, all the hip-hop programs on the station are blazing my tracks. I didn't pay for advertisement. No payola or marketing stuff. It spilled over to a Rutgers station with a stronger signal. The urban director got emails from major labels asking about me. I sold CDs with ease, off- and online. People said they heard me on radio, and my name was everywhere. For someone with few resources, that was a great start! I didn't expect word to spread so much from this little station in the middle of nowhere. But it had a huge effect, especially in my hometown market.

K. Banger works it wherever he goes. He speaks to everyone, spreading word about his music for the price of opening his mouth! Rolando Cuellar (Roland Entertainment) says networking and word of mouth helped him meet people who helped his first artist, Baby Jay, get special opportunities, like performing at stadiums and getting a top Texas energy company to sponsor several of Baby Jay's appearances in partnership with their presentations. Cuellar explains:

> I met a representative with the electric company at a networking event. I told him what I was doing with Baby Jay and all his accomplishments. Next thing I know he called and introduced me to his boss. We created a hip-hop/rap song about energy conservation. You never know who can help further your company and artists. I really didn't think anything would come to pass with this company, and look what happened! A great relationship began, and we became the first indie label/hip-hop artist to partner up with an energy company. So I present myself and my artists to everyone, especially those who I feel can benefit from our vision.

Technology has made word of mouth a lot simpler. Once some people get on your side, they can spread it electronically. John Szuch (Deep Elm Records) says word of mouth has gotten his artists far. He explains:

> Support from fans and friends of Deep Elm helped us grow over the years. We've never called music supervisors. It's always been through friends of friends. If you have patience and can build up a network through referrals or word of mouth, people will refer you. Word of mouth from your fan base for releases always gets the best kind of things—when you have people coming to you that heard good things about you.

Street Teams

Indies turn to street teams to spread the word about an album to potential fans. Street teams can effectively generate an early buzz on a release before its street date. Tony Brummel (Victory Records) says:

> They do anything from various promotions on the Internet; going to retail and setting up displays; securing in-store play; filling out stock checklists for us; giving us reports on what programs they see other labels' product in; compliance for listening stations that we pay

for, especially at the chain level. The big thing is going to concerts and passing out posters, stickers, or samplers and doing everything in their community to promote our records.

I think that many indies forget that music lovers have lives off the computer, too. With everyone promoting online, there may be less competition for fans handing out postcards and praising a band in person. Ryan Kuper (Redemption Records) says street teams are great for niche labels. Bands with loyal fans work well for labels to spread the word. They pump that first week of sales up as much as possible. Jay Woods (New West Records) is a big believer in having people talking up a record in stores:

> *We don't have the luxury of a big staff or having RED at our beck and call. So we constantly try to recruit people to be our eyes and ears for us in the stores. There's only so much you can do over the phone. Part of it is an imaging campaign and letting people know. There are thirty thousand new records out this year. How do you think ours stand out in thirty thousand new pieces? That's our challenge. You've got to let people know they're out there.*

Show great appreciation for street team members. Continually encourage people to sign up to join at gigs and on your website. Create a separate newsletter for them. Let them know news first. Make it personal. Thank individual members for specific things. Give them free tickets to gigs, advance copies of new releases, a song no one else has, and any perks you think of. When fans feel special, they work hard. Create a community, as GrooveLily did when they began their Petal Pushers (PP) program. Valerie Vigoda says they create a sense of community to make the fans feel special, because they are. They work together to spread the word. Vigoda explains:

> *The Petal Pushers turned into their own vibrant, growing community of friends. They have gatherings and parties. There is an active online discussion group, and we make "exclusives" available to the PPs as often as we can. We put one very avid Petal Pusher in charge of the program. He's the point person—asks each PP how they'd like to be involved and encourages them to do what they're comfortable with: postering, flyering, contacting media, giving sampler CDs out,*

*helping at the merch table at gigs, and in some cases, promoting shows.
A small group of PPs funded our bumper stickers, which say "Petal
Pusher Powered!" People enjoy being part of a community, helping to
spread the word about music they like. All we do is show appreciation
as much as we can and try to channel their incredible energies!*

Jesse Fergusson uses marketing companies to organize Def Jux's street
promotion. But it works best when the street teams love the music. If you
have the budget, hire companies to put street teams together in any market
across the country. If you can't afford it, get fans. Indie artist Ansel Brown
started a successful street team with his fans on MySpace that led to him to
join former NFL Defensive All-Pro Sean Gilbert's indie label, IPAK Records
as their flagship country artist. The street team grew from MySpace and
spread the word about Ansel and his music in many areas. He explains:

*What an incredible development the street teams have been for me
on MySpace. I was asked by Charlotte out of Texas if I wanted
her to run a street team page for me, and I said sure! It had a little
traffic and was neat, but nothing significant. Then I was asked by
other friends on MySpace if they could start one in their states. It hit
me—street team state divisions could be a cool way to get more help
and allow others to really participate in my dream! We started asking
for volunteers, and bang! Before you knew it, we had people from
ten states step up and start their divisions. It has grown to over thirty.
I was looking for leaders—not just fans! Boy did we find them! Street
team leaders collaborate with one another and work with one another
to really have impact! They have even gotten me radio interviews and
other opportunities—even starting a blog talk-radio show that airs
every week on blogtalkradio.com. My job is to keep them growing
and contributing. That way they stay onboard and grow the whole
thing with me. A little TLC and faith in them goes a long way!
I absolutely adore all of them!*

Send street teams to any place that a potential fan might go. Give them
T-shirts to wear at music events that fans of your genre attend. They
can give out samplers, stickers, or any swag with your name and website
on it. They can also talk up your music with the enthusiasm that only a
passionate fan can generate to fans of similar artists. Onno Lakeman (Red
to Violet) says:

We have given people T-shirts and flyers for UK festivals, and it works. In the U.S., we did the same during events so that thousands of music lovers visiting the festival see someone wearing the shirt and handing out flyers.

Street teams create awareness. Where might potential fans shop? Fans can bring promotional material to retail stores that music lovers may go into. These stores don't have to sell the CDs, but they might give out swag to support the music, if enthusiastic fans approach them. Tony Brummel agrees:

That's a big alternative marketing area for a label like us—a lot of alternative-type accounts that might be interested in our artists will do things for us, outside regular music retail. For example, we continually supply skateboard shops, surfboard shops, places like that, with free music, T-shirts, and giveaway items. In turn, they'll give out our samplers, put up posters, and play the CDs in their store. They don't sell the CDs. We still want sales to be in music retail.

Licensing Music for Use in Media

There's a strong market for licensing indie music for use in many areas. Artists can break after having their music on TV, in films, in commercials, etc. As Jay Woods says:

There are two ways to make money in the record business: One is selling music. The other is to license material. That's a viable part of what we do. We have had little leverage, and now we have a little more. The more we have, the more serious music supervisors take us. It's taken some time. Part of the reason Cameron [president of New West Records] stayed in L.A. was to be in the middle of that stuff. We have gone to music supervisor soirees and service those people. Most of the stuff we've had licensed for films or TV comes from meeting people over time.

There's more need for musical content than ever. While TV and films are obvious, there are a variety of needs for music in advertising, video games, and nowadays, for Internet sites, corporate videos, web programming, etc. Jeff Price (spinART Records and Tunecore) says:

Master use licensing allowed us to stay in business for so long. Another entity or corporation pays the label a fee to license the rights to one of its songs that it controls, called the master, to a movie, TV show, or commercial. Indie music is everywhere today, in every movie and TV show.

There are unlimited possibilities. Anywhere you hear music playing, from elevators to airlines to stores and much more, there are opportunities to make money from music. More and more labels are seeing the value of pursuing licensing opportunities. Often visibility attracts people who want to use your songs. Bill Werde (*Billboard*) adds:

Once upon a time AM and FM radio had more diversity on the airwaves. Nowadays, I think to some extent, Grey's Anatomy is the new radio. If you can get you song on the right TV show, and it plays at the right dramatic moment, it could be a big break for you. We see it on the Billboard charts all the time. The week after the show airs, you see the spike in sales. Brands are looking for more ways to further integrate themselves into what they perceive to be a credible experience and want to connect with passionate music fans.

Why would music supervisors want indie music? Because you can act much faster than larger companies and will take less money than major labels will for their music. Getting a song from a major publisher at the last minute can be futile, with miles of red tape to get permission. And, they drag out negotiations to get as much money as possible. Daniel Glass (Glassnote Entertainment) says, "Our first opportunity was for a ringtone campaign. It was very successful and gave us a lot of exposure online. On a major label it would probably have been negotiated to death and never happened." Indies work fast. If someone offers you decent money, you're more likely to jump at it. Just make sure a lawyer checks the agreement! Kelly Vandergriff says song placements helped to skyrocket the popularity of Five Times August. She explains:

The first song placement we got was pure luck; a music supervisor for MTV found Brand's music on CDBaby.com. He used one song, then we sent the new album at the time and he used five more. I think he handed copies off to his music supervisor friends, because we started getting calls from more and more, requesting to use the music. The first one we got was in November 2004. Then five more in January and Febuary 2005. Then it seemed like a different show was playing a Five Times August song every month! During this time, MySpace hits jumped through the roof, and our digital sales shot up. It's been extremely helpful. But just like with MySpace, it is starting to get saturated and mean less.

A key to licensing music is to develop relationships with people who license music. When they get to know and like you, and your music, they request your current songs or call if they need something specific to see if you have one that fits. Make an effort to get to know people who need musical content. When you prove yourself as fast and reliable, and show you have great music, they'll come back when they need more. Vandergriff says they really work it:

We develop relationships with them by going to L.A., New York, or wherever they are, taking them to dinner and letting them know how much what they do helps unsigned artists make a living. One music supervisor told us no one he'd placed had ever offered to take him to dinner before. All in all, the first album had thirty-seven song placements, and the latest one is also getting placements.

Getting music into film and television can generate a good revenue stream and provide exposure that can launch a career. Werde says:

One of my favorites in the last few months is Ingrid Michaelson, who doesn't have a record label deal but [her own Cabin 24 Records] is distributed through RED. She got music onto an Old Navy commercial during sweeps week, and everyone in the world knew they could Google the lyrics and find the music. She's done phenomenally well. Ingrid also had song placements on Grey's Anatomy. She's taken this commercial and TV approach to getting her music out there.

Ingrid Michaelson, who's sold over 200,000 copies of her album independently, agrees that getting her music licensed helped accelerate her career. She says she never expected much to happen because she needed to work and couldn't tour. So she thought, "I'll put my stuff out there and see what happens." Three songs from her album were used on *Grey's Anatomy*, and the show's producers asked her to write something specific. She wrote "Keep Breathing," used to end the 2007 season finale. All this from posting songs on MySpace! Things escalated when Old Navy used her song "The Way I Am." Michaelson says:

> *The Old Navy commercial was part of the whole upward swing of my career. It was luck that somebody came across my profile on MySpace, heard my song, and liked it. I didn't expect it to blow up like it did. That song was like the baby on the record. It only played for two weeks. There was nothing to identify me or the song. It was all about people seeking it out, which is incredible. Sales improved vastly. At first it was more digital sales, but it's become more physical.*

Many indies say licensing music helps them stay independent. Valerie Vigoda says, "We've been featured on daytime TV shows." Jonatha Brooke wrote a song for a Disney movie and has songs on TV, too, from contacts through friends and networking. And of course, having great music helps! John Szuch says licensing has helped his labels and gives his artists an extra revenue stream. He explains:

> *We've been licensing music since the second season of* The Real World *on MTV. Someone on that episode was a fan of one of our bands and wore their T-shirts. A producer got in touch with us. We sent some music and met folks at MTV. For a long time, we allowed them to use music for free. We absolutely don't allow that anymore, for anyone! Over time those people got jobs in different places, and we built up a network. Licensing is an active part of our business. It's very competitive, and a 24/7 job. You need to be available any time to provide music for a music supervisor or someone in the editing room. They call or email us saying what they need, or "Here's the scene. This is what we're looking for." You can send twenty songs and might not float their boat. What they want or will like is pretty subjective. Sometimes we hit a home run with someone who loves a song from one of our bands and wants to use it in a commercial. In our licensing deals, the label keeps the portion of funds for the master use. The band*

keeps the portion assessed for the synchronization use. Licensing music is a continuous form of revenue for bands. After we license something, it will eventually come out on DVD—an additional way to make money for us and the band.

Music supervisors cruise websites such as CDBaby, MySpace, and Facebook. Some websites offer opportunities to post music, and people looking to license can peruse it (more in Chapter 20). Mark Carpentieri (MC Records) warns, "As a label, it depends on how much you own of the masters and songwriting. It becomes more difficult for the person trying to license music if they have to split things up." Always check with a lawyer before you embark on seeking licensing deals for your artists' music. If you plan to pursue licensing opportunities, alert your lawyer so it's covered in the artist agreement. It may not be worth your time. Stephanie Furgang Adwar, Esq., says:

> *Labels in general own the masters. If they don't own the publishing, it's not in their interest to try to get synchronization licensing. However, many labels, all of the majors, have publishing arms that do just that. If a label holds onto the publishing, as the publisher, they have an obligation to utilize the music and maximize the income stream as much as possible. It is in their interest at that point. The [people who want to use the music] may not want the master use. They may only be looking for the synch license and decide to rerecord it in some other way. Master use is using it right off the record—use of the master itself. That gets paid for. The label owns the master under most agreements. They are allowed to license the master for use. The artist will get the percentage that is set up in the terms of the contract. If there's no provision within the contract for master use licensing, then the money goes straight to the label. In publishing, the standard is usually a 50/50 split between the publisher and songwriter.*

There are also opportunities to license your music in foreign markets. Many are found online. According to Rick Purcell, Esq., associate counsel at MasurLaw:

> *In addition to the obvious advantage of an additional revenue stream, licensing deals provide independent labels with unique*

opportunities to reach new audiences in foreign markets that may not be accessible via traditional channels. Where traditional media in foreign markets, such as radio, may not be receptive to new artists from other countries, licensing an artist's music for use in film, television, or advertising can bring the music to a new audience. Such licensing deals are particularly effective when the artist is matched with a related product or media due to potential audience crossover. For example, an American rock band can benefit from being licensed for use in a foreign advertisement for an American motorcycle commercial. Furthermore, many licensing opportunities exist for independent labels due to budgeting constraints that make licensing from major label artists prohibitive.

In my book *I Don't Need a Record Deal!*, there's a huge chapter with detailed information on how licensing works for film, TV, advertising, ringtones, and much more. I interviewed dozens of music supervisors and others involved in the process.

Just Darn Creative

There are other income opportunities and promotional approaches for your label. Find ways to tie yours into things outside the box. John Szuch says, "We're experimenting and will offer our entire catalog on a high-resolution DVD. We're always looking for new ways to get music into the hands of people who love it."

Rolando Cuellar saw a market in schools for his artist Baby Jay. While he doesn't have to do it, Cuellar is relentless in his pursuit of getting Baby Jay in front of young people. He works hard to find schools, events, and other places to reach his target audience. It's greatly increased his mailing list, which benefits sales. He explains:

The first school that booked Baby Jay was in Houston. A teacher wanted to raise money for the Cure Autism Now Foundation but didn't know how. I told her about Baby Jay. She was very impressed. He helped raise over a thousand dollars with his performance. The first two years, Baby Jay did not charge. It was more a promotional campaign to bring awareness to schools about his mission. He got an honorium. Now gets paid for every school presentation/performance. Students throughout the country have heard about Baby Jay. Bringing his message to a young audience will help his career in the long run. Students will grow with Baby Jay and follow his career.

Since he has a huge fan base in colleges, Rich Hardesty takes his act to Jamaica for spring break. He got spring break companies to pay for him and provide free trips to raffle off. He invites his mailing list to join him in Jamaica. Many do! Hardesty says:

When I played my first gig in Jamaica, there were kids from across the country. I stacked my suitcase full of CDs and bumper stickers. My marketing plan was to get them out with the website on it to all these kids from different parts of the country. I hired Jamaicans to give them out. A big spring break company put me at the most popular bar. There were about three thousand people. It was so successful they sponsor me every year.

Hardesty's mailing list expands with each trip. He created an opportunity for a free vacation and great promotion. His mailing list increases with new fans from new markets. Creativity brings opportunities. Think outside and under and over the box. Where can I pitch music so people who might like it will hear it? Be vigilant. Great opportunities can spring from anywhere you put energy. If you have great music, find a home for it, and vacation homes for yourself as well! John Szuch says:

You never know what will do it for your artist—whether it's a big write-up in a magazine, or Perez Hilton putting up a link, or some crazy video that everybody loves, or a celebrity in the audience at a show thinks your artist is great. You never know what's going to take off. There's no formula. That's why you try as best and as much as you can. Try every avenue, and hopefully something takes off. Go out and make it happen! Take risks and see what happens. If you really believe in the music you're putting out and love what you do, then you'll do those things and make those sacrifices, because where there's a will there's a way.

CHAPTER 16

Getting Publicity for Your Product

M any labels point to publicity as the best tool for fueling an artist's career. Whether it's in print or online, getting your name out helps to brand you or your artist's name. According to Derek Sivers, founder of CDBaby:

> Press is the single biggest factor—the difference between musicians who are selling thousands and those selling none is the ability and the persistence of the musician to go out to the media with an interesting angle and an interesting twist and get stories done about them. Anybody can get the world's attention if they can find the unique angle in what they do.

Jesse Fergusson says, "Here at Def Jux, publicity has been very effective. It's free advertising." When people read about your artist, they're more likely to at least check out the record or attend a live show. If they like the music they may buy it. Songwriter David M. Bailey agrees. "When I go to a town, if there's a good article written with a photo, that's tangible proof I was there. I can extract quotes." A good record review generates sales. Dan Zanes (Festival Five Records) says, "There's an article in the *New York Times Magazine* that I think put me on the map. Everything changed."

Publicist Karen Leipziger, of KL Productions, says, "People need to be made aware. Publicity can make the right people aware in the right way." It lets potential fans know the record exists. Getting PR requires knowledge about the media, a good plan and press kit, perseverance, and most important, music worth promoting. Hiring a publicist or having one on staff is always advantageous, or attempt it yourself. Mark Carpentieri (MC Records) says:

> My background is PR. It's so important to get attention to an artist's music. You're trying to get your artist exposed to people who wouldn't know that artist and go buy the record—discover them. That may be the biggest challenge a label has.

When you start out, put more energy into smaller publications that offer a better chance of writing about your artist. Try for major ones, too. Just be aware of what you're up against. Ellyn Solis, founder of Vermillion Media, does a visualization with artists:

> Picture your favorite big-time journalist, like David Fricke at Rolling Stone in his cubby at the magazine, surrounded by hundreds and hundreds of mailers filled with CDs. Picture them as towers surrounding him. Those are just from this week, and he is currently on a deadline, because he just scored an interview with [a big-name artist]. He then has to spend the weekend going through this pile of mail and sifting through what is going to be important in the magazine. If you do this visualization correctly, you will quickly understand that you, as an independent artist, fall very low on the totem pole in David Fricke's priority pile. That's not to say he won't listen to your CD. It just illustrates the sheer numbers game you deal with when sending your stuff to a national, long-lead publication. Most of the time, these publications write about major label and big indie label releases. Your precious time is better spent working outlets that have the print space to pay attention to an independent artist release.

Hiring a Music Publicist

A good publicist knows editors at publications and producers of TV and radio shows and knows which are best for publicizing a client's product. Publicists give you a professional introduction to the media. Only hire one that specializes in music/entertainment and has relationships with appropriate writers, etc. Their job is to maximize your artist's chances of getting covered by the media. Jonatha Brooke says, "The benefit is hopefully you're seen enough. You hope it's worth it, because it's really expensive to pay a publicist every month. We committed to it." A publicist is a good investment if you can afford one. Mark Redfern, publisher/senior editor of *Under the Radar*, advises:

> Find a publicist who has worked with other good bands and who is trusted by journalists. You want a publicist who is friendly, truly gets the music, truly gets the magazines that they are pitching to, and who can be persistent without being pushy. If I have a good relationship with the publicist, I'm more likely to check out their albums first.

Should you hire a publicist or have one on staff? If you believe that good exposure for your artist would substantially increase sales, it can be worth it. If your artist's contract allows, the cost of an independent publicist may be recoupable from their royalties. If you hire one, start before your street date. Karen Leipziger agrees:

> The more lead time someone has, the better chance they have for someone to pay attention to them. A lot of publications have long lead times. You should ideally get a publicist three months before the record comes out. If you start contacting people the day an album comes out, it's way too late.

How do you find a good publicist? Word of mouth is best. Ask other indies for recommendations. See who's getting great exposure. Call their label—ask for the publicist's name. Ask journalists whom they like working with. Hire someone experienced with your genre. I once hired one to work a hip-hop act. Although she was confident, she didn't know jack about hip hop. She tried hard but wasn't familiar enough with those who wrote about it. Before hiring a publicist, ask for references.

Putting Together an Effective Press Kit

If you can't afford to hire a publicist, prepare to work hard and be patient. It takes time, but you CAN reach the media. It takes a lot of research to find appropriate people to approach, and a good presentation. Sometimes you can find a publicist to pay by the hour to guide you, instead of paying a huge monthly fee. For example, publicist Ellyn Solis has a consultation service called PR Lady (www.publicitylady.com) that offers hour-long PR consultations. Solis explains:

> We assess our clients' PR needs and then provide the tools necessary to do a campaign on their own. Most publicists charge high monthly retainers, including my company, but if you only have a limited amount of money and want to roll your sleeves up, it can be done DIY. PR Lady has been very successful because we tailor the campaign to your exact needs and cut out a lot of extraneous effort on their part that might not be necessary. Remember that PR is a skill, but with a little bit of knowledge, time, and finesse, it can be acquired quite easily.

A basic press kit contains a bio, photo, and cover letter. Include music, even if you burn a CD-R. Jesse Fergusson says, "My recommendation for a press mailing is four months prior to the street date. Give print media plenty of time to listen to the record and argue about it with their editors." Timing can mean the difference between getting press and anonymity. I asked Anslem Samuel, music editor at *XXL* magazine, what common mistakes people make pitching him. He says, "I'd say one of the main things is thinking that you are the only one reaching out to me for coverage and not understanding the lead time of monthly publications. Keep your verbal pitches brief and to the point." National magazines work on long lead times. Solis advises:

> If you are going to send your stuff to long-lead publications, include information on your CD that will expedite the amount of time it takes to get educated about you. It is important to include as much information about you as possible. In the case of bigger long-lead pubs, include your touring history, any sales inroads you might have made in the past, and where you can be found on the Internet, beyond MySpace.

Getting material to the press in advance is key for publicity! Mark Redfern says, "If a press release doesn't list a release date then I take that as a red flag meaning that the album is already out or the label is so small that they aren't planning much of a release and have limited distribution." If you want to make money, take your music seriously and give publications what they want. Meanwhile, create a buzz in every corner you can. Anything you do in advance of the release helps. Karen Leipziger explains:

> Start letting people know way ahead of time what's in the works so there's interest in the project before it comes out. There is so much music being put out, but much of it isn't very good. All these people are fighting for the same limited space. A label and publicist not only try to get to the right person but try to get that person to pay attention to it. If you want to get it into the "to be listened to as soon as possible" pile, generate interest ahead of time, so when somebody sees it, they'll open the package and listen to it.

Written Material

Imagine what it would be like to read through a large assortment of press kits every day—tedious. After a while, artists can start to seem alike. So when journalists get a kit that jumps out at them, with written material that makes them laugh or want to know more, it stands out. Anslem Samuel says:

> The question I want answered from any person pitching me is: "Why now?" What specifically is going on with you or your artist that warrants coverage at this particular time? There are countless artists whose music I like, but if the timing isn't there I can't do anything until then. And by timing I mean having something in the marketplace to connect any coverage with, be it an album, huge single or video, recent signing, or deafening buzz—locally or nationally. Truthfully, having dope music is only half the battle. That leads to the second mistake: "Where's your music?" You can talk me to death about what you've done, who you know, etc., but it all means nothing if there is no music to back it up. Email MP3s, send links to MySpace pages, or snail mail CDs, but I have to hear you to make any decisions. And folks, indie or major, have to understand that making those decisions takes time as well. Just because you hit me today doesn't mean I had an opportunity to listen to your music or the music of dozens of

*others today. So if I ask to give me a week or two while I finish
closing the magazine that I'm currently working on, please adhere
to the timeframe rather than bombard someone every other day.
I listen to everything eventually. It just takes time. That's why
concise pitches help.*

Create a biography (bio) that tells the story of the artist, no more than
two pages, double-spaced. A bio should be interesting, presenting a clear
picture of the artist in a way that makes a journalist want to read it. If it
sounds like a résumé, it's boring! A bio is written to entice media people
to write about that artist. Dig for interesting facts about your artist and
include them, even if they don't relate to music. Ellyn Solis adds:

*Most journalists complain bitterly about how every bio is boring and
reads like a sales sheet. I think what makes a bio great is something
that is interesting about the artist beyond the music. Every bio says,
"this artist is different and unique"—that's what makes it boring!
If you are involved with the Peace Corps or if you became an artist
after serving two years in Iraq or you are a transgender woman,
now a male that is fronting a metal band, that is what makes you
interesting. Find what is unique about you as an artist, and make
that your bio.*

Keep it fresh! Dick Renco (Trout Records) says, "We keep the bio
updated with what is happening." Karen Leipziger recommends, "Include
an interesting description of the music—not just saying it's great, but
something that makes it sound unique and specific to get people
interested." Make journalists want to know the act! I once used a funny
play on words with the band's name in the opening paragraph of their bio.
We got write-ups because I made journalists laugh. The rest of that bio
was facts about the band. Journalists loved reading that bio after all the
bland ones and thanked me by writing about them. If you feel you can't
write a stand-out bio yourself, hire someone. Jim Sullivan, Boston arts
and culture reporter for www.NewEngland.com, formerly music writer at
the *Boston Globe*, says:

*The problem for a music writer is cutting through the glut of stuff.
I get a lot. When I was on the Globe staff, I got even more.
It's difficult for a writer to choose, when there's so much music*

screaming for attention. What gets mine? Be enthusiastic, but don't oversell the band either. Having other press helps. If I see that Paste *or* Pitchfork *has gotten on the band, that piques my interest. If I ask for a follow-up disc, include a note in the package reminding me I requested it. A lot comes in, and it helps to be reminded when I open the mail.*

Include press clips about the act. They let a journalist know about any buzz on them. Mount them on paper, with the publication's masthead. Enlarge or shrink their size, depending on what looks better. If you get a bunch of short reviews, consolidate them onto one sheet, or include them on a quote sheet. Short blurbs that appeared in a publication can also be included on that. If the artist is doing many live performances, a gig sheet lets the media know. Paul Hartman, editor of *Dirty Linen*, emphasizes, "Please don't send two pounds of paper—every single newspaper calendar listing, etc." Less can be more effective. Sullivan agrees:

Always look for that new angle for what makes the band different. Keep it fairly brief. There's a lot of stuff to go through. When a writer is hit with pages of material, it can blur sometimes. A new band must strike a line between interesting the writer with what's exciting about the group without overwhelming them, like including quotes from places that aren't well-known. With the rise of the Internet, there are quotes that can be snatched from everywhere about anybody. Because of this, the importance of them can be devalued.

A cover letter should accompany the press kit to introduce your label or the artist. This is a sales pitch and should be written to convince the media to write a story or a review. If you can catch their attention with the cover letter, they're more likely to review the rest of the kit. Organize your written material. Michael Mollura, associate editor of *Music Connection*, advises, "Everything should be easy for an editor to sift through. If I have to go through pages and pages of material just to get contact information, it's a problem."

Publicist Ellyn Harris , founder of Buzz Publicity, emphasizes, "Make your press kit look clean, and have contact information on *everything*. Make it easy for someone to contact you if they want to." Paul Hartman adds, "You would be surprised how many people don't put their address anywhere on the CD." Without contact info, no one can send you a tearsheet of the article or let readers know where to buy the CD.

Your Story

"Have a story" is a very common catchphrase. Great music does not make a story, but how you market it can. Print magazines can't let readers hear the music as they read articles. Music magazines want to write about interesting people. So while your music should be great, it's your story that gets media coverage. Where have you played live? Who else has written about you? How many CDs and downloads have you sold? Is radio playing your music? Are you getting online attention? How much action is on your MySpace page? What's going on *now* that makes your act exciting that others would want to read about? That's all part of the story the media folks look for. Anslem Samuel explains:

> Be able to answer the question of "why now?" regarding your coverage and conveying that to editors in a concise way. We don't just cover people because; there has to be some reason why. In terms of new artists, if you're making noise in the marketplace on your own, that will be recognized, but if you're not, it's about doing things on your end to make that happen, keeping lines of communication open, because a no today doesn't mean no forever. You just have to be open to criticism. Not everyone is hating, especially if they give advice on what can be better. Also if I see some talent but just the timing is off, I'll keep an ear open for you. Just shoot me an email as things develop, and if the timing comes together it'll happen. Make hits (notice the plural), have personality, know your story and how to sell it. The only thing better than great music is a great story. But having both is the best of both worlds.

Keep in touch with media people as your story grows. What might be a no today can turn into a yes tomorrow if a top blogger recommends you or you open for a name act. Instead of being a pest for coverage right now, develop a relationship with the writers you'd like support from. Be polite. Express appreciation if they respond, even if it's not the answer you'd like. Keep them posted when you get a bump in your story. Then the writer might be familiar with your name and be more likely to write about you when there's something interesting to say. Meanwhile, find ways to generate a story around you that can create interest. Ellyn Solis recommends:

If you get involved in some philanthropy, any charity that interests you, preferably on a small local scale in your hometown, it is a great way to garner attention and feel good at the same time. It doesn't mean doing the yearly walk-a-thon. It means getting involved in a cause that inspires you to write a song, donate proceeds from your CD release party to that charity, traveling to a city to promote that charity, etc. This is the age of philanthropy, and it can't be said enough that when you get attention on that level, it is far more fulfilling and long lasting. It also makes all of the regular effort you make much more worthwhile.

Photos

When people open a press kit, a photo gets attention faster than words. Photos should capture the artist's personality. Send one with a note that others are available, and include contact info on photos. Put a sticker on the back with contact info and the names of everyone in the picture so the writer can identify them in a caption if they use the photo. I'm told it's common for photos to arrive with no identification other than the name of the band. Make it easier for the writer! An interesting photo with energy has greater impact. Karen Leipziger, of KL Productions, says, "I've seen newspapers and magazines run photos of artists because the photo was interesting. They didn't care what the music sounded like if it was a cool and interesting picture." Michael Mollura says:

Headshots don't really work. Have photos that are clear, with an intention that fits into the category of music they're playing. When there's a contradiction between how a band appears and how they sound, it's distracting and doesn't help their cause.

When looking for a photographer, check out several. Don't settle for just anyone. Some photographers are more artsy than others. Some emphasize movement. Some take flat photos. Get good photos the first time by being careful about who shoots them. Network to find a good photographer you can afford. Have a variety of images. Put lots of photos on your website so people can download them. Make them high-resolution photos—300 dpi in a size that makes them easy to download. This allows a magazine to take them right off your website. It's cheaper for you—no copies or postage! Often the listings editor of a newspaper that lists an artist's gig will pull an interesting photo to use beside a listing. Make it as easy as possible for publications to publish photos! It's a win/win situation.

Press Kit Presentation

Create an eye-catching press kit. While many people will look at an electronic press kit, it can still be helpful to send something in the mail. Media folks get tons of material. Be creative to make yours stand out. Keep material as short and to the point as possible. Quality is always better than quantity. The less you send, the faster they can go through it. Ellyn Solis advises:

> I do think it is valuable to send information to journalists, but expensive press kits, in my view, are a waste of money and resources. It is better to establish an email relationship with someone and then ask if they would like to receive a press kit. Then send your beautifully done one. You will need less of them, and they won't go to waste. You can do a lot of it yourself. Printers and computers spit out beautiful work these days, so it is no longer necessary to go to a graphic designer to build a press kit. It should have your band logo, a beautiful folder with a press release about your tour, CD, etc., and some key information about you as an artist. You don't need a long-winded bio—just some compelling information that will get interest from that journalist. Of course, don't forget the music! That's the most important element. We like to send out a press release and let them know if they want to receive the CD, please let us know. We work with a lot of independent artists, and this system really cuts down on waste and saves money.

Folders that open up to show a pocket on each side hold the components of your press kit easily. Spruce them up with stickers or paste-on labels with the artist's name. If you have a nice logo, print it onto stickers that can be placed on the covers. Be creative in putting your kit together to make it attractive, which catches attention more quickly than the music inside. And no matter what format you use, include a business card. Most folders have a slotted space for one inside. More and more

211

people are trading the folders for clear plastic sleeves and putting the materials inside them in a neat, organized, and attractive way. Some editors nowadays prefer a concise one-sheet with a summary of that all-important story. Mark Redfern advises:

> Some publicity firms put a little sticker on the actual CD that includes the release date and a list of three to five bands that the band sounds like, which is the absolute best way to handle things. Based on the influences I can tell right away whether or not a band might be up our alley and a good fit for our magazine. Also, it's helpful when labels don't lie or exaggerate when comparing their band to other artists. There's nothing worse than putting in a CD because the press release compared the band to some of your favorite bands to find that they sound nothing like them.

That said, these days more and more people just use the Internet to get material to the media. Some editors would like a CD with a Post-It note directing them to all your info and photos on a website. You can have an electronic press kit on yours and/or create one on Sonicbids (more in Chapter 19). Every editor and writer is different, so don't assume that one approach fits all. Have a website and hard copies ready.

Press Releases

Send regular press releases—an announcement of something newsworthy, such as the release of a record, a new band member, or a showcase. Include a catchy headline at the top. If it announces a specific event, include all pertinent details (date, time, place, cost, etc.) in the first paragraph. Don't use adjectives to describe too much. Mark Redfern says:

> Make sure the press release that accompanies the album is very clear about two things: (1) which other bands the artist sounds like and (2) the album's release date. When I'm looking at a press release I never read the bio part. It's best to have a little self-contained box on the press release that lists influences and who the band sounds like.

A press release is an announcement of news and should read like that. Keep it short, preferably on one sheet. The less you write, the greater the chance it'll get read. Build excitement about the artist. Whenever he or she has an event or something special, send a press release. If the artist has a special gig, note how to get on the guest list. Jim Sullivan says:

> *If it's local and designed to work with an event, show, etc., be sure to get all the pertinent information such place, phone number, time of set, website, who else is on the bill, ticket price—some very basic information. Don't put it right at the front. But have it stand out in the email so if the writer likes what he sees or hears, that info doesn't have to be tracked down elsewhere. A surprising number of people just put things about the band and don't include the basic stuff.*

Many artists send a postcard for all gigs to media only. They'll also send a press release. It enables journalists to become familiar with the artist's name. I've had instances where I met journalists who were familiar with my artist but didn't know why. It was because everything I sent made the name stick. Nowadays, people occasionally fax press releases instead of mailing them. Another alternative is an email press release.

Compiling a Good Media List

To work the media effectively, study it. Read publications. Learn names of editors, writers, and reviewers. Get familiar with their formats, and gather media resources early. Find as many publications as possible, and pick up free local papers and scan all magazines to see if there's a place for your artist. Do they review CDs or gigs? Be creative about formulating reasons why the media should want to cover your artist.

I begin by going to magazine shops and bookstores, looking through each magazine to note which did reviews, used photos with captions, and had columns covering my genres (as well as who wrote them). I discreetly wrote down names, addresses, emails addresses, and phone numbers of possible writers or editors to approach. You may find a whole bunch of publications you never knew existed when you research.

Be diverse. Besides straight-out music magazines, there are many that specialize in related aspects of music. If your artist is a good keyboard player, think about approaching *Keyboard* magazine. There are loads of guitar magazines, too. If he or she is also an engineer or does technical work, check magazines that cater to audio engineering. There might be an angle for a story or some kind of mention. Getting even a mention can lead to sales and enhance your press kit. As in everything else, be creative about reaching the press.

The Musician's Atlas (www.musiciansatlas.com) has a city-by-city list of local publications—newspapers and other publications that support the local music scene. Use them when your artist plays in a specific city. Talk to folks wherever you go, and get names of more publications to add to your list. Check local TV shows to see if there's a place for your artist.

Always get the names of specific folks to send your press kit to. Don't just mark it "Editor" or "Producer." Call each publication or radio and TV station. Ask who's the best person to send a press kit to about a music act (be as specific as possible). Publications list their writers and editors on their mastheads, and television shows usually list producers in the credits for each show. See who handles stories or reviews about music in your genre, or who does great stories in general. Always check the correct spellings of names, and make sure they still work there before sending anything.

Opportunities for Media Coverage

Be aware of options when planning publicity strategies. Some publications are easier to crack than others. Ellyn Harris advises, "Start with local and regional press—weeklies, dailies, wherever they are. If the artist is from that region, they're much more likely to be interested in talking about them." Begin with the most local and work your way up. Each clip enhances the artist's story. The more you get, the more opportunities come. Be realistic. Make sure you pitch the right magazine. Don't waste time with inappropriate ones. Lydia Hutchinson, editor and publisher of *Performing Songwriter* magazine, says:

> One thing that I tell artists who are trying to get exposure for their independent CD is to gain an understanding of the sheer number of CDs that are out there vying for the same, limited editorial space. And as hard as it is to stomach, the odds of just getting a review are going to be tough (here at Performing Songwriter we get over three thousand indie submissions a year, with space for ninety-six DIY reviews at this point). But once there's some understanding of that, hopefully the publicity effort can be approached as sheer business.

Understand the fact that each page actually has a certain cost to a publication and that editorial choices might be made based on other coverage that is in that issue. And before you send anything in, educate yourself on the publication: Who is the target market? What are the number of pages allotted for reviews? To whose attention do you send your release? What are the check-back procedures for that publication? The bottom line is, once your product is finished, the sacred, creative part is over. Now it's time to approach getting it heard as a business.

Nowadays, a lot of PR opportunities are developing on the Internet and replacing or complementing offline media (see Chapters 19 and 21). It's important to do your best to pursue them all. Wherever you can get your name helps strengthen your overall brand.

College Newspapers

If you have trouble getting your first clips, try college newspapers. Visit nearby schools and pick up their papers. See who does stories or reviews about artists similar to yours. Call the paper and ask who'd be good to contact and how to reach them. Or someone may know of a journalism student looking to get his or her feet wet reviewing a CD.

Invite a local college paper to send someone to your artist's gigs. Treat them well! They could write your first clip. Send the appropriate writer a CD and ask him or her to review it. Remember, students write for those papers. Most aren't jaded and might like to write about your artist. Make them feel important. It might seem trivial to get reviewed in a college paper, but a clip is a clip and adds value to your press kit. Being in a college paper can stir interest in the CD, since students buy lots of music.

Newspapers

Newspapers, which reach a broad audience, are a great avenue for getting your artist's name in print. Start with local and free ones. Depending on your angle, you might interest them in an event in their city, a human interest story about local residents, or to review a gig. Newspapers have different sections. Figure out which editor to contact. Sections focusing on a more localized news format are easier to get into. Have a variety of photos. You can get press just from a very cool photo. Dick Renco explains:

We make sure we have good-looking photos, and don't send the same one over and over. These guys [Trout Fishing in America] are visually intriguing. Newspapers don't really care about music. They care how their paper looks. Send an intriguing photo with a great line and you'll do better than if you had five hundred words with no picture. We're always surprised and delighted when we move into a market and compete on the same night with a major artist on tour but end up getting the ink in the paper, or the interview.

Some newspapers have large entertainment or listings sections to announce gigs, another place for a good photo. Since newspapers deal with current events, timing is critical. Also, they deal more with events and topics than personal profiles, so they'd want to know what your artists are doing, not who they are. Approach the editor of a special section and have an angle that may interest that person. Mark Carpentieri says:

One of the nicest ways of getting PR is working locally. Any time a local band has a new CD, that's usually worth a photo and mention of the date, and things like that, by people who champion local music, whether it's the weekly entertainment papers or the daily paper with a once-a-week section. Any time you have anything like that, I think people want to root for you.

Another possibility for exposure in newspapers is news services, such as the Associated Press (AP) and Reuters. Their stories and reviews are made available to members across the country—most newspapers. Anyone receiving them may choose to run them in their local newspaper or other media outlet. Getting a news-service story gives you potential access to newspapers across the country. A reporter might interview a band that's doing something special or touring their region. You must, like with any publication, give them a reason to write about you.

Human interest stories are good to pitch to a news service. There has to be an angle for a a story on your label or artist. People want to read about something interesting, not that an artist they've never heard with a new CD. Create a fresh idea and find someone to write about it. If your artist hasn't done something interesting enough outside his or her music, try for a review that could be published in a variety of newspapers. Send a CD to a music editor at the news service with a good description of the music at the top of your press release.

They have offices in many large cities. Check the Internet for locales of AP and others. Call the one nearest you and ask who'd be most likely to write about what you're offering. Pitch them. At large AP offices, people assign writers to stories. When you read local papers, pay attention to which articles give credit to a service. Track down those writers. You may have to approach several until you find one in sync with your needs. When you do, cultivate a relationship.

Magazines

Fanzines might be easier to start with. They're often devoted to a specific genre of music or one artist. Some are more organized than others. Depending on your music, fanzines offer the potential to increase your sales and create a huge buzz around your artist. Ellyn Solis says:

> Pitchfork is the gold standard as far as fanzines, but it is hard to get their attention. I still think that local fanzines, on- and off-line, are helpful for one very important reason: You want to get ink, and that is a great way of doing it. The list is hundreds long these days.

According to Jim Testa, owner of *Jersey Beat Fanzine*, "Lower end fanzines are usually sold in record stores, directly to fans at shows, or at any cool store (a clothing store that caters to skate punks, for instance, might have a fanzine rack). Bigger fanzines use distributors, which go to bookstores, record stores, etc." These day, many fanzines are on online. Don't write them off because they aren't as professional as commercial magazines. Testa says you can benefit from using a fanzine because:

> They are affordable. My fanzine may reach fewer readers, but those are people who are already interested in a certain kind of music. Dollar for dollar, it's at least as good an investment as advertising in a mainstream magazine with astronomically higher ad rates, where only a small percentage of readers may be interested in the music you are marketing. When dealing with smaller or newer zines, record labels can often trade product for advertising, which benefits both parties. Fanzines help you find your target audience. You directly reach the audience you want.

Look for coverage in one that caters to fans who love your genre, or a band in your genre. If you get a publication hot on your artist, its readership may support him or her, too. Since every fanzine is different, the potential for increasing your artist's fan base from exposure in them varies. Solis says she loves *Under the Radar*, an independent music and entertainment magazine that's distributed across North America and select countries worldwide. According to publisher/senior editor Mark Redfern, they only write about bands they actually like, not who they're told to like. He explains:

> Under the Radar *is independently owned, so there isn't anyone in some corporate boardroom somewhere telling us what to do. We keep advertising and editorial completely separate and are never paid off to cover certain artists. Our articles are often in-depth. We don't write fluff pieces and have a history of helping break new bands, including those from other countries.* Under the Radar *was also an early supporter of such artists as Bright Eyes, Death Cab for Cutie, the Decemberists, Doves, Rilo Kiley, TV on the Radio, Yeah Yeah Yeahs, and [many, many] others. Each issue contains between 140 and 190 reviews, so we have one of the biggest reviews sections of any American music magazine. Our critics don't pull any punches and write honest reviews. We've recently also branched out to cover film, TV, comic books, video games, DVDs, and books; but our main focus remains independent music.*

Many labels try to get into *Billboard* magazine. I asked Bill Werde, its executive editor, about the difference between consumer and trade magazines. He explains:

> *If you want to reach out to all the decision makers, if you want to get your music into a mobile campaign, a branded entertainment space, or into the hands of a party planner or a DJ on a radio station,* Billboard *magazine is the place to go for that. The difference is, do you want to reach the decision makers who are going to green-light a project or reach the consumers who are going to buy the music? Our main goal is to expose the best and brightest and most successful ideas, business strategies, and music. We want to hold those things up to the light and let people learn from them and deliver access to the folks that are making decisions and show what their thought*

process is. We want to take you inside deals and show you how they're structured and why they're structured that way. It's basically pulling back the curtain a little bit on the business, which is both changing rapidly and constantly. www.billboard.com is for the consumer. It has 4 million unique visitors a month and growing. That's for music fans.

Consumer magazines are designed for fans of music and help sell albums, since their readers buy music. Trades get you more industry attention. *Billboard* comes out weekly, so everything in it is very current. It's news about the music industry as opposed to a vehicle for giving artists exposure. They report on all aspects of the music business—everything important that's happening worldwide. You'll get a good education by reading *Billboard*. They have charts and articles for every type of music and an international section, too. If you want to get into *Billboard*, Werde says:

Read Billboard. *Look at the sections of the magazine—how it's structured, the kind of things we're writing and the ways we're writing about them. Situate yourself into a story like that. We love trends. If your artist is part of a certain movement that we haven't covered in a minute or doing something truly innovative, or if you're doing something different from a marketing, branding, touring, or retail perspective, and it's working for you, we're looking for the innovation and the success in the innovation. We do a page of album reviews, a page of single reviews, and a page on unsigned artists. We're always looking for really great new talent. The trick is to break through the clutter with a concise, well-organized pitch on who you are and what your sound is. Give some metrics for your success. If you don't have a story to tell, don't have a MySpace page with growing traffic numbers, you can't point to shows you've been playing that have an increasing audience, if you can't show that growth, it's hard to justify writing about it.*

There's not just *one* person to pitch. Look in the masthead. It lists editors for all the sections. Look at the different departments and figure out which one your story fits into. Then find the editor and contact him or her. Werde advises, "It's helpful if you take the time to figure out who the right person to approach for something is." *Billboard* comes out weekly and covers industry news, so be conscious of the timing.

I've emphasized that for most consumer magazines, stories are written well ahead of publication. Timely ideas won't work without a long-term angle. Study potential ones carefully before sending material. Magazines offer opportunities for feature stories, reviews, blurbs in a column, and interesting photos as fillers. Be realistic and work your way up from small to large magazines. KL Productions' Karen Leipziger advises, "Don't expect to get the cover of *Rolling Stone*. Contact publications that make the most sense for getting coverage." Jesse Fergusson offers hope:

> *A lot of smaller music magazines aren't as big an organization as they'd like you to think they are. Send something to the attention of the music editor. It can help. As long as you have some credibility as a label, they'll pay attention. It might take a few times, but they will. Follow up as much as possible.*

What do consumer magazines look for? They want something that would be of interest to their readers. Spell out the story—what would their readers find interesting about your artist? The first paragraph of a cover letter or press release should grab them. National magazines write about nationally known artists, or those buzzing loudly on the way up. A national story provides the biggest edge for getting into a national magazine, if you contact them soon enough. Mark Redfern says:

> *The most important factor for choosing one artist over another is whether the album is good. Then we need to consider if an artist is a good fit for the magazine, in terms of their musical style and sound. For example, we don't even consider metal or hardcore bands. Obviously more established artists get considered first. If it's a band who we've covered before, we're likely to cover them again. Another big factor is the release date. We only print four to five issues a year and always want our reviews section to be timely, so our ideal is to review records that are due out after our issue hits stands, so our readers can read reviews of albums before the albums are released. But we usually also review a lot of albums that are already in stores by the time our issue streets, but they have to be albums that have at least been released in the last month or two. We also take into account which label the release*

is on and which publicist or publicity company is working the release. If it's a label or publicist who we have a good relationship with and who we can trust, then we're more likely to review their releases.

Some magazines have reviews for niche markets, such as *Dirty Linen*. Paul Hartman describes it as "the bimonthly magazine of folk and world music, which includes Cajun, Celtic, blues, bluegrass, singer/songwriter—a whole spectrum of music not covered by mainstream media." He likes a CD with a one-page bio and one page about the songs if no booklet with details accompanies the CD. Photos are optional.

Television and Radio

There are opportunities for free publicity on television and radio: interviews, news features, video exposure, talk shows, and segments of a specific show that spotlights interesting or different stories. These forms of media are hard to reach in the beginning, although it's not impossible to do so. News shows need timely stories, such as a specific event, and an unknown can get a break if not much news happens on the day of his/her event, and the producer needs to fill a time slot. Luck can play an important role in getting on TV or radio. Smaller cable or public-access shows are the easiest to get onto. Radio shows, especially specialty programs, those on noncommercial stations, and those in smaller markets, do interviews with artists.

Approaching the Media

To begin to get press, send a CD with a cover letter to all magazines that review music, addressed to a specific reviewer or editor in charge of assigning reviews. Or, send a file or link to a page that one can go for more info and to hear music. It depends on the recipient's preferences. Mark Redfern says:

> *I prefer to receive music via actual CDs. It's a lot easier to keep track of all the music we're sent when we get psychical copies. Often when I'm sent downloads I ignore them, unless it's an artist I already love and I'm dying to hear their new album. I only have so much space on my computer. Sometimes I download albums onto my desktop, never listen to them, and delete them later for space. Digital downloads are more likely to be discarded in the future, whereas we'll keep any CD*

that we like, and we often keep copies of anything we've reviewed and even some we haven't reviewed, in case we want to revisit the bands later. I hate reviewing records via secure online streams, as you can only listen to the music when you're logged onto the Internet, and often you can only stream one song at a time, which interrupts the record's flow.

The letter you send, whether by mail or email, should provide relevant info about the release date, price of the record, and address or telephone number for ordering, as well as info about the artist and a photo. Include stickers, T-shirts, key chains, or other merch you have in the package. Gregg Latterman (Aware Records) says:

If an artist is touring, I won't wait for a publication to request the music or photos. I'll contact someone and let them know I'm sending materials. It's much more effective than sending a press release telling them to let you know if they need anything. In a lot of cases, when they see good materials, they may decide to do something if it's strong. Ultimately, it's about the music. If the music isn't there, none of the other stuff is important.

Before pitching the media, identify goals and possible angles for a story. The greatest CD can be ignored if it doesn't grab attention. Since journalists are bombarded by material, send something fresh. What makes your artist different? Why should someone want to write about him or her? What's intriguing about the artist? Jim Sullivan says:

Email is the best way to reach me for the initial contact. Include what the band has built so far and what kind of press or radio attention it's got so far. It wouldn't hurt to include what genre you fit into, what your unique factor would be. This can be anything from the way you sound, how you came together, a unique approach to recording or touring.

Emphasize what would be of interest to readers. Put it together in a package that shows you take your label seriously. Michael Mollura says:

I look at every package that comes in. At our magazine, major label artists go through a different system than an indie artist. A label that an editor doesn't know should contact him first to establish who they are so he knows them when he gets the package. Indie labels send me emails to let me know what they're developing.

Email or fax journalists to say you're sending material so they can watch for it. Make the message short and friendly, so it will make them want to open your package. Capturing their interest can mean the difference between their listening to your music and tossing it aside. Bill Werde says the best way to reach *Billboard* editors is by email:

I hate press releases and don't do much with them. I feel if I'm getting one, everyone else is getting it. If you send a press release it better be a situation where we're going to break that news before it goes to anyone else. Otherwise, send me an email with what's unique about your story. Tell me why it makes sense for Billboard *readers to know about this. People tend to forget that. They think, "Look at me, I have a great album."* Billboard *readers are looking for the next great story of a great album—the way a great album actually succeeded.*

Following Up

Don't send out a great press kit and wait for reviews and features to come in. You need to follow up on everything. Develop a system for keeping track of whom you sent press kits to and make follow-up calls. It can be tedious and confusing when you speak to many people in one day. Maintain accurate records to keep things sorted. An efficient system makes the process smoother. Approach journalists with a personal touch. Build those relationships! Ellyn Harris says:

The tricky part about doing your own PR is being able to sell yourself. If you have a really good salesman type of personality and can sell your artist with enthusiasm and sincerity, then you can do it. That's what PR is—selling with enthusiasm. It is time-consuming.

Keep track of the media with a comprehensive list that includes the names, addresses, and phone numbers of all the writers and editors you need to contact. Find your own system. Some of you may be comfortable with an informal one. Others might prefer a very detailed format for recording info. If you intend to keep your label going, develop good habits. Your system should be one that can be passed to employees as they take over various projects. Ellyn Harris advises:

> Set up your own campaign. Make a list with all contact information—
> address, phone, fax, email—of the publication. You can put them on
> a call sheet. When you make each call, each mailing, each contact,
> note that and make a plan to follow up.

Index cards are a great way to sort info. For Revenge Records, I wrote the name of each publication/media outlet on a card, with contact info. Then I recorded all pertinent info about that publication, including the names of journalists/editors; music genres it covered; its schedule; whether it did reviews, features, short news stories, or other types of columns; whether it ran photos with blurbs. I recorded all details when approaching or following up with a publication, such as best times to call and any quirks about it I learned in my interactions with them.

   I recorded my progress on the back of the cards, listing dates when I called and their responses. I noted when a publication said to call back. I kept a file box with Monday through Friday sections. If I had to call back within a week, I'd put the card in the appropriate day. You can also use press call sheets to record information like Harris recommended. When designing those sheets, leave enough room to make notes. Keep a master list on your computer so it can be easily updated. I've used a date book for notations about when to call individuals back.

Making the Calls

Start building good relationships with your first media contacts. This can mean exercising patience when a person doesn't return calls or follow through on promises. Be persistent, but don't come across as a pest. A friendly, polite follow-up phone call won't offend anyone. Polite persistence pays off. Ellyn Solis advises:

> Follow up is key, but please don't spam these very busy writers. You
> would be better off following up once in email and then just keeping
> that person informed about your career development. Don't be a pest

and always be polite, even if you feel like the journalist is blowing you off. You have to develop a very thick skin about dealing with writers. They are inundated on a daily basis, and time is very limited. Be cognizant of that fact and you will get much further than you think in making that person aware of your music.

Media people are busy. Speak to an editor's assistant, if there is one, to see if your package arrived, and if the editor listened to the music. Try to develop a relationship with that person, who can help you get in the door. If the package can't be found, send another, to that same person if possible. Before calling, prepare to say exactly why you're calling, says Ellyn Harris:

Ask how they like to be followed up with. Email or phone? I call first because I like person-to-person contact. I'm good on the phone. You'll probably get a machine. Be prepared to leave a message. Have a script to use for their voicemail so it's quick, to the point, and well said. Tell them what they'll be receiving and why they'll be interested in receiving it. Visualize their office with piles of CDs and press kits. Make yours stand out and let them know it's arriving. Otherwise, it may get stashed in the corner. The more personal attention you can give your package, the better it is. They're busy and not dying to talk to new people. Be polite.

Send material in a distinguishable envelope. When you call someone who hasn't seen your package, being able to describe it—for example, "the package with artist stickers," or "in a hot pink envelope," or "addressed in big purple letters"—makes it an easier target to locate. Asking someone to look for a standard mailing bag makes it harder. If you send an attractive package, they'll more likely notice it. According to Israel Vasquetelle, publisher of *Insomniac* magazine:

Packaging is everything, from the envelope you send your music in, to the included literature about your band, cover art, and jewel case. Think of packaging as dressing for success. If you were going for an interview to try to land a big corporate position, you would definitely dress your best. So why do so many artists send out poorly packaged music? Some artists don't even think about packaging. They figure the music is good enough, but it's the packaging that may grab enough attention to get them to pop it into the player. The question is: "Is it appropriate and professional?" If you ask yourself that simple question when deciding on packaging, you will make better decisions.

Journalists are busy. Show respect for their time. If you get who you want, ask if it's a good time to talk. And don't call too much! If a journalist says he can't do something, don't argue. It's counterproductive. Continuing with a hard sell adversely affects relationships with them in the future. If they can't do a story, thank them for their time. You may have another artist down the road. If you don't leave a bad vibe the first time, you might get what you want later. Jim Sullivan advises:

Email is the best way to follow up. Phone calls can be intrusive. The key is to be persistent but not be a pest. It's a fine line to know when to push or to back off. There are no easy answers about how to know that. Keep in mind the writer is probably juggling a lot of different things, so it can take time to listen to a band's material. As a writer, I have guilt about having a lot of music that's waiting to be played that may be very good that just isn't going to be gotten to because of time constraints.

Getting obnoxious or angry is never productive, even if it's justified. Smile to yourself before calling to create a good mood. Always be polite. No matter how pissed off they make you, sound friendly and appreciative. Don't complain about how many times you called. Thank him or her for speaking with you. Some things are just in the nature of this biz and must be tolerated with good grace. If you need media coverage, prepare to bend, flex, smile, and accept what you don't like. Get over any attitude about media people being difficult. They're inundated with requests and can't respond to everyone as they might like to. If you get their attention at all, be grateful. Michael Mollura advises:

Email is the best way to follow up. I do 98 percent of my communicating through email. Find out the style of each editor or reviewer and how they like to be approached. Different editors have different styles. It's more comfortable to find out first via email. If somebody sends me an email asking if I got their package, I'll go see if I got the package. An email gets into the line of fire.

KL Productions' Karen Leipziger advises, "Be consistent, and have repeated contact. Some people prefer email, but some hate it. Part of this is getting to know people and what they prefer as a way to reach them." Working hard and being persistent enables you to successfully work the media. Valerie Vigoda (GrooveLily) says:

> Try to give people a good story. Sometimes the media will take a press release or bio and use it word for word. We make sure our photos are exciting and eye-catching. We're lucky right now to have a Petal Pusher–turned-publicist: A terrific young woman with lots of charm and enthusiasm. We find enthusiasm gets results just like experience, sometimes even more (as long as you're also organized and follow through). Attitude is everything.

Don't be discouraged. Even if someone turns you down, be patient. Come up with fresh ideas periodically. Be polite and friendly. Persistence helps you eventually get what you want. Ellyn Harris, who was instrumental in getting the Grammys to add two categories for dance music, encourages:

> Be brave! Think outside the box. Contact everyone you've ever met in the entertainment business. Tell them what you're doing. Everything that's been the most fun for me are things that everyone said, "You can't do that." It's the mentality I used to get a category for dance music at the Grammy Awards. People had been trying for ten years. I followed through with my passion for the music and didn't let the ball drop. We got two awards categories. Don't be afraid. If you think things through creatively, just try it. Don't say no to yourself before someone says it to you.

Advertising

There are loads of places to advertise your product, if you have extra cash. This route needs careful thought. What are your objectives? Don't incorrectly assume that advertising will result in a write-up or airplay. If that's your main reason for taking out an ad, think twice, unless money isn't an issue. But there are benefits to advertising, as long as you keep your goals realistic. Now there are online advertising opportunities that are more affordable than print or radio.

You can advertise the release of your record or a special gig. If your act is youth oriented *and* you have a photo showing the artist(s) looking hot/ stylish or other traits that attract kids who buy records, stimulate interest by including one in your ad. If a publication covers your genre specifically and its ad rates are realistic, advertising might help the most in reaching your target audience. Some publications have rates for many levels of ads, from business-card size on up, and reach audiences who buy very specific kinds of music. Include your website in any ad. Have samples of your music on your site so they'll want to buy the CD. Ryan Kuper (Redemption Records) says:

> *There are certain magazines that I feel are more suited for our material. Their demographics are what we are trying to hit. I definitely believe in print advertising. I have found that the monthly half-page, full-color ads I have placed in magazines like* Alternative Press *have been very effective. These ads usually feature one or two acts and possibly some tour dates and information about what is coming out. I think they help sell records as well as generate general interest in the bands and the label. Sometimes buyers see the ads and think, "This label's got it together. This ad coincides with reviews, and I've seen in other magazines and I'm hearing it on the radio. This is a cohesive push." For the same reasons, I place banner ads on a lot of websites as well.*

Some people believe that radio ads are a good way to get your music on radio. If your act is playing a decent venue, consider advertising it. Any ad you make should have your music playing clearly in the background. Radio ads can be pricey, so make sure the station reaches your audience. Certain hours are much cheaper than others—like those in the middle of the night. Lots of folks listen to radio at those times, so it may be worthwhile. If you have some sort of budget, you might consider taking out a late-night ad on an appropriate radio station. Being an independent allows you to act quickly and take advantage of last-minute opportunities that major labels couldn't. For example, Daniel Glass (Glassnote Entertainment) was excited the day I interviewed him because being independent, he was able to take advantage of a last minute opportunity that a major label couldn't have accepted quickly enough, saying:

> *We had a big ad in* USA Today *for Secondhand Serenade, which we took advantage of being independent. Somebody fell out of that*

ad. That ad costs more than three people make here in a year. We couldn't afford it. But, we were able to make a decision quickly and we were able to get the ad done in minutes, turned around, and the ad is in the paper today.

Publications that lose an ad need to fill the space. A much cheaper rate is better than not getting anything. Major labels have so many channels to go through before they could accept an offer, so most of the time it would be too late. Any indie can see it as a great opportunity and get out the credit card right away. Advertising helps develop a relationship with a publication or radio station. People in sales generate profits made by those media outlets, so they often have good relationships with those you want to reach. When negotiating an ad, it can't hurt to ask if the salesperson can introduce you to someone who might review the record or write a story or to the music director of a radio station. The salesperson may or may not accommodate you, or may string you along until receiving your money. Politeness combined with persistence pays off, but recognize when someone has no intention of anything beyond running your ad.

CHAPTER 17

Getting Radio Play

Radio play offers an opportunity to reach listeners who might buy what they hear. It's probably the best vehicle for selling records, but it can be the hardest to ride. There are different levels of radio play, and indies usually work their way up. Getting radio play is difficult at best, but it can be achieved with a combination of hard work and great music. Daniel Glass (Glassnote Entertainment) says:

> *Radio is very important. We're in love with the online element of Clear Channel radio—clearchannel.com. They embrace independent music. We're doing very well at XM and Sirius. It is so refreshing. If you ask me what the greatest thrill is, it's the first time you hear something you've been involved with on the radio.*

Commercial Radio

I don't want to discourage you, but I must be honest. Commercial radio is tough to crack. Majors put lots of money into radio promotion, and they get much more priority. People at commercial radio stations say they add an average of three to ten songs per week. That's it! Competition is heavy. But it's not hopeless. Indies *do* get commercial radio play. Incredibly hard work will be necessary. Ken Weinstein, president of Big Hassle Media, says, "Commercial radio is gravy and not to be counted on. I'd spend money elsewhere."

There are different levels of commercial radio markets. Those in larger cities are considered primary ones, while others are considered secondary or tertiary. Most commercial stations play one format. The most common formats are CHR (Top 40), Adult Album Alternative (AAA), Album-Oriented Rock (AOR), Hot Adult Contemporary (AC), Country, Modern Rock, Urban, and R & B.

The main players at a radio station are the programming director (PD), who programs shows, and the music director (MD), who listens to music and makes recommendations. At smaller stations, one person may do both jobs. Commercial stations are businesses making money from selling airtime to advertisers. Advertisers want to be on stations playing the most popular music. To please them, playlists are often limited to music by artists with high visibility. Beth Krakower, president of CineMedia Promotions, works with titles considered "special projects" or "classical crossover" (movie soundtracks, Broadway cast albums, reissued titles, and an eclectic range, fitting into noncommercial radio formats like classical, cabaret, jazz, and classical crossover) and advises, "Remember that commercial radio's purpose is to make money by selling advertising. Because the stakes are so high, commercial radio stations are not in the business to break bands."

DJs often don't have freedom of choice. On most commercial stations, the PD chooses a pool of records. Unless they host a specialty show with more latitude, most DJs can't play what they love without approval. Commercial stations add songs each week to be played in rotation—they'll be played at regular intervals. Heavy rotation refers to songs that haunt you because they're on so frequently. Light rotation is regular play but at longer intervals. The bigger the story on an artist, the heavier the rotation. Songs grow on people when they hear them over and over. Hearing them occasionally has much less impact.

Commercial stations prefer CDs with a story; they want artists that tour heavily, sell records, attract media, and get airplay on other stations and on charts. They don't want unknown artists. Develop a story before approaching them. Competing with the clout of what a major label's money buys is tough. Your great music is up against the perks majors give. They have gigantic marketing/advertising budgets, throw parties, and offer all sorts of freebies. Don't worry about payola. I've heard stories of exorbitant legal gifts. Eric Speck (Ace Fu Records) says:

> *Radio at the same time is entirely insignificant and the most important thing to sell records. For major labels it's still a large*

mover to sell records. For independents, it's incredibly hard to get your music on commercial radio. Now most stations are programmed on a national level so it's even harder to get significant spins by region if independents don't have big-budget radio staff or connections with the national programming directors of these radio chains, so to speak.

Major labels spring for promotions, freebies for stations to give away, and send artists to events the station sponsors. But don't despair! Many indies do get commercial airplay. Lisa Worden, music director of KROQ, a top commercial alternative rock station in L.A., says, "It doesn't matter if it's an independent label. We look for the best new music to expose our listeners to and try to pick stuff that we think they'll really like." Many commercial stations play at least some indie music. The dynamic for getting airplay has been changing in commercial radio, explains Laura Duncan, assistant program director/music director at WTTS, in Indianapolis:

Nowadays, there are many different ways a consumer finds new music. Just as the dynamic for artists getting their music heard has changed, the methods used by radio stations to audition new music must adapt. Traditionally, a push by record company promoters has been the main method used by radio stations to not only listen to new music but to learn about the artist. I spend hours on a weekly basis investigating various websites to find the newest sounds and attending live shows to hear how artists translate their recorded music to a live audience. If all of the elements are in place and the sound fits what we feel is a desired by our audience, we give the artist or song a chance.

Sometimes an indie with fantastic music can create its own little machine and cut through the crap. With lots of hard work, perseverance, creativity, very radio-friendly music, and luck, an indie label can get commercial radio play. Lisa Worden says with many stations, it's about the music. She adds:

It depends on the station. I think other stations get bad raps. Advertisers do not determine what is played on a radio station. I think that's a false impression that's out there. [What determines it is] hits for the radio station—what the listeners want to hear.

Preparing to Work Commerical Radio

Give yourself the best shot of getting on radio by not approaching stations in ignorance. Make them take you seriously with a professional pitch. Stations like short songs. If necessary, do a radio mix. Radio prefers a CD single. If you have an album or EP, indicate the song you're pushing. To get on radio charts, all the stations must play the same song. Don't tell them to choose what they want to play—they probably won't.

Commercial radio stations see what records are selling and playing on other stations. Broadcast Data Systems (BDS) tracks radio play with computerized technology, so stations learn what's being played and how often. Many stations hire radio consulting firms that help choose the records played. Call the stations for their names. Get them excited about your music. If you persist, you may find a station to support your music. Dave Roberge (Everfine Records) did:

> We have had some radio play at a commercial station in Chicago. They embraced a couple of independent artists. I have the highest regard for a station like that, competing against the bigger stations out there but is still taking chances because they know what people want to hear. They don't want the manufactured pieces of crap anymore—they want a sense of discovery. That station is providing it. But, they're few and far between. O.A.R. is drawing between two thousand to five thousand people in every market. The kids are going crazy for them. Any radio programmer that doesn't see that as a legitimate thing would have to be crazy, but that's how it works. It's about coming up with promotional dollars and getting onto radio that way.

Tell commercial stations the artist's story, with press clippings, a tour schedule, radio play in other markets, record sales, chart positions, etc. A full press kit isn't necessary, but a one-sheet is. Like the one for retail stores, it must include a short bio, marketing and promotional work, and whatever might convince a PD to play your record. A well-presented sheet can make a difference. Send as little as it takes to tell it—make each detail count. Laura Duncan adds:

> In addition to receiving the CD from the artist, a letter of introduction is desirable. Include some brief introductory information and a

web address that includes answers to all questions that may arise. Investigating the radio station that is receiving the CD is also a good idea. I can't tell you how many times I have received a hip-hop CD. While the music might be great, WTTS is an Adult Rock radio station. The artist just wasted time and money sending me music that will never be played.

What catches radio's attention? Duncan says that presentation is key when you're introducing an artist's music to a radio station's representative. Many say they open attractive packages quicker. Packaging is the first impression. If it doesn't show that you take your music seriously enough to dress it nicely, it might not get heard. It may not be right, but packaging influences how people assume the quality of music will be. If your package looks good, they're more likely to read your one-sheet and listen to your CD. If it doesn't look professional, it gets ignored.

Always keep in mind you're competing with major label artists, with major label budgets behind then for great artwork. Radio stations get dozens of CDs every day. No one has time to listen to everything. See how your CD compares to others in retail stores. Then get real! Ultimately, it's the music that matters. But it won't matter if they don't hear it. Your main objective should be to get them to listen. MDs say packaging can set one artist apart from others. Make sure your packaging is competitive. Then your music can convince them. Duncan clarifies:

Submission of music should be considered an element of an interview process. First impressions are hard to overcome if perceived to be amateurish. This is the introduction of not only the music but also personality, work ethic, and pride. I have received CDs with handwritten titles scribbled directly onto the disc with permanent marker. This generally tells me a lot about the artist without even hearing the first track. A nicely packaged CD will not get an undesirable song played on the radio, but the music has a better chance of being auditioned if it is presented professionally.

Contacting Commercial Radio Stations

Radio stations often have specific hours each week when the MD meets with label reps and promoters. Call for the day and times. Many stations require an appointment. CDs can also be mailed to stations, followed by a phone call. Ask at what hours the MD takes calls. Be persistent. When speaking to MDs, thank them for their time. If you can afford it and have a great record with promotion on it, a radio promoter may help. Promoters have relationships with people at stations. But with so much competition, they often give greater priority to records they're paid more to promote. It's hard to find a good one. Talk to other indie labels. Be very explicit about your agreement. Watch the semantics in it. Promoters might be seeking a bonus for "getting the record played." That could be interpreted as a single play. Specify that it must be in regular rotation.

Begin in what's referred to as softer markets first. Those are smaller ones, tertiary ones, that may not be tapped as much by the majors. There are many in smaller cities. Use *The Musician's Atlas*. It lists stations in most cities that play at least some indie music and includes the format and type of music. You can also find stations listed with their websites in *The Indie Bible*. Be persistent about developing relationships in the markets you're after. Getting airplay in smaller markets is the first step to larger ones. Alert the person you're sending a CD to. Duncan says:

> *I prefer to be contacted via email or MySpace to give me a heads up that a CD is on the way. I always make a note of it and look for the CD to arrive in the mail. If the artist has taken the time to reach out, I will take the time to listen. I receive over forty CDs a week and try to listen to each and every CD, or at least get a feel for the product by auditioning portions of the CD.*

After you send a CD, follow up. Lisa Worden says, "There's a fine line between being persistent and bugging. I always tell people, follow up with a couple of phone calls or emails, and if you don't hear back, there's a reason." They'll contact you if there's something good to say. Be polite when you leave messages. NEVER sound impatient! Be professional. Music directors complain about people who call and act annoying. Politely call and be friendly if you leave a message. Give your name and ask if he or she would consider playing your CD. Don't demand or sound pushy. They probably won't return your call, but if you call again and get them, they might remember your professional message.

Even if commercial stations don't play your record right away, start developing relationships. Be realistic. Don't expect airplay before there's at least a small story about your artist. Report progress as your story builds. Email is probably best for that. Persevere, but be patient. MDs are swamped and can't speak to everyone. Reaching them takes time. When you finally do reach the MD or an assistant, be polite. Show respect for everyone's time. A relationship based on respect may get you airplay or a return call. Duncan says sometimes great music just isn't right for a station:

> There are times when good music gets passed on. It is my belief that a terrestrial radio station should not dictate the tastes of the market but reflect the tastes of the market. Each market is different to some degree. I have heard many songs that I adore personally that just don't reflect the tastes of our market or our audience. Those are the songs and artists that I listen to on my personal time and scream about passionately to anyone who will listen.

If your music fits the format of a specialty show, contact the DJ who programs it. If you're putting out dance music, get friendly with DJs from mix shows. If a record does well on one, it pumps up the artist's story and the PD may consider it for light rotation. What promotion can you offer a station? Would they like your artist to give a live interview or station ID? Can you do a ticket giveaway for a gig? Can your artist get involved with events promoted by the station? Commercial radio play is possible if your music is great and you work the system slowly.

Noncommercial Radio

College and public-access radio stations are indie-label friendly. Noncommercial stations don't depend on advertising. While major labels covet airplay, too, most noncommercials are more concerned with the music. Their listeners are are often passionate fans of music, wanting to hear new and creative music instead of the same songs repeated. They pay attention to music, unlike those who just listen passively to the music played by commercial stations. Beth Krakower says:

> With consolidation of ownership of commercial radio, there are fewer and fewer opportunities at commercial radio for these projects. Most titles that I promote find their own on public, community, and college radio stations.

Noncommercial stations like breaking new music. Rita Houston, MD for WFUV, a powerful public radio station in New York City, says she listens to almost every record received, noting, "We want to be the place that discovers a gem." She recommends patience for any indie label wanting airplay and advises:

> There are things labels can do to help a radio station along. I like getting a package that has a little bit of information about the artist along with the CD. I don't need [a full press kit], but when you're listening to something, you need to have a little perspective on it. That could be what the artist is about, or who produced the record, or what inspired the album.

Houston says a bio helps her see where a CD fits into her station's format. WFUV is artist driven, so Houston's not as interested in singles. Noncommercial stations like albums and choose their own songs. In terms of follow-up, Houston says, "Persistence is the prize in life. I'm impossible to get on the phone because there's only so many people I can talk to every day." She takes calls from those who have developed good working relationships with her.

Noncommercial stations are more likely to give airplay. How do you find them? There are loads in *The Musician's Atlas*. Beth Krakower advises visiting the websites of national networks of the main public radio outlets, www.npr.org, www.pri.org, and www.pacifica.org. Most DJs choose what's played on their shows. Although noncommercial airplay isn't as powerful as commercial radio, it can start a buzz to build your foundation. Krakower agrees. "Particularly for certain demographics, public and noncommercial radio is a great first step to begin creating a story for your project before approaching commercial radio." Dick Renco (Trout Records) agrees:

> It takes three to four years to break a market if you don't have immediate radio support. If you have radio support, it's almost immediate. We found stations through research. The guys were working in Arkansas, Louisiana, and Texas. Part of our plan was to find out independent public radio stations that had either specialty programs or at least programming.

Can an artist break with noncommercial radio? Absolutely! Rita Houston says, "In our format, which is AAA, it's mostly public stations that are leading the way and breaking new artists."

Working College Radio

The DJs at college stations are more concerned with the quality of music than its popularity. Since they're volunteers, they try to be true to their reputation for playing the newest, most cutting-edge music available. Fortunately for us, they look to indie labels for that music. Rudy Chavarria, of Rude College Promotions, says, "The bottom line for college radio is the music. If it's brilliant, they'll love it. You just have to get them to listen." Rev. Moose, vice president of content at *CMJ* (see below), explains what he sees as the technical difference between commercial and college radio:

> *College radio is usually owned or licensed by a college or educational institution. The classification that the FCC applies for is not only a position on the dial but also in the type of programming that's allowed to be aired, how frequently, when and for whom, community services, where ad money comes from, what scripts are allowed to be said, and everything else. There really are no rules for college radio. But traditionally speaking, the key elements as far as differences in programming for those stations is that they're a little more relaxed than commercial radio programming, which is run as a commercial business, and their whole intent is to sell air time, commercial spots, and rake in a lot of money for their owners. College radio doesn't have to focus solely on how much money they're going to earn each quarter and can focus more on the value behind their programming.*

Dealing with college radio folks can be exasperating. They're hard to reach because they're students, with classes or commitments. Many have scheduled hours at the station but are not always there when you call. It's harder to develop lasting relationships because staff changes as they graduate or quit. Stations may play a different genre every two hours. It depends on the DJs. Ken Weinstein advises:

> *College radio and commercial radio are very different beasts. Definitely work college radio. It's a key part of the artist-development puzzle. Anything noncommercial is easier to work than anything commercial, and it's great for exposure and for starting the story.*

Is college airplay worth coveting? Indies I spoke to were mixed about its value. Jesse Fergusson (Definitive Jux Records) says, "We work it—I don't know how helpful it is, but it's the only radio promotion we can do."

The general consensus I got was that college radio is a good vehicle for developing visibility for an artist. It keeps their name out, but no one was sure that it sold records. Robb Nansel (Saddle Creek Records) says:

> *I think college radio is necessary. Just because a record is doing well on college radio charts, I don't think there necessarily is a direct correlation to record sales. But you have to get the record out there to those people.*

To work college radio, compile a list of stations in the region you're starting in, especially stations that chart. CMJ (see below) is the best place to start. There are also listings online. Rudy Chavarria recommends you first fax teases:

> *We'll fax quotes about the record to all of the radio stations that are reluctant to add the record and a list of the people that are giving us a lot of love. Then they see the record is onto something and will open the package and give it attention. Email has taken the place of what faxes used to be. Less people send faxes. People like seeing one because it's something they can hold.*

Send a CD to the MD, who'll put it into a bin that all DJs can use. Contact them to see if they'll accept an MP3 file instead. When stations play it, call nearby retail stores, let them know, and send a copy. Cultivate street teams in colleges. Get students who are passionate about your music to promote it. Chavarria says, "Students can flyer retail stores, student unions, fraternity and sorority houses. Use postcards with the album cover on the front. If someone gets it at a party, they can fold it, put it in their pocket, and have it." Dave Roberge says:

> *We've tried to make a conscious effort to not do what we call a full-out radio promotion campaign for a particular single. We've done an awareness campaign, where we want to just make people aware of the band. So we focus on the CMJ Top 200 stations. We send information about the band. If the band is in their area, we invite them to the show. We try to set up remote radio opportunities to give away tickets and create loyalty at the stations. We send music but don't ask them to spin a certain track, and we'll give ten tickets to the show. It's about creating champions of the band right now.*

Target individual DJs. Send a CD and get to know them. A nice element of college radio is the relationships you can develop. Students are friendlier, so you can cultivate support. Get to know key DJs, and if they like your artist, they'll spread the word. Send postcards with the CDs so they have your website and other info handy if someone inquires about it. Ask for support when your artist plays nearby. Offer an artist interview. Rev. Moose advises:

> I think people buy music after repeated exposure to it. Exposure to music does come out of college radio. And it always has. Pre-Internet, it was the only place you could preview the songs. College radio used to be the only outlet to hear some things. There are a lot of different media outlets for music now, online, as well, so college radio has taken on a little bit more of the role of being the tastemaker than it has being the audio preview. That in itself is just as key in making sure people know what they want to be listening to or hear music they might not have been exposed to.

Developing relationships with college stations can get you lots of love! The students are volunteers because they love it. Contact several at each station to create fans at them. Give away tickets if you have a gig in their area. Make them feel like they're part of your artist's team. Many like that! Treat them as special. Find out how they prefer to receive music. Often the music director will decide whether it at least meets the minimum criteria for being on the station. He or she might recommend it to others. Then it's up to the individual DJs to play the record. Eric Speck says:

> Radio is important on a community level, especially if you rally a strong college radio base for your records in the strong stations like KEXP, KCRW, and other great community-based rally points where there are pockets of mostly underground culture. It's more important for getting your album into that scene than selling records. It does reach kids who will then be tastemakers and spread it. Reaching avid music fans will hopefully mean they'll spread the word.

Building relationships in college radio now can help your label in the long term. They're often plugged into music communities where they can help spread the word or help your artists get gigs. When I had my label, some of the DJs at college stations got local stores to carry my records and then plugged them on air. Many of the people working at the stations go on to get jobs where they might be even more helpful to your label, if they like you and the music you put out. So don't just send the music. Get to know them and see where the relationships can go.

Satellite Radio

New technology may change the face of traditional radio. Since things change so fast, I won't go into broad details. But satellite radio seems to be growing fast, and there are more opportunities to get airplay with satellite radio. According to Lee Abrams, former chief programming officer of XM Satellite Radio (www.xmradio.com):

> *Airplay on Sirius XM (the resulting company following the 2008 Sirius and XM Radio merger) is like obtaining airplay on most radio stations. Each station/channel has a program director. Service the PD with CDs, and use your best salesmanship to get added. Labels need to think out of the traditional radio/records relationship envelope. Sirius XM will do many things that terrestrial radio is incapable of or traditionally rejects.*

Sirius XM offers hundreds of channels for all different genres of music. People subscribe to get the service. Sirius XM satellite radio has grown and expanded its reach. Each show has a producer. You'd have to contact the people you feel play the kind of music you're looking to get on air. While many of the shows may not have the same impact as commerical radio, audiences for satellite stations are growing. If you develop relationships with shows that are increasingly gaining more listeners, you can cement them for the future. It's another seed that can be planted.

Radio Publications

There are trade publications for radio, and just as there are different levels of radio stations, different trades cater to them. *College Music Journal* (CMJ) (www.cmj.com) is for college stations. *Friday Morning Quarterback* (www.fmqb.com) is the next rung. *Billboard* (www.billboard.com), *Radio & Records* (www.radioandrecords.com), and *Hits* (www.hitsmagazine.com) are trades for major commercial radio. The UK has *The Radio Magazine* (www.theradiomagazine.co.uk). Each has reviews, charts, and other features. Sending a press kit with a CD can get your record a review. According to WFUV's Rita Houston, "What the trades allow you to do is build a story on a national level. Most programmers, myself included, read the trades cover to cover every week. That's another source of information for me."

CMJ is the authority on college radio, providing resources for marketing and promoting at college level. Rev. Moose says they started with what's now known as the *CMJ New Music Report*—a weekly industry trade magazine. He adds:

> *The* New Music Report *is the aggregator of the entire U.S. and Canada's college and noncommercial airplay for each week. What we do is we weigh each station to [see how much reach each has], note they're playing this X amount of times, and that translates into a number. We tabulate all those numbers and give you an overall representation of the nation's airplay for that given period. That gives you the ability to see not just what these stations are playing on a regular basis but also compared to the national level. If your artist plays one specific type of music and you see that forty radio stations play bands that are similar to yours, but not yours in particular, it's a great focus to be able to go to them and say, "Hey, you guys should be aware of this artist."*

Charting in the *New Music Report* doesn't carry the same weight of other charts. But, as you appear on more station's charts, it increases your artist's visibility, and other stations may request a CD. CMJ has opportunities to advertise using their packages. Rev. Moose adds, "If you're interested in reaching the college radio programmer, we already have their attention." CMJ also has *CMJ New Music Monthly*, a consumer magazine.

Rev. Moose says CMJ provides music to radio stations with the CD compilations packaged with the magazines. They also have marketing campaigns targeted at the college market if you have the budget. I spotlighted *CMJ* because it's the most accessible at the beginning. Other trades offer similar services, including sending your CD to radio stations that report to them. Getting onto a CD sampler that goes to radio stations allows many DJs to hear your music. College radio is the most likely to play what they like on a sampler. CMJ has a conference every fall, filled with people from college radio stations, all kinds of industry people, artists, and much more. It's a good opportunity to network, apply for an artist showcase, and make great contacts. Rev. Moose says, "I think the biggest benefit of attending the conference is the networking capabilities. I got my first job out of relationships I made at my first CMJ Marathon."

Just as you would with other magazines, try to develop relationships with trade magazines and push to get reviews. Radio trades advise advertising in them. Many indie labels feel that unless you have a particular situation that would make your record more likely to get radio play, consumer magazines are where your budget should be focused. Talk to other labels to see what worked for them, and try to get free reviews.

Creating a Plan of Attack

If you want radio play, design a realistic strategy. Start by building a foundation of smaller stations. Work up from noncommercial stations to smaller commercial markets, and then to larger ones. Keep building your story. Your artist should be known before approaching primary stations. His or her story must be impressive to crack that level.

Unless you have a big buzz, start with public and college radio stations. As you work colleges, coordinate performances at or near those giving you airplay. When there's a gig, ask the station to interview the artist. Get the college paper to cover it. Work this foundation so your story attracts more stations. Mark Carpentieri (MC Records) puts a bounce-back card, without stamps, in each CD to see what people think. Stations return them or respond by email. He adds:

> I ask who's filling out the card, as there are lots of changes. We ask what radio charts they report to, what cuts they like, their email addresses, is it appropriate for another show, how many hours a week do they play this kind of music? For blues music, a lot of the people who host shows may come in for two hours for their show. They're not as easily reached as trying to track the programming director at stations where you call at certain hours.

However you get music to stations, follow-up must be done. Keep accurate records each time you call, similar to how I recommended keeping track of publicity. Use a sheet listing stations, with contact info and space for notes. Index cards work, too. I made notes of what each MD said and the date. Always thank the MDs or DJs for their time. If you want radio play, be prepared to make the calls—many of them—over and over. Send a one-sheet with the artist's story. If you have swag, include that, too. Some stations like T-shirts and caps. Sending something a little more original than what everyone else may send can make you stand out.

If phone calls get time-consuming, find an enthusiastic intern/fan to do radio promotion. As you get more airplay, inform stations that aren't playing your record yet. Tell your distributor. Be patient. Rita Houston says, "If you have fans and are out there working your butt off, building a story, then radio's going to have to follow you. Get to work!"

CHAPTER 18

Getting Retail and Club Promotion

I f you want your records to sell, get off your butt. Active promotion builds your label. If you can't hire independent promoters, work the record yourself. You have to. Nurture those all-important relationships. When club DJs and people who work in retail know and like you, your foundation gets stronger.

Working Retail Stores

Once you have product in stores, create a system to keep in touch with them. Take notes when making calls, about what they think and when to follow up. I'd also note personal stuff they share. Bringing it up during later calls creates a personal connection and builds the relationship.

Be persistent, not a pest. Calling at less busy times, once a week to see how the record is doing, reminds them to stay aware of it. It also shows stores you're serious about marketing your product—you're not an indie that leaves product and disappears. Always thank people for their help. Even if they're indifferent, say their support is appreciated. Even if you have distribution, stay on top of stores. When they sell out, nudge them to reorder. Let your distributor know a store needs more. They should keep track, but don't count on it. They'll take you more seriously from those efforts.

Let stores know your artist is available for in-store appearances. Ask folks you deal with in stores if they'd like an autographed photo of your act. Have the artist(s) sign a bunch with something like "Thanks for your support." Ask if the person wants the autograph made out to him or her personally. Sometimes a clerk is more likely to hang one that's autographed to him or her. Some folks check out a record if they like a photo. Determine what retail promotional materials are best for your music.

Getting Visibility in Stores

You can get in-store visibility with placement on display racks or in listening booths. Andy Allen (ADA) says, "Make sure that when somebody walks into a store, they find the music there. The easiest way to do that is to have it in front where people can see it." People may not intend to buy your record, but if it's in their faces, they might. If people hear a song on the radio, seeing it on a rack reminds them. Folks use listening booths to hear CDs they're not familiar with. A review might pique interest, but people still want to hear it. Jonatha Brooke says:

> We know where our markets are really strong. The distributor helps us figure out when positioning in stores and record booths will be cost effective. If you're willing to spend the money up front, they're valuable tools, especially at the beginning of a record cycle and when you're touring.

These promotions are the most cost effective when you have other promotions going in the market and there's already an awareness created on the artist. They aren't free. Labels pay stores to position their product on racks and get into listening booths. CDs don't end up on displays by accident. That space is bought, like ads in a magazine. It can be expensive, but indies say it can get good results. Most store promotions are bought through a distributor. If you have one, they'll generally put up the money and recoup it from sales of your record. Some stores pressure labels to use their programs. Robb Nansel (Saddle Creek Records) explains:

> There are stores that won't take your stuff unless you get into their program. A lot of stores have automated ordering systems.

If they take one CD and it sells, all its computer knows is we had one and will order another one. It can take weeks for that one reorder to get in. So they never really have stock. The only way to get a big buy-in is to buy into a listening post. Then they'll take fifteen, and when they sell, the computer may order twenty more. The computer is smart enough to do that, but not smart enough to know that if we sold one in a day, they should get more than that.

Labels can get onto racks and into listening booths without going broke. Some stores are cheaper. Start with smaller markets. Develop relationships with people in smaller stores. Sometimes a friendly, personal approach makes a difference. Managers of a mom-and-pop store can sometimes support you if they choose, with lower rates or more. I've finessed my way onto displays for free when a space wasn't already bought. That's where good relationships help. Personal thank-yous were very effective for getting stores to go the distance for my label. Practice smiling! Research by talking to stores and other indies. Mark Carpentieri (MC Records) says listening posts can work well for a good record:

Are they worth it? It depends on the program. Some are worth it. Some are really expensive listening-post programs. Some stores do better jobs than others. I like listening posts in general. If you have an artist that's very visible, you can do the pricing positioning and it works. If your artist is not as visible, you want the curious person in the record store to hear the record because they don't know the artist and may not want to spend fifteen bucks to find out.

I spoke earlier of the benefits of giving away CD samplers. Some stores find two- to four-track CDs to be a great promotion and will distribute them to music lovers most likely to buy your music. People may listen in listening booths, but when they take a CD home, they digest it more thoroughly. Then they go back and buy the album or order it online. You can get business from value-added stuff given out to potential fans. Points of purchase (POPs) displays can also help increase sales. They're set up near cash registers to entice shoppers to buy other products as they pay for items they've already decided on. Some labels say they make up small posters to distribute to stores.

Some labels do co-op advertising with a retail store. The store agrees to order a specific amount of product and arranges an ad specifically for it in a local publication. The ad includes info about the product, the label, and the store. John T. Kunz (Waterloo Records) says, "The ad is co-opted with the store. Quite a few artists do well with our advertising." If you have them, include in your ad that people can get a free sampler, link to free digital downloads, or other added-value swag if they go to the store you're advertising with. Make sure to include logos, contact info, and your website in the ad. Mark Carpentieri finds these ads helpful:

> We do tons of co-op advertising, a lot based regionally. I like to combine touring with the ad—get the most bang for the buck. If the artist is playing [a specific city], do an ad in the weekly and maybe tag in Borders, so you're helping your artist and yourself. It's a win/win situation compared to just doing a straight ad announcing that the new CD is available. Co-op advertising is the most expensive for the least buy, because when you're talking about a buy-in, it's usually about a handful of stores for a lot of money. That's why we combine it with tour dates to get more out of it.

If you deal directly with the store, usually it places the ad for the label and covers your costs out of what they owe you from sales. Distributors can also arrange them. Unless it's a big release, I don't think the titles in the ad matter as much as the fact that you're getting your name and website out. Combine it with an in-store performance or other event. Decide what kind of marketing and promotion works for your music and budget. What's available depends on the regions and types of stores you work. Large retailers are less likely to have the kind of leeway a smaller store might. Find your strongest markets and work them first. As sales increase, you may have more latitude to buy into bigger programs.

Sometimes there's a spot in a listening booth or on a rack that hasn't been bought. If you have a great relationship with folks in that store, they might cut you a great deal or just add your CD. Since it's empty, if they believe in your music they may want to help. It's happenened to me! When you're friendly and have great music, and stores see you're working hard, they may reach out and help when they can.

Merchandising

Labels and artists can make good money marketing merchandise to fans. If your label signs artists, get some rights for merchandising in your artist agreement—If you plan to do something with it. It's not fair to take rights you won't work for. But if you help the artists make the merch, get a cut. Kelly Vandergriff (Five Times August) says:

> Even at high-paying college shows, we sometimes make more money in merch. And, at shows where you're not getting paid but a few hundred dollars, merch sales can really help cover your tour expenses. We sell way more shirts and posters than CDs, because you can't download a shirt!

Merch is a staple for many artists, and it can support them on the road. T-shirts, buttons, wristbands, caps, headbands, koozies (can holders), posters, stickers, etc. are sold at gigs, in record stores, and by mail order. Valerie Vigoda (GrooveLily) says:

> A large portion of our income comes from merch. We've found that giving people an incentive—free sampler CD or bumper sticker with purchase, for example—makes a difference, as does having other people besides ourselves hawking the merchandise at gigs. Fans make the best salespeople.

Merch can be a great promotional tool. You may give away as much as you sell. Folks in stores like free stuff. Some will wear a T-shirt if they like the artist. Onno Lakeman (Red to Violet) says they designed T-shirts that people like to wear. Instead of it having a typical promotion, it says, "Here I Am " (the name of their single) in big letters. Their name and website is on it, too. He says:

> I like that the person wearing the shirt gets attention and our band's name and site is also promoted. Sometimes buyers of the CD get a free shirt. We also send out giveaways for radio, to stores who ordered our CDs, reviewers, people who entered our contest on the site, and TV giveaways. It's a nice way to offer something extra that is promotional, too. It works. We get great feedback from people who have won the shirt.

Depending on the genre, merch sells well at gigs once a core of enthusiastic fans develops. Have everything available by mail order and advertise it in your mailings. If you have a website, plug your merch there. Once it sells, it's a double benefit—you make money and the artist gets free promotion. Rich Hardesty incorporates merch into his business:

> *At shows, I get good-looking girls and guys that want to sit there and get a free CD of the show and a T-shirt. Sometimes I pay people. We have a marketing table. I have a big, long shotgun case with my CDs lined up on the inside of it when it's open. On the tray part of it there's swag—stickers, picks, autographed pictures, and the free Jägermeister stuff.*

Dance Clubs

When I released dance music, I'd find out the best DJs for my record, what clubs they worked, and their hours. Arriving early, before a club gets crowded, makes it easier to get in free. I'd introduce myself with a friendly smile, saying I was just going to drop a record with the DJ. The DJs were great. If they liked a record, sometimes they played it. I'd get their phone numbers and the best times to call. Often I'd get an answering machine, leave a short, friendly message, and try again the following week. Never sound annoyed, no matter how many unreturned messages you leave. Getting angry won't get it played. Persistence might.

Another way to reach DJs is through record pools—groups of DJs who pay to get free records. The person running one solicits free product from labels and promises that members will play them in clubs and at parties. Most record pools have charts of what their members play. Servicing a pool gives you a good chance of ending up on that chart, but I don't think it sells records. I serviced many with my first few dance tracks and got little. Many labels like them, but I found DJs more likely to play a record they buy.

Should you service record pools? It depends on the individual one. To be fair, servicing pools can get more club play. I found record pools useful when they supported my label in other ways. When one called for records, I'd make an offer: Get my product into retail stores in their city and I'd service them. If they agreed, I'd send two copies for them to test. I developed long-term relationships with stores in an assortment of cities that ordered many of my dance records. If you give pools free records, get your money's worth!

Live Performances

Live venues offer exposure and a place to sell product. Depending on the venue, your artist can be exposed to potential new fans. Music lovers get passionate about an artist who grabs them during a live show. When artists interact with fans, it stimulates sales. Artists who keep in touch with them have a greater chance for longevity. Loyal fans will buy each album that's released.

Getting Live Exposure

Touring is a great way to sell records. Many artists now bypass it by sitting in front of their computers to find friends on MySpace. There's no comparison! That's where you meet fans in person, not electronically, and where you can show them the best love. I personally can't imagine how any artist who loves to do music wouldn't want to get out and perform in front of live fans. Ingrid Michaelson believes a huge part of the music business is the live show, which has become more important, especially with illegal downloading. Because of this, doing live shows has become a much more important way for an artist to make a living. She explains:

> Playing live is one thing that can never be replicated. You can make DVDs, people can watch you, they can steal your music. But there's nothing like the connection you make with people when they're at a show and you're all in the same room together. That's something that nothing can duplicate. And now record labels are trying to take touring money!

Many musicians hesitate to put a tour together. Schlepping gear to a club can seem like so much more energy than clicking on a computer, but they lose out on a lot! Eric Hutchinson explains:

> I think that touring is undervalued. That's how you make fans and find out about your own music. To not go out and tour is really robbing yourself of growth, both fan base-wise and musically. Touring generates interest, especially these days. That's when you really

separate the men from the boys. Can this person really get out there and actually perform? That's the one thing I like about American Idol. I don't agree with most of that show but do like that people have to get up there and cut the mustard, with nobody helping them out that way. When someone sees me for the first time, they say I'm an entertainer. It's not just about playing the songs. I talk a lot between them. It takes a lot of energy to haul yourself out of your house and go to a venue, that might be cramped, and overpriced. You have to respect the audience, if you expect them to come back again.

Juni Fisher (Red Geetar Records) agrees. The touring aspect of her career began when she got a call to perform for a major western festival—a very selective one that everybody wanted to get into. Fisher says a friend of the booker, who's a well-known western artist, was asked to listen to a pirated copy of her first album, since the booker couldn't believe she'd produced such an album on her own, while under the radar. That got her taken more seriously and opened her to touring. She says:

The artist confirmed what the booker heard and went on to recommend me to another really good festival. On a leap of faith, two small venues, both connected in some way to the first festival, booked me, one as an opening act and another as a solo. At this point, getting from Tennessee to California for those gigs cost almost as much as I was paid, but I was in heaven. I was getting paid to play! Over time, word of mouth was my friend, and the next fall, I decided that going to Albuquerque for the Western Music Association Convention was a good investment. There was definitely a buzz going on when I got there, and they found out I was booked for two of the four biggest and best western music festivals in the country. I met a lot of folks there who remain good friends to this day.

Sometimes artists or labels have to create their own gigs. Sue Baran (Push Play) says she wanted to get Push Play a good gig in New York City. She tried to get them booked into the Fillmore New York at Irving Plaza, a large venue. The Fillmore wouldn't book them because they didn't think they could fill it. Baran insisted they could, so she privately booked it herself because they didn't have an agent. They proved the promoter wrong by packing the place. I asked her how; she explains:

Drive! That's all I can say. We worked MySpace, got out there to all similar types of concerts and introduced Push Play, signed autographs from promo cards I had printed with the band's picture on it. I marketed it by sending out posters to all our street teams in the region, and we were relentless! Hours and hours and hours of hardcore work went into it.

Baran's hard work with getting Push Play into good gigs and filling them led to them being signed with Creative Artists Agency as their agent. Soon after, they booked the band to play the Nokia Theater, which holds 2,500 people. Creating the huge buzz with fans and keeping them active on their MySpace page (more in Chapter 21) is getting Push Play into a higher level of touring. All of this contributed to strong album sales, both physical and digital. Touring allows an artist to build a relationship with fans and promoters that can help with getting more gigs. As the record label, you're not responsible for booking your artists' tours, unless you have a 360 deal and get a direct cut. But, the marketing potential makes it not worth ignoring or just leaving to the artists. Daniel Glass (Glassnote Entertainment) is thorough about getting his acts on the road and giving them repeated support. It helps him sell lots of records! He explains:

Our touring policy is so specific, detailed, and anal. We call the promoter, club, radio stations, retailers, and the local magazines before the show, when the show is happening that night, and a day or two later to see how the experience was. That is getting us a major reputation. People like that. They're in shock, expecting us to only call before. We call after also. People recommend us because they think we're thorough. It tells our artists and the retailers that we care.

There are many ways to get live exposure for your acts. My book *I Don't Need a Record Deal!* goes into details on building a following and finding venues. Read everything you can. *The Musician's Atlas* and *AtlasOnline* (www.musiciansatlas.com) are great resources for touring. They have city-by-city listings of clubs, radio stations, local press, and many others to help plan and promote a tour effectively. According to its publisher, Martin Folkman:

Whether in print or online, The Musician's Atlas delivers comprehensive company and contact info that makes it easy to book more gigs and sell your music more successfully. The Atlas *connects you with more than twenty thousand talent buyers, programmers, music journalists, publishers, and other vital industry contacts. In-depth listings supply critical details. The* Atlas Online *is packed with 40 percent more contacts than the print edition—with new qualified listings and contacts added every day. The easy-to-use system enables subscribers to search the extensive* Musician's Atlas *contact databases by any number of criteria, such as company and contact names, music genres, and zip code.*

A more recent great resource is *The Indie Venue Bible* (www.indievenuebible.com), which is put out by the same company that publishes *The Indie Bible* (more in Chapter 19). David Wimble, its publisher, says:

The Indie Venue Bible *features thousands of clubs, restaurants, coffee shops, house concerts, theaters, halls, churches, and bookstores—any place you can land a gig! There are also thousands of venues listed in smaller towns that have been ignored by mainstream venue directories. For example, we have listings for over three hundred cities and towns in New York State alone.*

A different kind of service is Online Gigs (www.onlinegigs.com), an online subscription service that automates the administration of booking acts. It's better to begin regionally and work out in a circle; then you're not jumping all over the place. Or sign up with SonicBids (more in Chapter 19). Once your artist starts touring, provide whatever tour support you can. Jesse Fergusson (Definitive Jux Records) says:

I send promotional materials four weeks ahead of time to the venues— posters, stickers, CDs, photographs, bios—so that they can publicize the event with ammunition from the label. We don't make money when an artist tours, but if there's press about the event, we might sell more records. I set up retail support on tours, as much as possible, and in-stores in some towns.

Do PR for your touring acts. Tap into street teams—give them posters and flyers to distribute. Study the markets. Work it—radio, retail, and press— for each city they play in. Touring builds the foundation for sales. Saturate the markets as well as you can. Valerie Vigoda advises:

Even if you're playing at a festival or other soft-ticket event where your income isn't based on the number of tickets sold, don't rely on the presenter to do publicity. If you ask them for a list of media leads and follow up on those, you'll be way ahead of the game. The presenter will be happy you're taking the initiative to bring a crowd to your show.

Tony Brummel (Victory Records) adds:

It's always in a label's best interest, especially if it's underground-based music, to support your artist in the form of tour support. If you're trying to save money or don't have money, there are other areas to take those savings. It can be anything from buying a van, to giving money, to buying plane tickets, to making sure the band can pay their bills at home so they can stay on tour. That's how we sell records. Press doesn't want to interview a band if they're not touring; video won't play a band. Retail doesn't want to put a band into an expensive, higher-tiered program if they're not on the road. For us, it's about keeping our bands on the road all the time, as much as possible.

Touring isn't easy. Robb Nansel says, "Going on tour for any band is hard. It takes persistence. All our bands started by doing house shows, with maybe ten people. Those ten people eventually turn into twenty, then you're playing in a small club." When the record gets a buzz, there's greater potential for gigs. Get friendly with people who work in clubs. You never know how much influence a bartender has. Good relationships can get your artist in. Keith Grimwood (Trout Fishing in America) says:

We put a lot of miles down. We'd talk to other bands we'd meet and ask where they like to play. Ezra was very bold. He'd call up the Chamber of Commerce and just talk to someone in an area he liked on the map. We branched out. We'd look at other band's calendars. We chose bands that were similar and called the venues they played in. We began playing folk festivals in Canada and branched out to other states, a little farther each time. When Dick joined us, he connected the dots.

Talk to managers of clubs featuring artists with a name or large following. Offer to have your artist open for free. Some clubs will try a newer act if it costs nothing and they like their music. If you play with a roster of acts, ask to go on after one with a large following so you can potentially play to some of their fans and increase your mailing list. If there are clubs with open mics, encourage your artists to perform, or at least hang there, to meet other musicians and expose people to the music. Hip-hop artist El-P (Definitive Jux Records) says:

> *After Company Flow started to dissolve, I continued going on tour, bringing other artists. I still had the idea that I was doing artist development. I liked that I could bring someone in under my name, no matter how small a level it is, and grease the wheels a bit so these guys get heard on stage. When they have a record, they're not just coming out blindly. With a small label, if you're coming out completely blind and haven't laid any groundwork or created a buzz, you can't afford the big explosives.*

El-P says he markets all the acts on Definitive Jux through touring. Do what you can to get exposure. Damon Dash (Roc-A-Fella Records) did whatever he could to get Jay-Z out when he first started. He says, "We were performing a lot up and down the region. We saturated the 'chitlin circuit,' which is the region from Boston to the Carolinas. People were talking about us." Dash says Jay-Z ran on stage at a party at the Palladium during a performance: "Everyone went crazy for Jay. That started the attention and got radio play. We came with a buzz. We performed and were battling people. We generated a great degree of energy, so people were attracted to us." The record went gold. Dash says doing what it took to get attention was a lot of work, which created a successful label. He reflects:

> *You have to be able to put the work in. I don't think I could do that again, being on the chitlin circuit, performing every time we had the chance. We used to have to run on stage to start it out. It took a lot of energy creating it, but if you're hungry—yeah! If you want to go through all the underground outlets, we would go anywhere there was a mic and just perform. We'd battle anyone who wanted to battle.*

Rich Hardesty's niche is college kids, and students at the Indiana schools he started in are from all over the U.S. He says when they go home on breaks, they play his CD for friends. When they graduate, they move elsewhere. So his core of Indiana fans ends up all over the country. This allows him to play cities he's never been to and have a crowd. He explains:

> For example, I did a show in L.A. for the Rosebowl. Some alumni from Purdue suggested I come there and play in a bar because Purdue was playing. Alumni remembered me. Because of networking on the Internet—I sent out an email and posted it on my website—we packed the bar silly with my alumni following, people coming for the Rosebowl. The bar owner said he'd never seen anything like it. It was cool how the alumni support kicked in. They remembered their college days and wanted to relive it.

Hardesty attributes at least part of his success to his interaction with fans. "I have always been a people person, taking time to talk to the fans instead of ducking into the break room." He learned what worked best in his market. Since he tapes his shows, he used interaction with fans as another marketing tool. He explains:

> I'd say people's names into the mic throughout the show. They'd have their name on the live recording and think that was a big deal. People made copies for friends. They asked if they could. Live shows are what helped sell me. My live music is way different than a recorded CD.

Protect yourself or your artists while touring. Valerie Vigoda advises getting everything in writing and advance all the gigs well ahead of time. She says GrooveLily tries to book venues that are more likely to have a built-in audience and budget. Try whatever works for the artist, but get them on the road if you want to sell more records!

Getting College Gigs

College gigs can be very lucrative if you have the patience to go after them. It's a tremendous amount of work, but they can be worth the effort if your artist gets on a college tour. Colleges usually pay real money, which keeps your artist (or you as the artist) happy. If you ask for it, often they pay expenses. There's potential for exposure in their publications and radio stations, where gigs can be promoted.

To work colleges, start with directories or referrals. Pick an area, preferably one that's *not* near a major city. There's often more demand for entertainment. An artist can join National Association of Campus Activities (NACA; www.naca.org), considered the nation's largest organization for campus activities with nearly 1,200 member colleges and more than six hundred associate member talent agencies, performers, and other firms in the college market. Joining gives you access to their directory. They have conferences, and for a fee, artists can showcase, performing for people who book entertainment in colleges. It's expensive, but if your music fits the market, I'm told the money for gigs makes it worth the investment.

A smaller, less expensive organization for the college market is the Association for the Promotion of Campus Activities (APCA; www.apca.com). They also have conferences and access to the college market. It's not nearly as powerful as NACA, but it has some great benefits for a lot less money. Their national directory, which includes contacts for colleges and the people who book for them, is worth the membership fee.

Start at local bars near your targeted colleges. Invite people from Student Activities to come see you. When your crowd increases, let them know. Or, just contact the Student Activities departments cold. Don't send music until you see if they might be interested in booking you. Describe your music, play some over the phone, or send a link to your MySpace page or an MP3 file. Only send a package if they ask for one. Some colleges want videos. Get letters of reference when you perform for your college press kit.

If you want to do a real tour, organize it so it makes sense. Pick a city and book many months ahead of time (which colleges usually do). Work from city to city. Call all colleges in the region until you get at least one that can get you from the last college to their city. Do that around a region or around the country. Create a system like I mentioned earlier, to keep in touch with those you speak with. Be persistent, enthusiastic, and prepared to describe your music well, send a sample, or even play it on the phone. Don't just send packages randomly, unless you're rich. Make sure each person is really interested first.

CHAPTER 19

Joining the Digital
Revolution

S ince writing the first edition of this book, I've seen big expectations
about the Internet inflate and deflate. Now things look bright to
stay. People complain that the Internet will kill sales and careers.
Not true, says Bob Lefsetz, a music industry analyst who's worked with
many major labels. He writes the email newsletter *The Lefsetz Letter*
(www.lefsetz.com), read by many celebrities and music business honchos,
which gives his candid take on issues in the music industry. He says:

> *The Net is the best thing that has ever happened to everybody
> but superstars. Everything you build comes back to you. Every
> effort you make enhances your career. Choices may not be as
> obvious, effects might not be measured instantly, but get in the
> game for the long haul and watch as dividends get paid. First and
> foremost, for the first time in history, you can know who your
> audience is. You can collect the email address of everybody who
> likes your music. Maybe give a track away for free for an email
> address. Maybe not all of the addresses will be valid, but if they're
> truly fans, they'd love it if you contacted them in the future. This
> is what Led Zeppelin did with their O2 ticket sale, this is what
> Radiohead did with their name-your-own price In Rainbows
> deal, this is what Trent Reznor does again and again. You have
> to harvest email addresses, so when you go on tour, when you've*

got something to sell, you can alert your fans! *And it's no longer only when you're on tour. You can sell T-shirts while you're home watching the tube. People who've never seen you live can order a T-shirt or keychain or autographed tchotchke. Hell, you can personalize all your merch and sell it at an exorbitant price. You can even ask your fans for money to record. True fans will give you all their dough. They want to support you, they're in it for the long haul. If your first emphasis track/single fails, the fan doesn't drop you; he redoubles his effort; he's even more committed, because you* need him!

Stop trying to take the easy way out. Looking for a sugar daddy, a bank. Start doing the hard work. Or get your spouse to do the heavy lifting. Or enlist a fan, who will do it all for free! *Doubt me? Then how about all those fans who establish websites in your honor. They'll do the authorized one* for nothing! *Just because music can be stolen doesn't mean you can't sell it. Hell, look at iTunes, it exists side by side with P2P. Sell vinyl, which can't be downloaded and traded. Even if people don't have a turntable, they want the physical object as a work of art, as a totem of their dedication! You're living in the best era for music creation and distribution in the history of mankind. By complaining, you're just showing your ignorance. Knowing how to play is not enough. Just like you can't survive in today's world without knowing how to type. Don't cling tighter to history and complain. Take a typing lesson, do* research, *take a chance!*

To get an interesting and honest view of the music industry, subscribe to the free *The Lefsetz Letter* (www.lefsetz.com). The Internet is a fantastic tool for branding your label and making money. Find ways to develop your online presence and push your artists to develop theirs. CJ Baran (Push Play) says:

> *The Internet is the most valuable source for today's musicians, enabling us to reach out to the masses and get our music out there. It is this reason why record labels are now experiencing such difficulty. The Internet has made it possible for every grassroots band to take advantage of mass marketing.*

This chapter teaches you how to prepare to market and promote online. The next two will show you how to market and promote your music electronically, once you have your foundation in place.

The Worldwide Electronic Marketplace

Things change quickly on the Interent. Six years ago, people were discouraged that Internet opportunities they'd expected weren't panning out. That's changed dramatically! Jeff Price (Tunecore) says:

> You can become famous without having to go through traditional media. Create your own fame by having five million MySpace friends, or a frequented weblog, or through having a gigantic email list, or by selling music with iTunes.

The Internet has become *very* valuable. Communicating by email is considered the norm now. Philip Antoniades, president of Nimbit (www. nimbit.com), a company that allows artists to manage, market, and sell digital and physical music, merchandise, and tickets direct to fans, says compared to five years ago:

> The Internet is a mixed bag right now. Email campaigns are less effective, as spam has become so much of a nuisance. Five years ago a band could count on emails to effectively market a gig or product. Now they need to rely more heavily on fans hitting their website for updated information. On the other hand, more consumers are comfortable with buying and discovering music on the Net than ever before. Right now the downside is that there are too many places to discover music and too much music available. I believe we'll see more "tastemakers" emerge on the net over the next five years so those who need to be led will be pointed in a more focused direction. The power of the Internet still lies in capturing your fans and driving them to your website, your store, and your content so you establish your brand. No matter where the business goes, if you own your customers and your brand, you win!

The more often your artist's name is seen, the more brand awareness that's created. It may take time to make an impact, but, as people become more familiar with the names they see, they'll pay more attention and get more curious. Jason Feinberg, president of On Target Media Group (www.otmg.net), says, "Low costs, few barriers to entry, a 24/7/365 global marketplace, and constant technology developments are creating an environment where anyone with a music product and some marketing acumen can find a fan base and promote to them."

Electronic Communications

One of the biggest benefits of being online is having access to email service. Email is a cheaper way to communicate than having to mail letters and packages. Emailing a music file can save a lot of money on postage and also on the cost of the CD. Eric Hutchinson really appreciates the value of sending emails and says:

> I remember as I teenager I'd sign up for real mailing lists and bands would send out postcards with their touring schedules. I can't imagine having to promote shows that way. You can get the word out about a show now in just a day and still get a good crowd.

Nowadays, many people only want to receive emails. Phone calls are out. Communicating via email is a quick and easy way to show instant appreciation. When someone gets you a gig, email your appreciation. If a fan does something to spread the word, email your thanks. Robb Nansel (Saddle Creek Records) says, "We rely on the Internet for communication. We're constantly interacting with people."

One of your most valuable commodities online is email addresses. Collect them! Respect them! It gives you access to fans and a way to reach them. Jeff Price advises:

> Collect email addresses. Find out information about your fans—their age, zip code, gender. There's software to do that, or just ask them when they sign up. An email list provides you with an easy one-to-one way to communicate with all your fans in a cost-effective, efficient manner. You click a button and can literally reach tens of thousands of people.

Email can be used to announce what's going on at your label. As you gather email addresses of fans, build a list to keep folks informed about what's happening at your label. Use email to notify fans about an artist's gig. Press releases can be emailed to publications. There are endless possibilities. One click and you reach those you want to online. There can be problems with having your emails go into people's spam boxes. As your company grows, it might be worth it to get a service that sends them for you. They comply more with email rules and are less likely to have things they send bounce. Phil Antoniades says these days, other factors are much more important than getting email addresses. He explains:

> Getting a customer to add you to their address book or white list [to avoid being labeled as spam] is more important. Handing them some kind of tchotchke that has your URL on it and keeping the content at your site current and interesting is more important. I think getting people's SMS text addresses is much more personal and effective.

Online Newsletters

A great way to keep in touch with fans is to create a label or individual artist's newsletter. Let fans know what your artists are doing. Announce anything new. Include any info they might find interesting. David M. Bailey says:

> On my site, we have a sign-up for a newsletter. I send about one a month with all the songs, lyrics, and tour schedule. I put anybody who writes to me or orders on the email list. I write them, not in a "newsy" way, but more like I'm writing a personal letter to a friend. I try to create a sense of togetherness. It's cool that we are all sort of in this together. I really feel that way about the people who have been supporting me.

Newsletters are a great marketing tool, depending on what you include. *Daylle's News & Resources* has many helpful articles, interviews, and information for people in the music industry and has increased my mailing list dramatically. It's now expanded into an e-zine! Sign up for a free subscription at www.daylle.com. I ask people to forward it to others and they do, because the info is valuable. Jeff Price advises:

> Think through a newsletter to decide what you want in one, and make sure it's not annoying or stupid. If they're thoughtful and provide information that a person who signs up for it would want to receive, with links for access to things they care about, then they're very useful.

If you do a newsletter, especially at first, try to include some helpful info that folks will want to share. As your fan base grows, it can be more about you and your music. Philip Antoniades advises:

> The key is to develop and nurture the connection between you and your fans. Your fans have to care first. Then you have to send something of relevance. You know your fans best, and your fans may know your market (future fans) better than you. If you don't have a clue, ask your fans. They love to help and want to be a part of your success. Employ your fans to turn their friends on to your music. Give something away in every newsletter. Do something trackable so you can measure the result. If your own cause is getting stale, pick up a cause your fans are interested in.

Getting Your Own Website

A website is the hub for branding your label and artists, where folks can get info and hear the music. When people want to check me out, I send them to my website. Tony Brummel (Victory Records) says, "Your website and Internet presence are definitely part of your overall branding." As people find your site, they become familiar with your label. When there are reviews and radio play, potential fans can go there for more info and to hear music. As an artist's name gets around, people check out their website to learn more, get photos, check their tour schedule, etc. David M. Bailey says:

> My website has been a monster for keeping the whole thing afloat. For an independent performing songwriter, there is no better tool than a website. My site is a command center for people who want to know what's going on day to day. My newsletters are posted on there. I have my treatment history for folks interested in where I've been medically, all the albums, and how to order them. I make sure new photos are posted.

Many artists opt to just use MySpace as their website. I firmly believe you need both. As a journalist, I find MySpace harder to navigate when I'm looking for specific info. Many professionals don't take artists without their own site as seriously. Eric de Fontenay, founder and president of Music

Dish LLC and publisher of MusicDish & Mi2N (www.musicdish.com, www.mi2n.com), believes there are many reasons that justify the expense of having one:

> For one, it is something you own. No one imagined that sites like MP3. com (the original) and Riffshare would disappear one day, but that is exactly what happened in the dot-com bust, which left many artists that were solely dependent on those sites stranded from their fans. Secondly, it's all about perception. Anyone can put up a MySpace page and upload some MP3 files, but professional musicians invest in a storefront. In addition, this is where industry professionals should be able to find high-resolution pics, your professional as opposed to fan bio, all your reviews, etc.

There are inexpensive options for having your own site. Musician Chris Vinson created Bandzoogle (bandzoogle.com), which allows you to build your own website and update it yourself, all with no knowledge of HTML. It's geared to the needs of musicians—very quick and easy to use and priced fairly. Check out the site for more details. There are many inexpensive web services at www.godaddy.com, including web hosting. If you want to be a serious label, be serious about your website!

The most professional direction is having your own domain name on your own domain. With the Internet becoming so popular, many names are taken. Register a domain name that's as close to the name of your company as you can get. Many online companies will let you easily search names and register the one you want. Godaddy.com is super cheap and great to use!

Creating Your Website

Word-of-mouth referrals are best for finding a website designer. Compare prices, quality of work, etc. Or use a service like Bandzoogle. If your budget is limited, try to find a student who wants experience and a reference. Tell fans you need help. Someone might do it for you.

A website should have many dimensions. Since a page on a computer screen is flat, its content should give it depth and make it interesting to visit. The home page lets visitors know who you are and what you offer. Content should be clearly laid out as a road map to the rest of your site. Study how others present information. Decide what folks might find interesting about your artists. I asked Philip Antoniades what mistakes musicians make when creating their websites. He says:

> They are too complicated for their own good. Musicians need to ask themselves, what am I selling here, and why are people coming here? Then make sure you create only the amount of content that you can keep current and up-to-date.

A good website gets info across in a creative style that's simple and clean. Don't distract visitors with too many graphics! Look at sites for similar musicians or labels for ideas. Make yours reflect the music you release. As it's being designed, decide objectively if you'd enjoy visiting it if it weren't yours. Ken Weinstein (Big Hassle Media) advises making sure you have "links to retail, news info, tour dates, and fun things (links, fun photos, films, etc.) that add dimension to the band's personality." A news section has updated info about your artists. Have very visible links for people to contact you and to order your products. Don't forget a link to sign up for your street team. Ellyn Solis (Vermillion Media) says it's most important to have:

> Accurate information. I see so many artists that spend all of this money on Flash players and all kinds of fancy bells and whistles and then forget completely about accurate content. Remember, websites should be updated daily for new news about your band, new photos, new information. Fans love the close contact of a website, and the more intimate you can make it, the better—make the site feel like you are having a one on one conversation with your fans.

Fans don't come to stale sites. Update release dates, tour dates, reviews, photos, etc.—regularly! Fans stop returning to the same stuff. Either learn how to update it, or find someone who can. Let fans of your artists know what's needed. You might find a free web person! Dick Renco (Trout Records) says, "As soon as we list a tour date on our website, ticket sales start happening and record sales pick up in that market." Panos Panay, founder of Sonicbids (www.sonicbids.com, more below), emphasizes:

> It's critical to keep your electronic press kit current. Most artists don't realize that things like where they're playing, press reviews, and biography updates are as critical as their music when it comes to how

they present themselves. Invest some time in the way it looks and in the pictures you put up. All these things make a difference.

Audio clips are important. You'll attract new fans by letting them hear your music. Have samples of songs or the whole album available. Your call. Ultimately, it's about the music, so let visitors hear some! Have MP3 files of songs handy in case an opportunity comes your way. Eric Speck (Ace Fu Records) advises:

Never post MP3 clips on your website. It's so annoying. Just post the full MP3. Some bands put too much on their sites. People forget that what makes art and music interesting is a little bit of mystery, which the Internet causes the decline of. People give so much information it can become boring and unimaginative. Get creative with what you post, and sometimes hold things back.

Put up fun photos and videos of your artists—of their most recent performance or playing in their downtime. Change them frequently. Make each artist's page personal, with blogs, and stories from the road or recording sessions that change often. Some sites have contests and giveaways. Juni Fisher (Red Geetar Records) finds her website helpful:

My website is an Internet business card, so to speak, and most important, a place online where someone can go see a photo, see recommendations, reviews, and show schedules in the privacy of their home. There is no sense of obligation involved in a website; they have not asked you for a press kit and CD—to me there is a degree of obligation to "get back to you" when they ask for that—and they can revisit after thinking about what they have seen. I have an Internet store there, and it accounts for a small percentage of my sales but allows buyers who may be coming to a show to look over the titles and songs without the pressure of standing at the CD sales table.

Consider having a message board. It builds a community and allows fans to feel like part of something. They can do anything from discussing feelings about the music to finding someone to go to a gig with. Fans who meet online meet in person as they follow their favorite artist. Someone in Germany and someone in Ohio who love the same artist can connect through message boards. Loyal fans link to each other and create momentum. As they post messages, others want to know about the artist. All of a sudden people are talking about your artist around the world, and you've done nothing except cater to fans who get the word out. Creating a community feeling motivates fans to support your artist and spread the word. Robb Nansel says:

> We have a very active web board so people can talk with each other. It's a community. People keep coming back for that. We sell our stuff. We do preorders on our site and ship two weeks before street date.

Let fans know how to buy your music! They shouldn't have to search for a way! CDBaby is a favorite place to sell music among indie labels. CDBaby's founder, Derek Sivers, brings his musician's mentality into its operation. He explains:

> CDBaby started because I was selling my own CDs and had a credit card merchant account. I told my friends that were selling their CDs by check or money order that I could process credit cards for them. I never meant it as a business. It was a hobby that became a living. I was a full-time musician. The last time I had a day job was in 1992. Now I get a thrill building something that helps thirty thousand musicians make their music.

CDBaby gives you your own web page with sound clips (just send the CD and they do the rest), a link to your own website, reviews, and all the text you want. You can sell physical CDs and they can also get you into Digital Stores. Most online stores are nonexclusive, so you can sell elsewhere, too. If you have a bar code, many report sales to SoundScan. The more Internet exposure, the bigger potential for sales. Chapter 20 has more details on selling music digitally and how to get onto popular selling sites. Whether you set up sales on your site or direct visitors to other sites, make sure people know how to buy CDs, digital downloads, and merch. People may be inspired to buy when they visit, so make it easy! Passionate fans become more passionate when you cater to their needs.

Getting Visibility for Your Website

Your website won't mean jack if only you and your friends see it. Put its address onto everything you give out—CDs, press releases, business cards, and your MySpace and other social networking pages. And, it's very important to put your URL in the tagline of all emails you send. This is a BIG one—make sure that any URLs you send in an email have the full address so that they arrive ready to click on. I get so many in emails starting with www and often get annoyed at having to cut and paste it. They must be hyperlinked! Make it easy for people to just click! For example, www.daylle.com often must be copied; http://www.daylle.com can be clicked. When your site is being designed, ask about getting metatags embedded so your site comes up in searches.

Dan Zanes says, "I made sure that my website was listed on all the websites for kids. Someone did it for me. He used metatags." The Internet gives indie labels more opportunities than ever to compete with larger ones on a more equal ground. We all have the same shelf space on the Internet! Since I believe in promoting online activities in real life, too, give out the postcards I discussed earlier, with your URL included, at gigs, to invite new fans to visit. Leave them in stores.

Online Media Support

More and more people in the media are checking artists out online. Often they don't want to talk to you when they want a photo or more info. It's easier if they can check out the artist first. Press releases get sent and tours get booked electronically. Therefore, it's important to have a good press kit on your site. Make it appealing to those who might write about or book your artists. Include a bio, tour schedule, an assortment of photos, quotes, links to press received, and whatever else could entice someone to write about, book, or promote your artist. As was said earlier, editors like being able to grab high-quality photos from a site. A good press release lures editors to download stuff without contacting you. Even if you have a press kit at Sonicbids (more below), it's good to have press info on your own site, too.

A resource that can save tons of time and help you to target the most appropriate sites faster is *The Indie Bible* (www.indiebible.com)—a directory of almost every useful music-related site on the Internet. It has resources for developing an online presence—the only comprehensive directory of Internet sites. Besides online-only magazines and radio stations, it also has sites for many that aren't just online. And, on- and offline contacts are included. According to its publisher, David Wimble:

The Internet offers thousands of places where today's recording artists can gain exposure for their music. There are hundreds of online vendors that will sell your CD, several thousand Internet radio programs that will play your music, and an endless number of online webzines that will review your music. Your music can now be available to the public twenty-four hours a day, 365 days a year!

There are many powerful music websites that can increase sales and get people to your site (more in Chapter 21). If a good music site or magazine wants a CD, send it. *The Indie Bible* provides info about each site to help you target appropriate ones. If you can send material and music electronically, even better! If your time is limited, recruit people from your street team to search for you. Don't send random CDs to every site. Research to find the best for your needs. If you have an announcement, send it in a press release to Mi2N (www.mi2n.com), a music industry news network that lists news from the music business. It's free!

Sonicbids

I mentioned Sonicbids above but must devote more time to this worthwhile resource. I spoke to its founder, Panos Panay, about why it's such a powerful tool and how it can best help artists. Panay says:

Sonicbids is the matchmaking site for bands and people who book or license music. We make it possible and easy for these parties to find out about and connect with each other. And hopefully do business. My mission with Sonicbids is to empower a middle class of artists to make a living out of what they do best. We have about 130,000 bands from about one hundred different countries. This year we had over sixty thousand gigs take place through the site.

Panay wants Sonicbids to be a destination site where any band in the world and anybody looking to book or license music can go and find out about each other and connect. Musicians aren't judged before being allowed to join. Market demand determines who gets selected. Panay wants people to have equal access and opportunity. Sonicbids offers many opportunities to find and submit to gigs all over the world. Many festivals and other venues only use musicians who submit through the site. To use it properly, Panay advises having a goal. He explains:

You can't just go into Sonicbids and willy-nilly submit to hundreds of listings that we have. You'll spend a whole lot of money, end up being very disappointed if there was no strategy behind what you went after, and be rejected. Have a plan instead of arbitrarily submitting. Do you want them to in close proximity to you? Do you want to expand your reach beyond coffee houses and clubs to play other kinds of gigs? Are you interested in licensing your music? Find some information about the venue. Go to its website. See who they've booked before. Make educated decisions instead of knee-jerk reactions to something that seems cool or thinking that if you submit to one hundred of these, your chances of being selected are a hundred times more. Be willing to deal with rejection as part of life. Make sure that after you submit through Sonicbids, you follow up with them. Don't rely on a mouse to do the job after you submit your electronic press kit. Too many people submit to a listing and don't follow up by any other means.

Panay says they have an active community of bands on Sonicbids. The average one does twenty-eight shows a year, all over the world. When you join, you can set up an electronic press kit in their format. Promoters love listing on Sonicbids because it's made simple for them. Panay adds:

We make it easy for artists to submit to venues in a standardized, organized format. It's very easy for them to manage all these applications online, as well as share the applications they get with different members of their team. All submissions go to what's like an email inbox.

CHAPTER 20

Digital Income Streams

S elling music digitally has opened many more doors for selling music. But you have to go through them to take advantage! Everyone wants to be on iTunes, but there are lots more sites that sell music. Take advantage of all that you can. Most aren't exclusive, so you can also sell directly off your site while still having them with iTunes, etc. John Robinson (Shaman Work Recordings) advises, "Know that the digital music revolution is here, so learn it, indulge in it, and be a part of it now!"

Leveling the Playing Field

The playing field for independents has leveled, and then some. The majors lagged behind in taking Internet activities seriously, while indies worked it with a vengeance. Now the opportunities have caught up! Bill Werde (*Billboard*) says:

> *Promotion and distribution in the digital age makes a much more level playing field. If I had any musical talent, I could make my own recording now for less than a thousand dollars. It could sound pretty good with inexpensive technology and recording. I could distribute it for virtually pennies. I could promote it on a MySpace page for free. These are huge opportunities for artists who once relied on the almost banking system of the major labels*

to invest in a career in order to get off the ground. They don't need that anymore.

I see several reasons for believing that indies have an advantage online. Major labels have much larger bottom lines than indie labels. While everyone prefers selling whole albums, indies benefit more from selling single songs. The majors are used to the big marketing budgets and big sales from having physical distribution into stores. You're all equal online! John Robinson says:

Digital Distribution has put the power back into the independent artists' and labels' hands. It allows you to put more focus and efforts toward online marketing. Marketing and promotion online can be more effective in this digital music revolution era and also less expensive. It is very important to corner your market online via email blast/list banner ads on popular related websites.

Majors are focused on selling music. Period. Indies work harder on building their brands and nurturing fans. And fans are the best engines for driving people to buy music online. So the tools are there. Jeff Price (Tunecore) agrees:

At this point, artists are creating their own music without the need for a major record label. They can do it at home and don't need to physically release product now. In the old days, music was discovered through commercial radio, television, and print magazines. The major labels were the gatekeepers to these media outlets. For example, if you were band, you couldn't just take a video you made to MTV and get it played. You'd need a label to deliver it. Now, anyone can broadcast themselves on YouTube. The barriers have dropped significantly. Everyone has access to distribution. The cost is minimal. If the barrier to entry is gone, the cost reduced to almost nothing, and marketing and promotion can be done online with no up-front overhead, there's no reason why anyone who creates music should not take advantage of the worldwide distribution component. There's very little risk. If you can scrape together thirty bucks, where is the harm? The online world has a much greater reach than the physical world. Now you're in digital stores where people anywhere can buy your music and read your blog.

Many musicians worry about people stealing their music. It does happen. But fans will want to support you. They also like having the artwork. John Szuch (Deep Elm Records) reassures:

> Although there's a lot of free downloading, I think there's a group of people that understand that's theft and they shouldn't be stealing the cheapest form of permanent entertainment and will still buy music. We've done well digitally. We do a decent amount of digital sales.

Independent labels are definitely getting active in today's marketplace. Will it last? Things change fast in this industry. But at least for now, Ryan Kuper, who began Redemption Records in 1990, says:

> Like many industries, the music business goes in cycles. Independents, with their ability to develop artists and quickly incorporate technology, are assuming leading roles again. I imagine, in time, many will be purchased by companies looking to replicate their success on a larger scale, but for now, they are in a sweet spot! Indies are certainly better off than their major labels counterparts who pushed a dying medium with an antiquated form of marketing. With the overwhelming amount of choices facing modern consumers, you must find your niche and develop it. Indies were always quick to identify those niches.

Protecting Your Rights Online

With all the great stuff happening online, it's easy to forget about legal issues in pursuit of exposure and sales. If you're active on the Internet, which you should be, talk to your lawyer and see if there are any legal concerns for your situation.

SoundExchange (www.soundexchange.com) represents the new revenue streams for recording artists: performance royalties from Internet, satellite, and cable radio services. John Simson, executive director of SoundExchange, says this revenue stream grew from approximately $3 million in 2000 to $140 million in 2007. And it's increasing with the growth of Internet and satellite radio services. Currently, SoundExchange represents over 31,000 recording artists, 3,500 independent labels, and the four major label groups.

SoundExchange collects and distributes royalties to performers and sound recording copyright owners, which is different than ASCAP, BMI, and SESAC, which collect for songwriters and music publishers. It takes its cost from the collection of royalties and distributes the rest to performers and record labels. The law requires that SoundExchange divide performance royalties between copyright owners, featured performers, and non-featured performers as follows: 50 percent to the sound recording copyright owner, 45 percent to the featured artist on the sound recording, and 5 percent to background musicians and vocalists on the sound recording. Simson says there's been progress on behalf of digital rights. He explains:

> Until recently, performers in the United States had no right to receive royalties for the public performance of their work. That changed in 1995 when Congress passed the Digital Performance Right in Sound Recording Act. This law is limited to digital, cable, and Internet streaming and U.S. performers do not currently receive royalties from over-the-air radio, as do performers in the rest of the modern world. SoundExchange and twelve other organizations have formed the musicFIRST coalition (www.musicfirstcoalition.org) in an attempt to get legislation passed to provide a terrestrial performance right for performers and sound recording copyright owners.

Stephanie Furgang Adwar, Esq., advises being careful once you get into promoting and selling music on the Internet. Ask your lawyer to make sure you have all the digital rights needed from your artist to avoid getting into a sticky situation. She explains:

> If you're setting up a site where the music will be or where you're releasing music, there are all sorts of issues with putting up other people's music, even if they're signed to your label. Your agreement has to have provisions in it that allows you to use the artist's music today, to sell digital downloads, place it on other people's websites, and so on. You have to make sure you're not using the site in a way to exploit music that you're not allowed to. Often indie labels go to other companies and make contracts with them to put the music up on their sites to sell. Your lawyer should make you aware of what that means for you as a label. You need experienced counseling from someone that knows these issues.

I'd like to assume that all music lawyers would automatically include terms in all artist agreements that cover all digital issues, but I've learned never to assume anything when it comes to business and legal matters. Ask before you give the contract to your artist.

Selling Digital Downloads

Digital marketing makes selling music easier. It also allows your promotional efforts to be tied more directly to sales. Eric Hutchinson says:

> The Internet has taken all the guesswork out of buying an album. Perez Hilton put my song on his blog with a link to iTunes, so someone could discover me and become a fan within a half hour. I've also gotten a decent amount of printed press. When you read an article in a newspaper, you think it sounds interesting, make a mental note to check it out when you're in a record store, and probably don't. Many things make it fall through the cracks. With the Internet, someone tells you about an album, you look it up immediately at your computer, listen to it, and download it in a few minutes.

Ryan Kuper (Redemption Records) says, "It's tremendously important to have good digital distribution. You cannot rely on physical anymore, as that segment dies a little more each day." There are many stores online and services to get you on them. They've evolved in the last few years. Jeff Price started Tunecore after running spinART Records, which he cofounded, for fifteen years. He saw a need for a more realistic model for labels and artists to access digital distribution. Price saw less and less music was selling, yet it was everywhere, and he got an idea:

> I thought, the music industry is doing well! It's the music-distribution system that's not doing well. So instead of making money off the sale of music, I'd help creators of music achieve success by giving them the products and tools to do that at an equitable price. The business model for physical distribution still applied to the deal terms. Telling people you were going to take a percentage of their money for each song sold makes no sense in the digital world. You deliver a file once via an Internet broadband line through a virtual server. Why should a company make an unlimited amount of revenue off

the sale by taking a back-end fee? In the physical world you have a [large warehouse. There are many other expenses involved]. It makes sense for a distributor to take a share of the money. But none of those expenses exist in the digital world. Why should that company get an unlimited amount of money off of each sale? So I thought I should reinvent the wheel and just do a fee-for-service model. You pay an up-front flat fee, the music gets distributed, and there's no back end. You get all the money. There's no exclusivity.

With Tunecore, you can choose what stores you want your music in and pay a small fee for each. They do have an annual administration fee. You can be in just iTunes or as many stores as you want. CDBaby offers a different model. There are no fees for members and they take a small percentage of each sale. Deciding which model to use depends on how many digital sales you expect. If you sell a lot, using a fee-only service may make more sense. But if you won't sell many at the beginning, you might be better off with a service that just takes a percentage of sales. Think about it carefully but do get digital distribution from one of the services. Digital does have its advantages! John Szuch says they're selling out their CD stock and switching to only selling music digitally. He doesn't think it's changed essentially how they market a band, except there's no returns! He adds:

We're still in contact with magazines and other media outlets. All the digital sites are helpful, too. It's kind of a changing of the guards versus a whole new world. There's many new digital media services that we send things to for reviews. Those have pretty much replaced all the zines that used to be out. Magazines are going away while other stuff is popping up to replace them. It's a new format of marketing but not radically different from the way we do it. Essentially, what we're trying to do is find people who would appreciate the music we love so much; people who will write about it whether it's on the web or in a print magazine or on a blog. It doesn't make much difference to us. We want to get out there, share this music, and make people aware of it.

Labels are concerned about people buying singles over albums. It is a strong pattern, but successful indies accept it. Kelly Vandergriff (Five Times August) says, "For so long, record labels put out albums with one or two

START & RUN YOUR OWN RECORD LABEL

good songs and the rest filler. I understand people just wanting to buy their favorites. For us, it has definitely been helpful." Rich Hardesty says he has eleven independent CDs and doesn't expect his fans, especially new ones, to buy them all. He says, "I like that they pick and choose a greatest hits roster of their own. Technology makes that an option." And Juni Fisher (Red Geetar Records) adds:

> Digital sales is a small increments of my sales, but I have found that sometimes someone buys one song and then a few minutes later buys the whole album via download. It takes no work for me to sell a download and no pressing a CD and having to ship it out. While it is not a big moneymaker for me, it is another tool to gain momentum in some markets.

CJ Baran (Push Play) says, "We were in the Top 100 of iTunes for the first two weeks when our first album came out, which is pretty unbelievable for a grassroots effort. Goes to show how helpful the Internet has been." Using a digital distribution service means promotion is up to you. Rich Hardesty does cross-promotions and marketing aggressively online. He says, for example:

> I have a jukebox on MySpace. I also have links to CDBaby. I send out a mass mailer and say, "Go get the new Rich Hardesty track fresh off the burner." The coolest thing about this is that the CD isn't even out yet but I am marketing it with one of the songs and making money at the same time. I still sell lots of CDs, but 90 percent of my Internet sales are coming from individual downloads.

There are suggestions for digital marketing and promotion on the Tunecore site. Price recommends creating iMixes as a way to attract people to your music:

> An iMix is a playlist of songs that anyone can make, give a title to and put into the iTunes music community, as long as the songs are available to buy at iTunes. Put together a playlist of ten or twenty songs, with three or four of your own and the rest by more popular bands in the same genre. Give it a really cool title. Then when people go to, say, the Led Zeppelin page on iTunes, they'll see iMixes there that feature songs by Led Zeppelin. If they click on the one that has your songs, too, people are more likely to discover

you. iTunes has a feature that's called Publish to Web. Once your iMix is live in iTunes, you can click Publish to Web and copy and paste the HTML code that iTunes gives you and post that playlist anywhere.

Many labels prefer to have a stronger distribution system, and there are many options. Kuper says indie labels have innumerable choices for digital distribution:

You can lock up with a solid distributor or handle accounts directly. iTunes still has the lion's share of the digital market. Napster, Rhapsody, and eMusic are great subscription-based companies. Beatport undeniably has the best electronic music and also offer higher-quality files for premium prices. There are many good subscription-based companies as well as mobile platforms to sell through. I use a company, IRIS, that deals with over 450 digital retailers in over seventy-five territories. It would be too time-consuming to deal with them all myself. They leverage their relationships with retailers to get my releases featured placements. That obviously helps sales. They work my releases in coordination with other promotional elements (press, radio, online, etc.). That model is no different from what a physical distributor did. For some well-positioned labels that can leverage a good deal with a distributor, they will keep the largest retailers as direct accounts and utilize the distributor for handling the multitudes of smaller retailers and mobile partners.

John Szuch prefers to sell directly off his own site. He likes the flexibility it offers, explaining:

We're selling downloads directly from our store. You can change your pricing, do sales or bundle deals. A bundle deal is a new concept we've been working with. You can't do this on iTunes or other stores like that. When buyers come directly to Deep Elm, we can sell six digital releases for $29, as opposed to the person spending $9.99 six times. We can offer you the tracks on the hardcopy CD plus a couple of bonus tracks. Artwork and complete lyrics for everything in our catalog are always available on our website. It's very important to me to always have the lyrics available. We won't put up a band unless we have complete lyrics for each song.

The technology is there to have a digital store directly on your site. Philip Antoniades (Nimbit) thinks it's the best way to go. His company, Nimbit, allows you to upload MP3s and sell them directly from your site or blog using the NIMBIT OMT sales widget. It also allows you to sell e-tickets. He advises:

> The silliest thing I see is when a musician does a great job of marketing and drives a customer to their website only to send them off to iTunes to purchase music. The hardest part was getting the fan to your site, now you send them away to buy from another place and you'll never get to know who the fan was? Be available wherever fans may shop, but when they reach your site, sell direct! Don't ask your fans to go to one store to get your tracks, another to get merchandise, and another to get CDs. They can all be sold easily through one store direct from your website.

Another company that can help you sell digital downloads on your site is Echospin (www.echospin.com). Cofounder Jon Lowy says you can set your own price, make your own rules, and keep fans as your customers. They have you send your album and artwork and choose what to charge for it. Echospin gives you back a simple link to place on your website, your emails, etc. Lowy says:

> When a fan clicks your link, the Echospin Delivery Wizard installs itself in seconds. Without needing to leave your environment, the Wizard lets fans preview all your tracks, collects payment, and then automatically downloads the music to their computer, saves it to their music folder, burns a CD, copies it directly to their iPod (without going through iTunes), and even prints out the album artwork and launches their default music player. Echospin only makes money when you make money and charges a lot less than Apple. You set the price, and Echospin charges a low flat fee for each sale you make. They collect payment (using their secure, built-in e-commerce capabilities), deduct their fee, and remit the rest to you. They even do free weekly Nielsen SoundScan reporting.

Echospin also allows you to sell your album on your MySpace page. As with all the sites I've mentioned, technology is growing and changing daily, so keep checking the websites to see what new and improved tools get developed.

Online Music Licensing Opportunities

In Chapter 15 I suggested creating a revenue stream from licensing music for use in a variety of media outlets. Even if you have no contacts, you can begin immediately after you have a finished recording if you tap into places that allow you to post music where people looking for music go. Remember, wherever you hear music played, there's a good chance someone is getting paid for it. For example, Trusonic (www.trusonic.com) licenses music to companies who have music playing when they put you on hold during a phone call, etc. The opportunities can be endless!

Online music licensing marketplaces, such as Ricall (www.ricall. com) and Pump Audio (www.pumpaudio.com), allow you to connect with people who need music content and have your music considered for licensing opportunities. They're both nonexclusive and don't take any rights to your music. You just give them the right to license it on your behalf. Ed Razzano, vice president of business development (North America) for Ricall, says:

> Ricall has a searchable database with independent music writers, producers, and record labels, as well as major label people. People with all categories of music can come to us to put their content up on our website. Music can be searched for by content, genre, year, instrumental, tempo, keyword, lyrical content, and almost any other combination. We work a deal with each content provider. Because of our agreement with the performing rights societies, we have to insure we have deals in place with the content providers, granting us those rights, etc. It's nonexclusive. The beauty of our system is it's all computerized and tracked. We can tell the musician how many searches their music comes up in and how many people listen to it, even if it didn't get licensed. That can help the musician see how much interest is in their music. We mainly take whole catalogs or an album, not one song.

Razzano says people who need music content like using this service because if they don't know the creator of music they want to use, or are a smaller entity without the ability to clear a song, they simply click a button and Ricall clears it for them. If they hear a song they want to use, they can download it as well. People often need music fast. If an editor is doing a session and finds the perfect song on Ricall, they can download it immediately and put it up against picture to see if it works with the visual. Ricall's system makes it easy for them to get the tracks they want, fast. Razzano says there are good opportunities for licensing besides film and TV. He explains:

> I think a lot of corporate stuff wants to just use a piece of music that inspires. They don't necessarily want a hit song or to go through the rigamarole of trying to find out how to license it, etc. There's also a big market starting to develop from what's called webisodes. They're sort of television episodes that exist on the Internet but also have a little bit of an advertising slant to them.

Another company that offers great online opportunities for licensing music is DMX (www.dmx.com). For over thirty-five years, they've provided music, video, and other services to some of the most identifiable international brands and a variety of services, including music-programming services for satellite and cable television networks in the U.S. and Latin America. Christopher Harrison, vice president of business development for DMX, says:

> DMX is now the only business media provider capable of delivering branded music content to commercial environments, private residences, and directly to consumers' cell phones via over-the-air downloads, personal computers via streams or digital music downloads, and via preloaded portable media devices. By enabling cross-platform consistency, DMX's commercial customers can effectively integrate their branded sound into their consumers' lives, delivering a uniform and branded experience wherever and whenever consumers want it.

Harrison says that DMX sits in between businesses that need content to differentiate and distinguish their brands and artists and record labels that want to expose their content to as wide an audience as possible, with compelling opportunities to both artists and labels. They create playlists for in-store play for many well-known stores, including H&M, Nike, and

Pottery Barn; restaurants, including Hooters and Olive Garden; and many other places that play music. Many of their clients are on the DMX site. He explains:

> For established artists represented by record labels, DMX is able to help promote artists through brand associations, such as the recent promotions involving All American Rejects and American Eagle Outfitters and the Pussycat Dolls and Mandee. Record labels that do not currently have a relationship with DMX and wish to have their music exposed to the millions of consumers who enjoy DMX's music through thousands of commercial establishments should email DMX's licensing department at legal@dmx.com. For unsigned artists, DMX provides a unique platform to be heard. Currently DMX has unsigned artists playing in thousands of businesses across a variety of genres, from country to dance to hip hop and beyond. Importantly, DMX pays unsigned artists just like represented artists whenever their music is played. Unrepresented artists who want the opportunity to be part of DMX's commercial and direct-to-consumer services should visit DMX's unsigned artist service Get U Played (www.getuplayed.com).

DMX also launched Sonic Tap (www.sonictap.com), its own D2C digital music service that delivers thousands of playlists for all occasions and situations organized by genre, style, and theme. Rather than relying on complex but unreliable computer algorithms to recommend music, each playlist is crafted by one of DMX's professional music designers to blend together the right music experience for any occasion. By now there are a lot more technology advances. As of this printing, they were working on making songs from their playlists available as digital downloads. Check out the site and see what you can take advantage of!

Getting visibility for your music online can also help you get noticed by someone looking for music. Music supervisors who cruise MySpace, Facebook, CDBaby, and other sites known for having lots of indie music have found many songs. Razzano suggests:

> Indie artists are more accessible now than they ever were. With sites like MySpace, those who need music have access to someone who lives in a small town with great music. And direct contact with them! A music supervisor can build a relationship with an artist this

way. The online networking places offer instant access to music. The Internet in general is an inexpensive way to market yourself. I think the days of mailing a CD are pretty over. You may want to mail [music supervisors and other people who use music] a postcard directing them to your site.

Mobile Promotions

With mobile devices improving and offering more services, having one has become the norm, rather than the exception. Therefore, the demand for mobile content keeps increasing. Selling ringtones can be a good revenue stream. More important, having your music on people's phones is a great source of promotion. There are ringtone companies, like Xingtone (www.xingtone.com) that allow you to have a ringtone store right on your site. But, it's only worth doing if you can sell a large number, to offset the monthly fee. They do allow you to give away fifty free ringtones a month, at no cost to you, so that could be something you use to reward your street team members or as incentives to buy your album. Whichever way you choose to go, make your music available for ringtones.

CJ Baran (Push Play) says, "All our fans have ringtones of our songs, so yes, it has been very successful and it is *very* easy to set up." Todd McGee is CEO/cofounder of AppliedSB (www.appliedsb.com), a web and mobile-based platform that's all about creating direct relationships between fans and artists. AppliedSB created Groupie Tunes (www.groupietunes.com) and offer indies all sorts of services for fans to get your music into their cell phones. For example, McGee says fans can sign up to get various text alerts from their favorite artists. Artists can send a message out to their whole fan base, or by state, zip code, or other demographics. Or put all your tour dates in at one time and it automatically sends a text message telling fans where you're playing.

Fans can buy mobile content, ringtones, and wallpapers through Groupie Tunes. McGee says if you want to sell ringtones:

You can go to the site, create an account, upload your music, sign online contracts, and start selling that day. Put one song or a whole album on Groupie Tunes. When you upload the music, you can specify the defaults with our ringtone editing tool that lets you cut out the part of the song you want used. What's cool about it is if someone doesn't want the default, they can use that same ringtone editor and cut the part of the song out that they want for their ringtone. You can move the slider back and forth and preview it. What's unique about our platform is when we find out what part you want, it's converted in real time. So an artist can play a song, finish it, upload it onto Groupie Tunes, and text fans to let them know they can buy it as a ringtone. Basically, you can create a mobile fan club. At a venue, you can tell people to turn on their phone, type in your keywords, and they can buy your ringtone right from their phone.

McGee says if you want keywords just call them. A keyword is a short code, an identifier for a track or piece of content. So when a fan texts that identifier to Groupie Tunes, they know which track they want to purchase. It's charged to their cell phone bill. McGee says "the carrier collects the money, they pay us minus their fees, then we pay the label. Ringtones cost so much because the carriers take a significant cut of the transaction, roughly about forty-five percent." There are no fees to get onto Groupie Tunes. They take their fee out of sales. You can put a link on your site, MySpace, and anywhere else you'd like to people to know about buying your ringtones, and it directs fans to your Groupie Tunes page where they can buy your ringtones.

CHAPTER 21

Effective Digital Marketing

D igital marketing offers a plethora of opportunities for marketing yourself and your music. But, it can be hard to know where to begin, and end. The biggest expense of taking advantage of so many opportunities is time. You could spend all your waking hours going onto all the different social networking sites and other avenues of promotion and still not make a dent. To do it properly, make a plan and prioritize your needs. Don't just jump from one site to another, without working anything well. But do find ways to work this new model for marketing and promoting music online. Ansel Brown has been very successful using the Internet. He says:

> *The new model is all about the personal connection between the artist and the fan. With unparalleled access to our fans via the Internet, independent artists are in a better position than ever to connect and build relationships with their fans. If done with heart, it endears us to our fans in a way that artists of the past would have only been able to dream about. We can be as close to a fan that is halfway around the world as we are to one in our own backyard. So, the new model is all about the artist/fan relationship and building long-lasting, endearing relationships like never before.*

Creating an Online Presence

With all the artists and labels vying for online attention, you must work to make your music stand out. It's not enough to just register on all the websites. While there's unlimited space for everyone online, you can get lost in it all. Plan your direction carefully and mobilize fans to help. It's important to brand your name online. The more people see it, the more curiosity can be generated, which leads to potential fans checking you out. Both labels and individual artists should brand themselves. Bill Werde (*Billboard*) advises Googling yourself to see how strong your Internet presence is:

> *If it's not what you like, take a long hard look in your own digital media mirror and ask yourself if you're really taking your career seriously. The first three results when you Google yourself should be your own personal page, your MySpace page, and your Wikipedia entry. If that's not there because you don't have a Wikipedia entry or it's not done well because you didn't take the time to do a MySpace page or you don't have your own URL, if those things are not there in place, you're not taking your career seriously. As someone who judges these things, I must say, if you're not taking your career seriously, why would anyone else? Your artist page should be great. It should have selling opportunities, music, pictures—all the things that are going to introduce you to the world as your calling card online. Your MySpace page should have the same thing—video, music, pictures, and your story. But the Wikipedia page is what everyone kind of forgets about. Yet inevitably it's one of the top three Google results. Sometimes the second. The people who might give you your big break as an artist may discover music in the industry by hearing something about an artist from someone. The first thing they do is Google the artist. If I Google you and can't find information, easy-to-listen-to samples of your music, if I can't get a quick snapshot of who you are and what you're about, and I mean quick, I lose interest. Try to make it as easy as possible for the people who can help you to know the things we need to know.*

I already discussed the importance of having a separate website, and being on MySpace is discussed below. Getting onto Wikipedia (www.wikipedia.org) is something many labels and artists don't take advantage of. You should! Wikipedia is a free online encyclopedia. Many people go there to get facts about a label or artist. Information is submitted on almost every topic. It has millions of articles in over two hundred languages and millions of page views each day. You can contribute to an article, but their team of volunteers must approve submissions before they go up. According to Mark Pellegrini, member of the Wikimedia Foundation's press committee, "Musicians benefit from having a Wikipedia article for the same reason anyone else does—increased exposure."

I like checking labels and artists out on Wikipedia. The format is straightforward and consistent. MySpace can be hard to navigate. Every page is different and varies in the info included. Wikimedia just has facts rather than the hype of other sites. Fans find that appealing, too. They can learn about you on Wikipedia and then go to another site to hear your music. Guidelines for creating an article are on the site. Pellegrini says they're touchy about people editing their own articles and limit them to people or companies considered "notable." Check the website for specific guidelines as to what does or does not constitute notability for a musician. He says they have recurring spats over what is or isn't "notable" enough to have an article. They want to keep to information accurate, so they prefer you not to do your own. Pellegrini explains:

> Just like someone tends to exaggerate (or lie) on a résumé, people are inclined to do so when editing their own articles. To that end, we have a guideline. It says, in essence, be careful when editing your own article. You might just want to avoid it entirely. Instead of editing your own article, we suggest that subjects of articles make suggestions on the talk pages or recruit a neutral party to make the edits. The benefit to musicians of doing this is that it assures that articles on them exist, that they are lengthy and informative, and that they are accurate.

A buzzword online is having something go viral, like a video or album or something about an act. That means word about it or links to it spreads like a virus spreads fast among people. When people like something, they'll pass it on. Jason Feinberg (On Target Media Group) explains:

> Viral marketing refers to the concept of letting fans spread your marketing message to their own networks, effectively doing the promotion for you. It is based on simple human behavior—we tend to share things we like. If an artist can create a compelling asset—video, audio, an image, a game, etc.—and encourage fans to pass it to their own social networks, it can generate a level and

type of exposure that a marketing professional would find difficult (or impossible) to do on their own.

Eric de Fontenay (MusicDish and Mi2N) suggests using your offline efforts to help online promotion. He recommends spreading the word about stations playing your music and trying to drive music requests to those stations and their sites. And you can use airplay to reach out to blogs that cover the station's local scene. Websites are becoming more powerful for breaking and promoting artists. Daniel Glass (Glassnote Entertainment) says, "There's a lot of cool websites. When we go to a conference, people interviewing us used to be radio stations. Now it's radio stations and different websites and social networks that are doing things." Juni Fisher (Red Geetar Records) says:

> *Nowadays we are all easy to find via our websites and a simple search. If someone makes the excuse that they did not know where to find me, they don't really want to find me, because last time I Googled myself, I found dozens of pages that pointed back to my website.*

To increase your profile online, Scott Lapatine, founder/editor in chief of the well-known blog Stereogum advises, "This is a little gimmicky, but if you cover or remix a song by another well-regarded band, you'll immediately be intriguing to that group's fan base." Rolando Cuellar (Roland Entertainment) says having Baby Jay interact directly with fans is very powerful. He adds:

> *They tell their friends and so on. Baby Jay has received emails from fans all over the world. When people here about Baby Jay on the news, in newspapers, etc. they can Google his name, and tons of articles/sites come up regarding Baby Jay.*

Besides Googling yourself to assess your online visibility, sign up for Google Alerts (www.google.com/alerts). Don't confuse this with the Google Alert (googlealert.com) site, which charges fees. You can have an alert for any keywords you choose. It lets you know when your name or the keyword is on a site. Create one for the name of the label, artists, and anything else you think of since it's free. Then get busy giving the alerts more to alert you about!

Planning Your Online Campaign

Create a flexible plan, since nothing stays constant on the Internet. Ryan Kuper (Redemption Records) says the "best" blogs and social networking sites are always changing:

> Those that are hot today won't be tomorrow. It's the nature of the Net. These things come and go. The same may ultimately be true with the digital music retailers, but so far they have proven to be more stable. As of right now, though, I like last.fm, uber.com, and still use MySpace regularly. I also like imeem.com and virb. com. My friends in the UK prefer beebo.com and my Canadian friends facebook.com.

Spend some time checking the best ones for your genre. Use an assortment of sites to brand your artists. It's also important that artists connect to fans. Artists who write back and interact with their fans regularly develop the relationships that fuel careers. Before you begin, make sure you're ready to commit the time. These fans are the ones who mean the difference between anonymity and getting your name out. Kelly Vandergriff (Five Times August) says it's all about repetition and presence, adding:

> The more people see your logo or face and hear the music, the more likely they are to buy it. We are on a ton of sites, from MySpace to PureVolume to imeem to iSOUND, etc., etc. Brad runs all his own pages and mainly just stays connected to the fans. He writes everyone back who writes him, and that means a lot to people.

If people see an artist's name in enough places, they'll eventually click and check out the music. Then the music can speak for you. Jeff Price (Tunecore) suggests that instead of pulling people to your MySpace page, put your media out in places where people can discover it. He explains:

> Nothing will help you more than the organic discovery of your media. By that I mean, put something on YouTube. Put some iMixes up in the iTunes music store. Get your music into last.fm, Pandora, Launch, or any of the other streaming radio services. The best thing you can do is create the media, whatever that

may be—an animated short, a flash animated video game, cover versions. Seed them out in the areas where people go to hunt and discover, as opposed to trolling and pulling in one person at a time on MySpace. Go to the places where you can put your things and hope people find it.

Deciding which sites to place music on and which to get involved in can be time-consuming, but nothing compares to the time it takes to maintain them. I barely have time to accept friend requests on the sites I'm on, no less be active on them. So be careful about how much you bite off. Jason Feinberg advises being realistic about the time you can devote to maintaining your online presence:

It's hard enough to get attention online, but keeping it is another matter altogether. I suggest finding the sites that most clearly hit your audience and maximize their value. Use every function, get involved in any relevant community, post as much content as possible. If you do this in a serial fashion, where you dole out new content on a fairly regular schedule, you can quickly develop a devoted following. The key is consistency; if you cannot deliver on a reasonably regular basis, you might actually end up doing harm by appearing that you have deserted the site. Also, it's important not to aim too narrowly (for example, using only MySpace), but don't try to use too many tools and then have each of them underperform. You have to find a balance where your time allows you to truly maximize each tool.

With all the new digital tools and marketing avenues changing the playing field, indies who have time and fans willing to help them can benefit as much as any label can. Eric de Fontenay says the principal impact they're having, at least for now, is in brand development and fan building:

Social networking sites for example are a great way to "data-mine" prospective fans, otherwise known as friends. Of course, in too many cases, artists stop at just data-mining instead of the real challenge—namely, turning those so-called friends into real fans. But this cannot be done effectively unless you have a comprehensive strategy that builds on synergies between differing digital tools and marketing avenues. If you are not using those tools to have your friends join your fan list, and then don't have a means to effectively manage that mailing list, then you've wasted your time getting all those "friends." The other issue is selecting the right tools and avenues. Each artist/band has different demographic and other characteristics, which will influence which tools will work best for them. And frankly, many of those so-called tools are a colossal waste of time. Do you set up a profile on a new site hoping to grow as it grows, or do you wait until a site becomes established before investing the time and effort? Of course, the tradeoff in this example is that if you start out with a new site, your visibility among the "first adopters" will be greater, while waiting to join an established site will put you in a much more crowded (and less visible) position among the many users.

I asked Mark Redfern (*Under the Radar*) which online promotional tools that artists use have the most impact on him as a journalist. He says:

MySpace really helps, because I can look up a new band I've heard about or read about somewhere, and chances are they have a MySpace page. Then I can go to their page and right away listen to a few songs by the band. So I rely a lot on MySpace. Blogs are good for hearing about new artists. Blogs like Stereogum often hype up exciting new bands before anyone else does, and so they can be a good source for finding new artists.

It's often better to work fewer avenues thoroughly than to do a skimpy job with more of them if you want to increase your profile online. Sean Michaels, founder of the blog Said the Gramophone, suggests not wasting time on mailing a CD to every blog you find:

Figure out which outlets might genuinely be interested in what you do, and then target them directly, personally. Don't be afraid of loosing your music into the wild—word of mouth is what gives fuel to new bands, and the only way to accomplish that is for people to be hearing the songs. Find kindred spirits—others who seem to be swimming in the same river as you, whether musicians, writers, or artists. Those are the people who will respond to what you're doing.

Jeff Price says it's less about sites and more about tools and propagating yourself across the Internet so you're everywhere. He suggests using widgets to make that easier and save time, adding, "reverbnation.com makes a tool that does everything—a widget on steroids." So I asked Jed Carlson, cofounder and chief marketing officer of ReverbNation, to explain how widgets work. He says:

> A widget is simply a "box" of information that is pulled from one website and placed into another. A YouTube video is a great example of a widget. It's a video that can be embedded onto another web page for people to see. ReverbNation provides a variety of music-specific widgets that artists or fans can grab and place onto other sites. We have widgets that are music players that can be customized in terms of color, size, and whether or not you want the music to play when the page loads or play when the Play button is pressed. They can live on other web pages, blogs, etc. We have other widgets that are the artist's show schedule or the "fan collector" that let's people join the mailing list. Our most popular widget is called the Tunewidget and has almost all of an artist's info contained in one small box, including songs, videos, blog, show schedule, fan collector, and photos. This widget is different from most and can be used as an electronic press kit for artists. We have many artists using it as a replacement for their MySpace player, including 50 Cent. The benefit of using a ReverbNation widget is that it can be shared by fans, which creates a viral way for other people to generate exposure for the artist onto other web pages. We track all of our widgets for artists so that they know where their content is spreading and who is spreading it. It's a great way to learn who your best fans are.

Carlson says they started ReverbNation because nobody was making artists and labels their top priority or providing necessary tools to easily develop a comprehensive attack plan for the Internet. Their tools let you take your music to those who might like it, wherever they spend their digital time, rather than driving people to the music. Carlson says their operating philosophy around the office is called "Artist First." They only develop solutions that first help artists. He explains:

> ReverbNation is your home base for marketing and promoting your roster of artists across the entire digital realm, including social

networks like MySpace and Facebook, as well as email, IM, blogs, etc. It starts with a profile page that is tailored specifically for labels. It has a Roster section that provides links and song samples of all of your artists, as well as a New Releases section to highlight the latest stuff. From your label profile you can create and manage all your artist profile pages with a single login. We create free widgets that you, your artists, and their fans can virally spread across the net to friends and fans. We even provide a free email service so you can send customized, targeted emails to the fans of your label or each individual artist. Finally, we track everything for you, including where the music is being played, spread, and shared, so that you can understand how each artist is growing in popularity.

We have tools to promote the label as well as each artist. We make it easy to employ a digital strategy for all of your artists from one hub, without having to log in to multiple accounts to do it. With our tools, a label can easily place music players, show schedules (with interactive tour maps), "join the mailing list" widgets, etc. onto all of the artist's web presences. Once placed, all the label or artist needs to do is update the ReverbNation profiles with new info (like a new song or a new show date), and it automatically updates all of their sites in real time. It's a lifesaver for artists and labels who need to save time so they can focus on making the music.

Bless their hearts! ☺ ReverbNation also has a revenue-sharing program with artists, called Fair Share, and share 50 percent of all their advertising revenue with artists. Carlson says you simply opt in to the program (it's free) and start collecting money based on how much site activity you generate each month. He explains:

We introduced this program in May 2007, long before other sites began tinkering with the idea of sharing their ad revenue. The big difference is that we never attempted to "negotiate" for lower rates with the artists. Because of our "Artist First" philosophy, we have always looked at artists and labels as our business partners. We never even considered giving them less than 50 percent. Sites like last.fm are now beginning to share about 5 to 10 percent of their revenue. In our mind, this is not a proper amount of compensation for the value that their content creates for a site like ours.

What's in the future for this site that's looking out for artists? Carlson says:

We are working hard to build new revenue opportunities for artists by connecting them more directly with brands. As selling music becomes more challenging, artists are going to need new ways to earn money online. It is our belief that the core asset any artist possesses is the relationship they have with their fan base. In the future, they will use the influence they have to make money by carrying other people's messages to their fan base. It is our belief that creating an environment where all artists can receive brand sponsorship will help them earn money from that influence that they have. We are building that environment right now. The key is to give artists many options to choose from in selecting a sponsor. We are going to deliver that for them.

I've found that the people running websites and creating web tools for marketing and promoting music are so much more determined to be advocates of the people they create it for than were people who created musician resources in the past. If all of this gets too overwhelming, and you have a budget, Eric de Fontenay advises:

The truth is that while online marketing is relatively cheap as compared to print or radio, it is extremely time-consuming. So in the end, the best use of an artist's time is in developing a team of specialized professionals that have the network and resources to get things done efficiently and effectively. Just like you need a radio promoter to get real airplay, or a publicist for key print coverage, in the end there is only so far you can build your career online without a supporting team.

Social Networking

Social networking sites have become the sites that fuel fan power. People are on them because they want to be, and music fans want to learn about new music. John Robinson (Shaman Work Recordings) says, "MySpace and Facebook are both very valuable to indie labels as you have a network of millions of people on these sites." From a marketing standpoint, you must be part of them if you want to increase your business. Fern Reiss, a marketing expert who is CEO of www.expertizing.com and www. publishinggame.com, says:

> Anyone who's involved in marketing anything these days needs to be up on Web 2.0, particularly social networking. The smart businesses owners are the ones who are there now, establishing turf and building community; once the larger corporations begin throwing money in earnest at this arena, it's going to become more and more difficult for smaller business owners to play. The different social networks have different personalities—so really, the network you should pursue is the one frequented by your customers. If you're doing traditional/ professional business, that's LinkedIn. If you're marketing to Europeans, that's Bebo. Orkut has captured most of the South American and Indian market. My personal favorite is Facebook, especially for musicians, and I'm betting that that's going to continue gaining in popularity amongst the general population as well because it's among the "stickiest."

Ryan Kuper says, "You would be silly not to maintain a presence on all of the biggest sites. It's free, and a lot of good can come from directly interacting with existing fans and smartly seeking new ones." Eric de Fontenay warns against joining more than four. Managing more could become a nightmare. He recommends looking beyond MySpace:

> MySpace may not be the most effective site for artists. Facebook, for example, is a more effective networking platform if you have a large and active email fan list and is known as a very useful tool in getting people aware of (and attending) events. Then there are niche social networking sites like blackplanet.com or Nextcat (for arts and entertainment industry professionals). Each country also has its leading social networking sites. Demographics may also affect your choice: While Facebook tends to have a younger audience due to its college roots, the average MySpacer is in his/her thirties.

Publicist Ken Weinstein (Big Hassle Media) advises that someone on your team needs to be in charge of keeping the band sites/pages current and active. "It's obviously really important these days. You can't slack." If you just put up a page and wait to be found, don't quit your day job! While people might accidentally find you, it's harder to make headway without putting in the time. Panos Panay (Sonicbids) says networking sites enable artists to create awareness that didn't exist before, but he cautions you to temper your expectations about what these "friends" mean. Jason Feinberg says a devoted fan base can be developed on almost any sizable social network, adding:

> The key is to truly become part of the community, not just promote to the community. Find users that share an interest, and get involved. It doesn't always have to be about music. Quite often hobbies and other lifestyles lend themselves to a certain genre or style; get involved with those groups and a fan base will grow organically. It also doesn't hurt to get yourself in front of the promo people at those sites in hopes to get featured placement—that's the most effective promotion tool on any social network.

Reiss advises zeroing in on what's going to provide the most payback for you and your business. Learn about the personalities of the social networks, and play them accordingly, unless you have lots of help with them. She adds, "Then, be sure you keep up with the groups you've created. Build this in as a regular part of your marketing strategy." Don't just join sites—get involved. Eric Speck (Ace Fu Records) says that for a while, MySpace stats were important. But now that so many artists have big ones, it's your online presence in your community that matters most. He adds:

> You should definitely be visible on Facebook and MySpace. You can go to random people who really aren't interested in your music just to bring up your numbers but that doesn't mean much anymore. There's no point to it. Focus on strategically using MySpace, and stop wasting time with people who aren't interested in your music. Only send a bulletin when you have something real to announce. Don't do it for trivial things. Getting a song licensed to a TV show is something people might want to know.

As of this printing, MySpace is still the most popular for musicians. John Szuch (Deep Elm Records) says he thinks MySpace is essential for any band because everyone assumes a band is on MySpace. Many of his bands rely on MySpace as a way of contacting their fans.

He adds, "You can listen to songs by the band, see photos, and forward the page to friends. It's always available online. All those social websites are essential for marketing your artist." Kelly Vandergriff credits getting onto MySpace early as a big help. They've sold over 100,000 downloads as of this printing. She explains:

> Brad started Five Times in August 2001. There was a site called MP3.com. It was a pre-MySpace site, only for music, though. Fast-forward three years to 2004 when MySpace started taking off. Brad joined that, bringing his MP3.com fans with him. Getting on MySpace early is why I believe he's always in the Top 10 artists. He was on before it was saturated.

Publicist Ellyn Solis (Vermillion Media) advises nurturing the relationships that start on these sites:

> The best way to spend time on those sites is to really appreciate the people who are your "friends" and consistently communicate with them. I love the blogging aspect on these sites, and for music artists, the possibilities are endless, especially if you tour. I think Push Play's site (www.MySpace.com/pushplayrox) is a great example of a band maximizing the social networking aspect of a site. Even if your music is nothing like theirs, take a page from their "playbook" and notice what they are doing right on this site. They are independent artists, but have built a very high profile in a very crowded marketplace.

I talked to CJ Baran about Push Play's site. He says his mom wanted their MySpace page to be different from any other pages out there. Their site stands out, and fans flock to it. He explains:

> She wanted all the fans to interact as much as possible, and I agree. That is why I am on MySpace for many hours daily. Some of the fans think I'm nuts, but I feel that while we are in this grassroots stage it is sooooo important for us to reach out to every fan who wants to connect. So I plug away. And it has helped us dramatically. We have fans everywhere wanting to come see us in concert, so we are going on the road and perform our hearts out in every state. Next year we plan to make it a global tour.

Our first stop is Asia, because our Asian street teams have been phenomenal in attracting fans. They are all so much a part of our lives now.

Baran has worked the fans, and they're working for Push Play. It's important to have a good MySpace presence. When people hear about music they might like, most look for it on MySpace. Eric Hutchinson has also made good use of MySpace. He says:

I use it to send bulletins to let people know about my touring schedule. I don't do many friend requests. I do like being able to do a show and get responses afterward, to see what people thought of the show. I can tell how well a show did by how many comments I have the next day. I don't mention it anymore. Fans seem to know that they can go to MySpace and get in touch with you. I'm thinking about getting onto Facebook, too. It's easier to navigate.

Ansel Brown has rocked MySpace. He views it as his conduit to the world and to music lovers in particular. By valuing his friends, he's turned into what some call a phenomenon on MySpace. Brown says it's just connecting at the friend/fan level, almost face-to-face:

I call them my "true friends," a term a friend came up with a while back when he said I was being true to my friends on MySpace. I look at MySpace as part of my job as an artist, so I spend a lot of nighttime hours answering messages from every friend. I cannot tell you the number of people who can't believe I actually write and listen to them. They become instant true friends when I do. I also found that my blogs on my children's work helped me connect in a very genuine way with my friends. My true miracle blogs get a lot of traffic, and they are spoken from my heart, so friends see more in me than just the music. I seemed to have a "busy"-looking site because of all of the comments I was getting, and the fast surge in song plays on my player all started getting me attention. At that point I started to communicate with other artists that had already been to the top of the music charts. They seemed intrigued by my quick success. Then publications, country music Internet sites, and radio stations all started regarding me as an up-and-coming artist. It was really amazing—the only thing

I had done was start the page, give it a good professional "branded" look, and I was suddenly legit.

Music journalist Jim Sullivan says if he's interested in a band he'll go to their MySpace page to get a taste by listening to the songs and reading the written material to determine whether he's interested. He adds, "MySpace has become pretty common currency—the easiest way to get a quick fix on a band." If Sullivan is interested in a band, he'll request a CD. John Robinson says "The best way to be effective on MySpace is to be consistent with blasting bulletins, leaving comments with banner ads that click back to your site, and definitely have all the information on your page easily accessible." John Szuch agrees:

If you have your MySpace page together, send out weekly updates, ask friends to share banners with people, and ask fans to forward your emails to someone else—that's the kind of fan base you want to create. That takes a lot of patience. We send out weekly emails to our e-list to let people know what's going on and send bulletins on MySpace. Our bands frequently keep in touch with their MySpace pages and their websites.

Rich Hardesty says he meets people from all over the world on MySpace. He reads their profiles to learn about them and sends messages to begin a dialogue and often sends an MP3 file. When he's at a venue, he enjoys when people say they're on his MySpace page. Hardesty sees his MySpace page as a website with extra bells and whistles and has used it to create a fan club and promote his gigs. He explains:

When I have a show, I go to the browse section and type in the zip code near the venue. I can choose from five to ten to fifteen or more miles from the venue. I click on new people and ask them to come to my show. It is amazing how receptive someone is if you just strike a convo. I usually put them on the guest list if they are new to my music. I post banners on MySpace each time I have a show. I post it on my own comment section, and send it out to all of my friends and ask them to do the same. Each person on MySpace who wants to get involved is a member of the fan club. For example, I send out a message to all: "Who has an idea for a design? Who would like backstage passes for a show coming up. If so, tell me who

I toured with in '06 on Jäger Tour and be the fiftieth MySpacer to respond and win." I recently did a concert at Ball State. I asked for people living in Muncie to respond. I gave them free tickets to the show and a double-disc live show. All they had to do was post flyers around campus. The show was packed. The sky is the limit when it comes to a fan club on MySpace. MySpace is a fan club. You can make something happen with very little effort. If a fan has you on their top friends or using your song as their default song then they an active fan in the club; it's a domino effect, especially if you have a good song. If no one is using your song for their default, write one that they can't refuse.

Eric de Fontenay suggests, "For a tour or show, focus on driving attendance by giving a special door discount to your MySpace or Facebook friends, for example." Don't be discouraged if you can't do everything to work the networking sites. There are benefits to at least making an effort. Juni Fisher says that MySpace is fairly new to her. She's just been using it a few months but has already seen beneficial results:

I have used it to search for and communicate with bookers for clubs and house concerts and have been able to reconnect with some old friends I had lost track of over the years. I also use the search options to gather up folks in parts of the country where I'll be playing. I post whatever show is coming in my "Juni Fisher is . . ." section. And it has worked!

While MySpace offers great benefits, don't overlook Facebook. John Robinson says, "It's all about networking with the college students around the country who are in tune with the genre of music you are dealing with and keeping them in tune with what is new." Fern Reiss advises getting involved in Facebook by making friends, joining groups, and when you get comfortable there, start your own group. She explains:

This is the easiest way to grow a mailing list, and, if done correctly, your numbers will grow exponentially. You have to be careful with social networking—it's a community, not an advertising forum. You can't post messages that are too market-y, and you have to allow others—even, sometimes, competitors or detractors—to post. But if you maintain a high-quality group with good content, and moderate it judiciously, you can grow a list faster via social networking than by almost any other method.

Second Life

Jeff Krantz is an indie artist who successfully created a huge buzz on Second Life (secondlife.com), an online site that allows him to do virtual tours. He created a huge fan base and ended up in *Newsweek*, without leaving his apartment. Krantz explains:

Second Life is a virtual, online world, run by it's own users. It's a giant digital universe where you can do almost anything you can do in real life, but in a virtual form. I have used Second Life as a way to connect with people from all over the world and develop a fan base in the tens of thousands who come to listen and watch my live virtual performances.

Krantz says he spent hundreds of hours at his computer learning just the basics of Second Life. Eventually it got easier. He's known as Hep Shepherd, explaining:

Second Lifers choose their character's first name but must select a last name from a list. Mine is Hep Shepherd. I met a woman named "Through Thesewalls Moody" who was buying herself a virtual cocktail dress. We started talking, and she wanted to hear my music, so I sent her to MySpace. She fell in love with one of my songs and immediately offered her help and support. We consequently developed a friendship in Second Life, and she took it upon herself to get me my first virtual show. In seven months I played almost two hundred virtual shows. Moody has never missed one! She promotes me, communicates with my fans, and books me gigs. I've spent hundreds of hours networking and developing relationships with other people in Second Life and was featured in a full-page Newsweek *article, covering my music and performances in Second Life.*

Second Life allowed Krantz to stream live performances to people and also communicate with fans and venue owners in ways he couldn't before.

He says tens of thousands of people from all over the world have come to his shows and have contact him directly about his music, all though the in-world IM system. He says:

> It helped move me beyond the standard musician-fan model as I have developed real friendships with a large number of supporters. It's like having ten thousand friends calling you asking, "Dude, when is the album coming out?" They are so supportive and feel a part of my success. As I release my debut album, I have a huge amount of preorders just from SL friends.

Krantz says the key is still in the music. If your songs are good, people want to hear more:

> Second Life doesn't guarantee you fans, but it does put you in front of 10 million people who are usually willing to find out who you are and what you are all about. Whatever happens after that is up to you!

Promoting Your Videos

Once you have a video, get it out online. There are many places to post it. Eric Speck recommends:

> There are a lot of options besides YouTube, which is the Holy Grail of getting a video onto a mass-media forum. You can get online features and things seen and started without an onerous marketing budget.

YouTube is a community that allows people to watch and share original videos on the Internet. With a camera and creativity, you can post one on YouTube and get people excited about your music. Jennifer Nielsen, marketing manager at YouTube, adds, "People have the opportunity to upload and share videos with people around the world and connect with a new audience." Like MySpace, the competition for attention is fierce. But if you have great music and can make an interesting video, it's worth taking advantage of this expanding promotional tool. Rich Hardesty says:

My fans love to see me jamming on my guitar up in the mountains of Jamaica with a Rasta man. Or watching my husky pull me on my skateboard, while playing the guitar. I also post location videos. There is a place up in Malibu in the mountains, a helicopter landing spot where I sing and videotape. I like diversity and don't just post myself singing songs on stage. Music is my life. Life isn't always on stage. But my videos show that everywhere I go, music follows.

Post your video on whatever sites you can. Let everyone know about it with emails and announcements at gigs. Encourage fans to forward it. Like everything else, you have to promote it to get it going initially. If people like it, they'll forward it, and it can become viral as each person sends it to more. Nielsen advises putting tags on videos to help users find the content they want to watch. "Bands should use keywords that best describe their music to help people find it." You can go to videos for musicians in your genre that have a lot of comments and invite people who might enjoy yours to view it, one at a time. There are also communities you can join. Nielsen recommends:

It's important to become a part of the YouTube community and understand what is happening on the site. Watch videos, subscribe to your favorite channels, participate in discussions, and upload entertaining content. This is the best way to become a part of the community and help yourself rise up. Members of the community watch, rate, and share videos on YouTube. We have an editorial team that chooses the videos to be featured.

YouTube has become a live calling card. When you're booking gigs, send promoters to your video to see you in action. It saves money on having to send out DVDs. Ken Weinstein adds, "MySpace is a great outlet for videos as well." Post on YouTube, get the code, and embed the video on your MySpace page so friends can put links on their own pages. Make sure to include contact info so you're easy to reach. Video director Steve Penta (White Light Productions) says:

A beautiful thing about videos is that they do get out, and access to them isn't limited. It starts with turning some people on to the band enough to do the YouTube search.

John Robinson suggests if your budget allows, outsource to a video promo company to launch a full-blown campaign. Otherwise, if you get a camera and are super-creative, you can post videos that get people excited about your music. Ultimately, if your fans like the video, they'll start the process to get it out to others who might enjoy it. As each forwards it, your profile increases. Nielsen advises, "Just get on the site and start creating videos that express your creativity and personality. You never know what will become a viral hit."

Why not yours?

Blogs and Podcasts

Blogs and podcasts are becoming influential for helping break music. John Robinson says, "They are some of the biggest ways music is being promoted and shared online. MP3 blogs and podcasts are definitely great for marketing, as they provide a free and inexpensive source of online marketing." You can make your own for your fans, promote them to potential fans, and also try to get into popular ones that others create. Ken Weinstein says:

> It's less about one or two resources and more about multiple impressions. Obviously a great review on Pitchfork is desired, but you can't plan for that. If Stereogum or Brooklyn Vegan pay attention, you are in great shape. But there are hundreds and hundreds of blogs and webzines, and they should all be serviced.

Be somewhat selective in which ones you approach with your music. John Szuch says, "Larger blogs and podcasts are effective, so many people contact us every day. It's hard to support everybody." You may need to begin smaller and work your way up, just like with print magazines.

Pursuing Blog Attention

Jeff Price says, "MP3 blogs are replacing music magazines as a form of discovery." More and more music fans subscribe to them. What distinguishes an MP3 blog from other blogs? Sean Michaels, founder of Said the Gramophone (www.saidthegramophone.com), says, "MP3 blogs write about music and share with their audience some of the music they're talking about. It's the Internet equivalent of your friend telling you about

a new band, or new song, and then giving you the song to listen to."
Jeff Price adds:

> An MP3 blog is an online diary. They tend to write about music
> and usually have links to the music they write about. Blogs are about
> niches. People troll the Internet to find the things they're specifically
> interested in. Do a Google search for MP3 blogs or about your genre
> of music and see what surfaces. Then email the person who writes it,
> introduce yourself, and attach an MP3.

Eric Speck advises, "You need to know which blogs are for which genre."
Jason Feinberg recommends MP3 blogs as having tremendous power for
getting artist recognition:

> Hardly anything markets music better than the music itself. It's
> even sweeter when someone whose musical taste you trust suggests
> it. And then it gets even better when that blog is considered a
> tastemaker—basically saying they have credibility. Everybody
> wants to be the first to discover and introduce others to a great new
> band; MP3 blogs give this power to any fan with good ears and an
> Internet connection. Some people are reluctant to give their music
> away via MP3 blogs, but the example I give over and over is about
> ice cream—I could describe a new flavor of ice cream for an hour,
> or I could simply give you a little spoonful. Which do you think sells
> more ice cream?

There are many blogs. Some have more recognition than others. I asked
Scott Lapatine, founder/editor in chief, of Stereogum (stereogum.com)
why he thinks it's become so popular? He says:

> We are lucky to have started when we did. I first blogged as
> Stereogum in January 2002, when the blogosphere was young,
> MP3s were gaining a lot of traction as a viable format for quickly
> distributing music to a wide audience, and easily shareable online
> video was in its infancy. Dedication was key. I treated it as a
> job long before it became a full-time career (though that wasn't
> the goal when I started). Of course, given that Stereogum was
> born out of my passion for discovering and sharing new music, it
> was only natural to devote a lot of time to it. Also important was

consistency—in style, grammar, design (this is more important than you think), and editorial focus. I wanted to be taken seriously and wanted the audience to understand what Stereogum was about.

Many people see top bloggers as the new wave of music industry A&R people. When blogs like Stereogum or Pitchfork recommend a new artist, people take notice. Gossip blogger Perez Hilton (www.perezhilton.com) told me he's actually negotiating to start his own record label through Warner Bros. because of the impact he and his blog have had on music. Like Stereogum, he began his blog for fun. Hilton says he never thought anything would come of it, and it took on a life of its own. He loves being able to allow people to know about artists they never heard of before, explaining:

> *It's inspiring. I'm so passionate about music and am thrilled that I get to put good music out there to the Universe. I'm not gonna put stuff up that's crap. There is no Payola Perez. I only post things that I love and enjoy and am passionate about—that I think is worthy enough of my website. I like to think of what I do as having an opportunity to share. And my readers have the opportunity to receive. I mention musicians almost daily. The response I've gotten from the music community has been the best. The music actually is what I'm most passionate about in life. I'm not passionate about what's going on in Lindsay Lohan's life, but I am passionate about music. I think even the cynics, or the haters, or whatever you want to call them, have grown to maybe not like me but at least respect me as someone who more often than not has an ear for good music. I love that because I love music. That all started organically. I never started mentioning music thinking that I would possibly get a record deal from it or that I would be filling concerts or that I'd do anything music related. I just did it like everything in my life—it just happened organically. I thought, "Let me start mentioning bands or artists or musicians that people aren't that familiar with, or they are but that I love and want to share with the world." Sometimes it connects with my readers, sometimes it doesn't.*

When the music he posts does connect, the artist can score a home run. Eric Hutchinson says a friend sent Hilton his music. Then she called Hutchinson and asked for some MP3s because Hilton liked it. Hutchinson's sister read this blog, so he thought it would be cool for her to see him on it. That was the extent of his expectations. He checked the night before and thought it wasn't going to get up. Hutchinson says:

> When I woke up there was one of these night-and-day differences. I was bombarded with attention. People who hadn't called me back were returning my calls. MySpace jumped to close to sixty thousand hits that day. Within the day the album jumped to #7, having not been in the Top 100 before that. I reached out to Perez to thank him, and that started our friendship.

It all begins with good music. Hilton says, "Eric Hutchinson really connected with my readers. He went from nowhere to #7 on the iTunes charts. It was really amazing." When you can get the attention of a good blogger, you get introduced to a bigger audience of potential fans. Search blogs out and study them to see which would be appropriate for your music. Matthew Perpetua, writer of Fluxblog (www.fluxblog.org), says, "I post one or two MP3s every day, and each MP3 is accompanied by a review. The site is pretty focused on the writing, really." Each blog has it's own style and flavor. Michaels says:

> Most music blogs suck. Their writers are chasing traffic, posting the same stuff as everyone else, with gratuitous tour dates, puff pieces, and cover songs. Said the Gramophone tries to avoid all that. We try to do just one thing and do it well: to write with spirit about the songs we love. Our writing can be weird, precious, nonsensical, poetic, or terrible—but we're just trying to find a vocabulary for the way music shoves and sways us. We were one of the first sites on the Internet to post music by people like Arcade Fire, Beirut, Feist, Miracle Fortress, Clap Your Hands Say Yeah, and Yeasayer. But more than anything we focus on songs, not bands. Not on discovering the next big thing but on discovering the next small thing—the next awesome four seconds of your life. And then writing about it with spark and spirit.

You don't need to only get on the very big blogs to make noise. Perpetua says:

Blogs can be really powerful on a small level, especially if the reader finds that they share the taste of the critic and are willing to try things they wouldn't ordinarily go for because they trust the writer's judgment. On a larger scale, I think blogs are more powerful in aggregate, but when that happens, it's really more of a word-of-mouth phenomenon that has little to do with the individual writers.

It's easier to get recommended on blogs when you take the time to understand them and what you're up against. Lapatine explains:

We are a national outlet covering lots of genres and can only devote so much space to unknown local acts. Discovering young, indie acts will always be key to our mission, but your band needs to be special for us to bring it to the readers' attention. I think most musicians who write in understand this, but at Stereogum we get hundreds of unsolicited requests a week to listen to someone's band. There is no way we could listen to everything, so the pitch is important. Keep it short and personal. If you are going to mass email a big group of bloggers, it makes it easer to ignore you. You'll want to mention what other bands you sound like; that's sort of a no-brainer, but it could be the reason I click over to your MySpace page.

Hilton says he's a firm believer that good songs should get you instantly, from the first second you hear them. He explains:

That's how it works with me whenever I post something. When I hear something new that I post, it's a song that I instantly liked. There's no convincing me. Sometimes a song does grow on you, but that's just because you're conditioned to it, because of radio. For example, the new Madonna song has grown on me, for a minute. But I wasn't the biggest fan of it when I heard it, and I'm still not the biggest fan of it. But now I hear it so much, I can get into it.

When you understand what each blog wants, it makes it easier to determine which ones to pitch. Pitchfork is considered another of the gold standards that people try to get involved with. Ellyn Solis says:

The best way to work Pitchfork is to forge relationships with every freelancer that is listed on their site. It may sound hard, but they have so many wonderful journalists that contribute to the site that it is in your best interest to get to know what kind of music they all individually like, and then if your stuff fits, you know you are sending your music to an interested party. Also, they launched Pitchfork.TV, a great outlet for music video of all stripes.

I asked bloggers what gets their attention. Perpetua says, "They should be very good, and hopefully a bit different from everything else going around. I mean, there's no one way to do it." Hilton says:

I hate checking MySpace now. Usually what works now is someone sends me an initial email saying to check out this artist. I'll respond back, "Email me a few songs." Recently I've been even more specific. I tell them to email me MP3s, because sometimes people send other formats and I have to download them. The thing about getting MP3s is you can preview them in the email. And if you don't like it you don't have to download it. It doesn't have to clutter my iTunes, and I don't have to download songs I don't like. That's my process. Send an initial email with no more than three songs. Obviously it should be the best three or the best one. I listen to every single thing that's sent to me. If I don't like the first song in the first ten or fifteen to twenty seconds, I'll listen to the second song. Then if I don't like that one, it's 50/50 that I'll listen to the third.

Lapatine wants to know why you think Stereogum specifically would like you. Do you read their site? Why are you a good fit for it? He explains:

If I get the sense that I'm reading a generic pitch going out to every music website, I'm less interested. And again, with so many pitches coming in, I only have seconds to decide whether to act on your request. The best way for an unknown artist to get the attention of a big music site is to first get the attention of a small music site. There are great homegrown music blogs that we read regularly, and perhaps that blogger receives fewer pitches or covers a specific scene that you fit in. Start small. Another good thing to do is become an active member of our community in a meaningful way by contributing consistent intelligent commentary, and get to be known that way. Then when you eventually pitch your band, we'll recognize you from the thousands of anonymous people who send in tips.

Generic pitches are a big turnoff. It's so important to send personal ones, letting writers know you're pitching them for a reason. And make it easy for them to access what they need! Michaels says:

One of the best, cheap things an artist can do is to create a "secret" press page at their website—just a plain, simple single web page, with no embedded videos or flash or anything. Just briefly introduce the band, give a couple of single-link MP3 downloads, and a link to where the whole album can be downloaded as a .zip if we'd like to hear more. Become familiar with our blog; we have three writers, each with different taste and style. Then you can write to one or two of us—either send us a CD in the mail or a link to that page. Make your note succinct and helpful—we don't need the press release, the "sounds-like" faff. We'll be judging you based solely on what we hear. Show us that you know our site and think that your music fits in; if it feels like a blind mass mailing, it probably won't make it into our headphones.

What mistakes do artists make that turn writers off? Lapatine says:

This sounds obvious, but make sure you get the name of our site correct. This happens all the time when bands copy and paste the same message to multiple outlets (sometimes it will result in the first line of your email being in a different font than the rest, which is a giveaway). Also, if you are merely pretending to be a regular reader, we will see through it. We get a lot of "Hi. I love your site, especially [Second Post on the Homepage]." Also, don't randomly promote your band in the comments section. It's spam, and disrespectful, and we will never listen to your music if you're trying to hijack the discussion. Also, no email attachments. Instead send a link to a your website or MySpace page or a direct link to an MP3 hosted elsewhere. Do not sign us up for your newsletter, or even worse, a regular email blast that doesn't even have an unsubscribe option. Make your personal pitch . . . if you don't hear back, try again in a few months. Don't email and ask for a snail mail address. I get way too many CDs, and I don't even listen to them. There is no reason you need to send a CD these days. I am less likely to listen to a CD than online audio; I am pretty much glued to my laptop all day.

Each blogger wants something different so check before sending. Perpetua hates when people send him overly elaborate packages for their CDs and hates feeling like you're wasting your money on unnecessary things. He advises, "Release a steady stream of new music—give people something brand new to write about as often as possible. Also, be a little mysterious. That always helps." Michaels says he has no interest in MySpace pages, explaining:

I don't listen to music by sitting and staring at my computer screen, watching the song stream. Send me a link to somewhere I can download a song, maybe with a short blurb about what your band's all about. Don't put the MP3 as an email attachment—we get literally hundreds of these each day, and attachments are an enormous burden. Give us a link to where we can download an MP3 or two or a zip of the whole album. Yousendit.com is fine. Even better is if you send us a physical copy of the CD.

Hilton advises you to work hard and get a gimmick, adding:

By that I mean be special. You can't be mediocre. Be unique and sound like nobody else out there. What I love about people that I love is that they have a very specific unique sound that makes them different. No generic crap. Try to find the people you can really trust, who will not be afraid to criticize you and will give you really good advice, Even with my closest friends, if I don't like a song, I tell them. I also give them very constructive criticism. Making music is a very subjective art form. If you want to be successful, you need to manage expectations and know what you want to get out of things and why you're doing them.

While blog coverage can really help put fuel into a career, it's just one piece. You must work everything you can. Eric Hutchinson has kept the momentum going. He says there's been a steady, trickle down from Perez and other blogs, but he's still pursuing his touring passion, explaining:

> *Besides Perez, I have a lot of other blogs that I show up on. I subscribe to Google Alerts and see them. My plan, which has been to tour, didn't change much. I tour a lot and create my own buzz. My manager calls it making friends door to door. I believe in that. You've got to go to each city, play the shows, and meet the people face-to-face. That creates the real bond. I'm interested in making long-term fans, not just the ones who download my songs because everyone else is doing it.*

Making Your Own Blogs and Podcasts

Some artists create their own blogs and podcasts. Blogs are written; podcasts are audio. They can be boring or a great promotional tool. Jason Van Orden (www.how-to-podcast-tutorial.com), author of *Promoting Your Podcast: The Ultimate Guide to Building an Audience of Raving Fans* (Larstan Publishing), advises:

> *As a musician, your lifeblood is your fan base and the relationship you have with them. One of the most powerful tools that I know of for attracting new people to your music and turning them into loyal fans is podcasting. Podcasts allow you to regularly connect with people in a powerfully intimate way that is extremely cost effective. As they hear your voice, look into your life, and experience your personality through the podcast, their connection to you is solidified. This connection is what brings them to your concerts and gets them to tell others about you.*

Creating blogs and podcasts can be time-consuming, along with the other gazillion things you must do online. My blog, Lessons from a Recovering DoorMat, seems to eat up all my free time. I advise blogging only if you enjoy it. If it feels tedious, it will be a tedious read, and you won't have readers! I enjoy writing mine, and readers feel the vibe. If it's fun, it can be worthwhile. Podcasts can be a personal connection with your fans since they hear you. Ellyn Solis adds:

I believe wholeheartedly in the power of the blog and the podcast. If you have time, it is never wasted to have an RSS feed available with an interview and some music for distribution and also an up-to-date blog on your website and on your MySpace page.

Everyone has their own opinion. Podcasts don't seem to be as helpful and accessible as blogs, says Jason Feinberg:

Podcasts can be a useful tool in getting eyes and ears on your music, but they can also be difficult to leverage. The medium itself allows for great promotion, especially on podcasts that utilize video and web links. The challenge is finding a podcast that has a sizable amount of listeners in your target audience and then convincing them to include your material in an episode. There aren't a lot of somewhat-successful podcasts—most either have a lot of listeners or just a few. The ones that have a lot of listeners naturally have many other artists pitching for coverage. Any time a podcast uses your material, it's smart to request they include a call to action—telling fans where they can find you or where they can find a free download of the song they just heard. Otherwise, you don't see a lot of results from just getting played one time in one podcast.

Be prepared to put some time into creating and promoting any blogs or podcasts you make. You've got tons of competition and must separate yourself from others so people notice yours and subscribe. Find an angle. Just talking about your music over and over can be boring. Recommend other music. Say or write about something unique and special. Come up with a very catchy title. I get many curious visitors because of my Lessons from a Recovering DoorMat title. People want to know what it is, and since I have good content, many stay. You have to give potential subscribers something they want. If you have a huge base of diehard fans, maybe they'll just want to know some personal details of your day-to-day activities, but it's better to give more. Van Orden adds:

A blog is a powerful tool that makes relationship building fun and easy. This tool helps you cultivate a relationship with your fans with minimal cost and effort. And as an added benefit, it helps you attract new fans as well! A blog is much more than the typical news page or online journal. It allows readers to comment on each entry (or post). It creates a "feed" that readers subscribe to for free to automatically receive the latest updates. Blogs are also a magnet for search engine traffic. Most of all a blog is a current, fresh, and personal conversation between you and your fans. It's easily consumed, linked to, and shared.

Link all blogs and podcasts to your website and social networking pages and in the tag of all emails. Register with blog and podcast directories. iTunes has the best one for podcasts, according to many experts. There are many more ways to promote, get keywords listed in search engines, and other technical things that I unfortunately don't have room to include here. But there's a world of resources available. If you decide to blog, I highly recommend subscribing to the posts at www.problogger.net. Read the archives like I did when I started mine. It's a wealth of free info. Its writer, Darren Rowse, has a book now, too, with many of the tips—*Problogger: Secrets for Blogging Your Way to a Six-Figure Income* (Wiley). Is it worth it for artists to write their own blogs? Jason Feinberg says he encourages all artists to actively blog, including using audio and video:

> *These days, we don't promote music as much as we promote an experience. Of course this includes music, but it also involves artist interaction. Blogs and other online tools have allowed artists to give a sense of transparent access to the fans, when in reality it is technology that is doing the heavy lifting. Blogs give an artist the opportunity to display alternate sides of who they are, and fans can react instantly and directly. This holds especially true when artists use video to take fans behind the scenes, on the road with them, or give them additional glimpses into their offstage lives. Fans so desperately want (demand, really) to see this, and if you aren't offering it, another artist surely is.*

Internet Radio

The Internet offers many online radio stations. Is it as helpful as regular radio? Jeff Price says, "Last.fm, Pandora, Launch, AOL, and Streaming Radio, have replaced commercial radio, to a big degree, for music discovery and sales." Ellyn Solis adds:

The jury is still out, but we work with a lot of Internet radio outlets. They really try to get good music on. I won't give up on it because I feel like it is completely the wave that is coming next. Between podcasts and Internet radio, it is really the only place people can go to hear new music. Regular mainstream, terrestrial radio is so homogenized, edited, and canned that an independent artist doesn't stand a chance of getting attention there, so any other outlet is helpful.

Eric Speck thinks streaming radio will become more and more popular, explaining:

Once iPods have streaming radio as an option, I think it will become more and more powerful. A lot of the Clear Channel stations are making their online sites a priority and developing online communities. Everyone is looking ahead to the digital scene grow. It's where people are looking to find and consume music.

A big advantage of Internet radio is there's room for all good indie music. Most don't discriminate between indie and major label music, so it's a good place for your music to speak and attract fans. Jeff Price says a lot of people listen to them. "Pandora is editorial. They don't let everybody in. Last.fm does let everybody in and has a much wider and bigger listening audience. There's also AOL, Yahoo, iLike, and more." John Robinson adds:

Internet radio is highly effective and will continue to become more effective at a rapid rate. Internet radio is boundless; it takes away all the guidelines of broadcasting limitations. As the digital music revolution continues to grow, so will Internet radio and so many other things.

One of the most popular Internet radio sites is Pandora (www.pandora. com). Its founder, Tim Westergren, says his passion was always music. He began his career as an independent musician and created the Music Genome Project™—an enormous collection of songs that are analyzed, one by one, along close to four hundred musical attributes by a trained musician. Music is broken down into its most basic components—every element of melody and harmony, rhythm, and instrumentation. An analyst gives a number to each attribute, and they make up a song's musical fingerprint.

I've created many stations on Pandora and have discovered lots of great new music. After registering, you can choose an artist you like and the Genome creates a personal radio station of many similar songs. They don't all sound alike. It knows what other music I'd like by the artist I enter. Westergren says, "When you type a song into Pandora, we look at that song's music fingerprint and connect it to other songs that are its nearest musical neighbors. Since the Genome is blind to popularity, you hear a ton of music on Pandora that you've never heard before." Not everything can get on. Westergren says the only criteria is the quality of the music:

> We consider the Genome a curated collection. We use about 30 to 40 percent of the stuff we get. Our team analyzes about fifteen thousand songs a month. We have to work to find those. The majority of music is not ready for prime time. I celebrate people who make music, but our job is to deliver radio stations that people will come back to and listen to over and over again.

Pandora isn't a social networking site like the others. It's just about listening to music. Westergren says commercial radio plays a very tiny amount of music, over and over again. Pandora plays the music of about 45,000 artists. Why try to get your music on Pandora? He says:

> The beauty of how the playlist works is that it's completely blind to popularity. Once a song is in, Pandora doesn't know if the artist is well known or not. So you're just as likely to play as a hit artist who sounds like you. On an average day, we have about a half million plays per day. About 97 percent of the songs in our collection play every day. So it's very different than commercial radio. No one artist would get a massive bump like an artist on regular rotation on commercial radio. But when Internet radio is fifty times its size, I think it will give birth to a musicians middle class. That excites me the most about it. When it gets larger, it will be an extraordinary promotional channel for musicians. We see anecdotal feedback from musicians that Pandora is having an effect. They may see a spike in iTunes sales. We did a survey, and people who use Pandora are

buying 50 percent more music than they did before getting on it.
That's a monster change!

There's no fee to put your music on Pandora or to create your own radio stations. Westergren goes around the country holding town hall meetings to talk about Pandora. He says people of all ages thank him for helping them discover new music that appeals to them. Every genre is represented, and music from the past and present is there. Right now is the time to get involved with several online radio sites. Stake your presence before they get more saturated with music. It's a lucrative, free resource for getting people familiar with your music.

CHAPTER 22

Some Advice from the Pros

This final chapter has advice from professionals who've been there and done it. They know how hard it can be to start an independent record label and how satisfying it is when you can do it for a living. Learn from them and others in this book to find your own way to satisfaction in marketing and promoting music successfully.

So much of your success will begin with how you approach it in your mind. This business is very competitive and can be tough. I was warned to be wary of everyone and to go after my goals at all costs, but I didn't like that mindset. I'm very spiritual and believe that what you give out, you get back. So I brought that belief into my world within the music industry and met the most wonderful people, and they gave me enormous support. I highly recommend not losing yourself, your values, and your integrity in pursuit of creating success. You truly can get everything you desire while having a spiritual mindset in the world of business, including the music industry. Or maybe especially here! My book, *Nice Girls Can Finish First* (McGraw-Hill), has specific suggestions for women based on the lessons I learned when I ran my label. I got taken seriously while still being nice!

There is a whole chapter in *I Don't Need a Record Deal!* called Mental Independence for a reason—you need as many tools as you can get to navigate all the emotions that fear, rejection, disappointment, and being ignored can create. Don't neglect YOU in the process of running your business. People may try to discourage you. You'll have disappointments. Some folks may let you down or even screw you over. Stay on a positive course with positive expectations. Succumbing to words of gloom and doom will bring you gloom and doom. *Expecting* to succeed gives you the best shot at success. I believe with all my heart that your thoughts create your reality. Make yours confident, successful ones! Just make sure you have GREAT music to market!

Henry Ford said, "Whether you think you can or you think you can't, you're right." Why not be right about making your label a business that sustains you and the music you love? Read on for more advice from the pros.

Daniel Glass, Founder, Glassnote Entertainment

If you don't know the one through ten, find people that do. A lot of people who want to start a record label have talent or great taste. So know what you're good at, but, more important, know what you're not good at. Surround yourself with a good business team, so you don't go out of business. And pay your bills, because your reputation can go like that! The other part is knowing what to do with it when you get something good. You have to get it on radio, into stores, and get your act on tour. And you have to get paid. Surround yourself with a great team. I surround myself with bright people. Knowing what is not a hit is a talent. No one knows what a hit is. Get financial resources or align yourself with someone else.

Ingrid Michaelson, Founder, Cabin 24 Records

You can't expect anything, but that doesn't mean you shouldn't try really hard. Put your music in as many places as possible, and align yourself with artists that you like. I have a great community of people in New York and a great community of people in L.A. It really helps to have friends who you think are talented. Everybody looks out for each other and helps everybody out. Write music that's really from you and not what you think other people want you to make. That's what happened with my first record. I made songs I thought I should make.

El-P, Cofounder/Recording Artist, Definitive Jux Records

Figure out why you want to start that label. Have an idea behind it. If you can't figure out within an hour why you want to start a record label, without the answer being "because I want to make money," don't start a record label. You're gonna fail because you're not gonna have what it takes unless you have a lot of money. There is a new generation of kids that came out of our little industry that isn't going to be so susceptible. There's a difference between fame and happiness and a modern-day trick of combining the two— the rare and elusive combination of being financially stable and being happy. It's a long-term plan, and not many people are willing to stick around for the long-term plan. You need patience. I have the word tattooed on my arm. Somebody, somewhere, has to eventually not want the buy-out and actually do what they set out to do or were destined to do. It's hard. We're getting the offers for the buy-out. I spent my entire career being offered major label deals, and I have not taken one. We put a record out ourselves that we made in our house; we did the artwork on our kitchen table. We were eating off of that record for two years. Once we realized that, the whole perspective changed for us. It became the license for me to actually follow this line of thinking.

Jay Woods, Senior Vice President and General Manager, New West Records

Be clear and realistic in your goals. It's an inside job. You have to ask yourself what are you really willing to do. You can't expect anybody to do it for you. You have to do it yourself. Dig deep and say, "What lengths am I willing to go to?" And expect the same from your artists, especially if they're developing artists.

Jonatha Brooke, Founder/Recording Artist, Bad Dog Records

Learn by the seat of your pants. You can only learn by putting your butt out there and taking big risks. I've learned if you don't take chances, you get nowhere. If you take chances, you're gonna lose your shirt, but hopefully it will come back at some point. It's worth it.

Sue Baran, Manager, Push Play

I always look to this one saying: "Never say die." The saying has kept me on the straight and narrow and has allowed me to plow through adversity. When Push Play performed to crowds of only fifty and they were a bit depressed, the saying always spewed from me. That with "going the extra mile" has helped me to achieve many personal goals and has helped Push Play to do the same. Luckily all five of us have the same mindset. That's why the recipe is so delicious. The sky is not the limit . . . there is no limit. Pursue, pursue, pursue. Get your hands dirty and your feet wet, and enjoy the journey, because that is really where the success is! And when you think you have made it, then pursue, pursue, pursue, all over again.

Damon Dash, Founder, Roc-A-Fella Records

Learn the business—exactly what you're entitled to. You have to have your business correct. Be knowledgeable of it—know when you're getting jerked or when somebody's trying to pull something where it's not as lucrative for you as it is for them. Get with some talent that you're 100 percent confident in—where you love them and are willing to invest everything in it. If you feel this way, then don't let anybody tell you anything different. I knew Jay-Z was the real deal. No one could tell us to change this or that. The reason we were so focused is because we were so confident.

Jeff Price, Founder, SpinArt Records and Tunecore

Understand what you're getting into. Identify your goals and objectives, and figure out the best path to get there. The worst thing you can do is not have a clue about what you're doing and go into it hoping for the best. You'll trip all over yourself.

Eric Speck, Founder, Ace Fu Records

You don't get into the music business to become rich. You're sometimes gambling on your passions and your taste. Sometimes it runs counters to what good business decisions require. It's a really tough balance. But that's the indie spirit—put out a record and figure it out. People always say they wouldn't know how to start. Just do it! You'll learn as you go.

Eric Hutchinson, Founder, Let's Break Records

Before you do anything else, absolutely make sure you really love it and are doing it for the right reasons. The American Idol *thing shows how many people don't want to work but want to be famous. In my experiences, just being after the glamour is not going to get you there. There's too many hardships that come along. Passion has to really be there. Sleep on it. There were so many nights I felt like quitting. Usually things look a lot better the next morning. There's going to be endless battles, but hopefully you'll win the war. Once you're established and you believe that you're passionate about it, the next step is cutting out the day job. If you're gonna do it, then you have to really do it. I see a lot of people with day jobs and don't have time for what they need to do. I stopped having day jobs. It puts a lot more pressure and emphasis on you to work in the music world and make money. Then you have the energy to keep going and write songs. Otherwise, you have a day job, get home at night, and don't feel like writing songs.*

John Szuch, Founder, Deep Elm Records

What's been key to my success is starting from absolute scratch, as opposed to working at another label and trying to start something based on what I learned there. It's wanting to do something, learning about it, and learning the hard way—doing some things right, doing some things wrong, understanding how publicity and college radio works and doing that myself. Really learning the nuts and bolts and trying to get a comprehensive understanding of the way the business works and what's out there. You can't do that overnight. It's helpful if you hire someone for college radio promotion to know what they should be doing. You have to be smart. You have to be careful. There's a lot of people who are not very trustworthy in the business, and a lot of people who are. So you have to pick and choose your friends in this business very wisely. I think it's good to be honest with people about what you're doing. Honesty is the best policy when talking to an artist about what you think you can do or help them accomplish.

Juni Fisher, Founder, Red Geetar Records

My advice to someone who wants to go indie is this: Find your unique voice and the unique niche where you fit. Go for it as if you are already successful, as if you are already there, and present yourself in a professional, confident manner. Better to be an hour early than one minute late for an appointment or sound check. Be polite to everyone, and take time to write a thank-you note for every gig you play. Get your notebook out and make a list of short- and long-term goals. Make yourself check that list, and check off a goal a week! Become your own best cheerleader: Study the bios and promo materials of the acts you wish to "compete" with. You need to match or better those acts. Value your music and your time, and don't play for free unless it's your choice to donate a show to a charitable cause, or if Joan Baez spots you in the audience and asks you to join her on stage. Once you play for free somewhere, why on earth would they pay you when you come back? Network like your livelihood depends on it, because it does. The adage "Find something you love, and find a way to make money doing it" is a great start. Become brave, even if it's scary, because in the end the brave move to the front of the line.

Kelly Vandergriff, Manager, Five Times August

Be prepared to work hard. And I don't mean forty hours a week. Brad and I work seven days a week, sixteen hours a day at minimum. We have to, because we're doing an entire record label's worth of jobs. Brad designs all his own merch, maintains and designs his website, MySpace, PureVolume, Facebook, and several other online pages. He maintains his own PayPal store and ships his own orders, writes back to every email he gets. And he also has to find time for writing and recording songs and touring and performing. I do promotion, licensing, our accounting, tour management, and until recently the booking. It takes dedication, but if there are four guys in a band, and all work at it all the time, there is no end to what can be accomplished. Look what Brad and I have done with just two people.

John Robinson, President, Shaman Work Recordings

Be a visionary and think long range and think BIG always! Never forget that there are no easy steps to greatness. Also make sure to build a solid team to carry out the mission. Your team is your foundation, so build it with permanent bricks. Team is everything, and timing is everything!

Gregg Latterman, President, Aware Records

Sign music that you can be passionate about. If you're doing it to make money, don't do it. You have to do it because you love it, or you'll never be successful. Try to find a niche in the business. Do things the way you want, not the way you think you're supposed to do them. Everyone should read all the how-to books because you need all that background information. Take all that and try to make it work. Be street smart. That's what this business is all about.

Dave Roberge, President, Everfine Records

You can't take the approach that things are going to start happening for you. In this day and age, you've got to make it happen for yourself. A lot of it is sitting back and watching how things work and trying to understand how the industry, and how the different players interact with each other. The first thing you have to do is learn the business that you're trying to break into. If you don't try to educate yourself and go into it with the "I am a sponge" mentality, you're going to hurt yourself. I see a lot of people come in and think they know everything. That's very difficult—every day the industry is constantly evolving. You have to be adaptable to change and innovative, to be on the forefront of identifying when that change is going to come. A lot of times, by being there, you can turn it into a competitive advantage.

Ryan Kuper, President, Redemption Records

Pick a niche and stick with it! Keep a general sonic focus until you can afford to make baby steps outward. Be careful to not spread yourself too thin by overcommitting to bands. It will only hurt all those involved. Remember that these acts are in your hands— think of them as your children. Remember who helped you along the way, and keep those relationships strong. Always stay alert to market changes and advances in technology that may affect your business. Establish a healthy relationship with your distributor and any third parties you hire to work for you. These people will work for money but will work harder if they like you and feel your passion. Understand all aspects of your business, and don't think you are above a conference, a book, or having a mentor. You never know what may be revealed to you.

Valerie Vigoda, Recording Artist, GrooveLily

Make sure you work with people you really, really like—because you'll be spending an awful lot of time with them.

Jane Siberry, CEO/Recording Artist, Sheeba Records

Do it slowly and carefully. Build from the bottom up. Don't hire too many people too quickly. Keep everything as uncreative in the office as possible so you have a solid structure. Don't budge under the pressure of "this is how it should be done." And honor more than anything the people coming to you to buy what they want.

Mark Carpentieri, President and Founder, MC Records

Before you start a label, try to figure out what you are presenting that no one has done before. If you do what everyone else is doing, it's not going to work. You have to come up with a different kind of artist, different kind of music, something that is not being addressed. If you're addressing that, then you've got a chance.

Cliff Chenfeld, Co-President/Cofounder, Razor & Tie Music

Disregard all conventional modes of thinking. I think where independent labels can flourish in today's market is to find niches and alternative means of getting music out to people . . . finding niches for artists who might not fit the cookie-cutter model that has been created to break the great majority of major label artists. There's a large number of artists who have the potential to sell anywhere from 50,000 to 500,000 records that major labels are not going to be interested in for a variety of reasons. It might be that they're not obviously commercial enough from the outset or that it takes four albums to get you there. Major labels may not have that patience. The thing to do when you're setting up your own label is to think about what openings the marketplace offers you. Don't think that because a certain music is the rage, if you can find the next band that sounds like them you'll be okay. The majors kind of copy and do that. The majors can repeat the success with four or five like-minded bands, but the radio stations are going to be inundated with stuff that sounds like that from major labels who they have to play ahead of you. If you're coming to them with the same kind of stuff that the major labels are giving them, you're by definition going to lose. You have to come to them with something different.

Rolando Cuellar, Roland Entertainment

Have a plan and implement the plan. If it's your passion, you won't give up. Stay focused and meet others who are in the same level and can come together to work together. Help one another and cross-promote. Also partnering up with nonprofits can help advance your artists' careers. Think outside the box, and be creative with your marketing. You have to take risks in this business, and if you don't you'll never maximize your full potential. All successful people take risk. Again, don't give up, or you'll never know your full potential.

Edward Chmelewski, President, Blind Pig Records

Do your homework. Know your market. Music aside and the quality of music aside, you've got to figure out who you're going to sell this to. What's the market for this? Who's going to buy it? How am I going to reach those people?

Ezra Idlet, Recording Artist, Trout Fishing in America, Cofounder, Trout Records

Do it! The technology is set up today for musicians to do this more than at any other time.

INDEX